Giving Goliath His Due

Problem w/ book is he takes Bible literally & then sets out to prove it

He discounts the North — Severia & credits David & Solomon all the time

Philistines were part of the "People" — invaded Egypt — then went to Canaan

(are from Greece) western Turkey (Anatolia) & probably Crete

Superpowers: Babylon, Egypt, Assyria

Giving Goliath His Due

New Archaeological Light on the Philistines

Neal Bierling

Foreword by
Paul L. Maier

 **BAKER BOOK HOUSE**
Grand Rapids, Michigan 49516

Copyright 1992 by
Baker Book House Company
Printed in the United States of America

Library of Congress Cataloging-in-Publication Data

Bierling, Neal.
   Giving Goliath his due: new archaeological light on the Philistines/Neal
Bierling: foreword by Paul L. Maier.
   p. cm.
   Includes index.
   ISBN 0-8010-1018-7
      1. Philistines. 2. Bible. O.T.—History of contemporary events. 3.
Excavations (Archaeology)—Israel. I. Title.
   DS90.B54 1992
   933—dc20   91-35152

Illustration Credits

The author acknowledges permission to reprint illustrations on pages 54–58, courtesy of the Oriental Institute of the University of Chicago, and on page 86 from Blegan, Carl W., and Rawson, M., *The Palace of Nestor, vol. 1, part 1,* copyright © 1966 by Princeton University Press. Reprinted by permission of Princeton University Press and the University of Cincinnati.

Other illustrations appear by the courtesy of

W. Aufrecht, 79
Biblical Archaeology Society, 42, 82, 98, 100, 102, 107, 129, 185, 206
Joel Bierling, 59, 215, 242
Neal Bierling, 21, 95, 105, 117, 222, 232
Israel Antiquities Authority, 60
Kibbutz Revadim, 93, 116, 122, 123
Lahav Research Project, 155, 156
A. Mazar, 114
A. Mazar and George L. Kelm, 109, 226 (L. Ritmeyer, artist), 228 (L. Ritmeyer)
Joe D. Seger and Hebrew Union College, 143, 153, 164, 168, 186, 214, 216 (Merele Joseph, photographer), 218 bottom
Ilan Sztulman, 14, 124
Tel Miqne-Ekron Excavations, 13, 20, 37, 41, 44, 46, 87, 121, 172, 218 top, 219
David Ussishkin, 209–13 (Gert leGrange, artist)
Michael Woods and Peter Connolly, 78
Yigael Yadin, 201
Louise Bauer, maps
Ray Wcisel, line drawings

Dedicated to my mother and father,
who many years ago instilled in me a love of
reading as well as a love of stories in the Bible

Contents

Foreword

With the possible exception of the Amalekites, the Philistines were the most implacable foes of the ancient Israelites and certainly the most durable. The pages of the Old Testament are filled with the accounts of their bloody clashes with the Hebrews, who were largely denied the Mediterranean seacoast by the pentapolis of Philistine strongholds at Ashdod, Ashkelon, Ekron, Gath, and Gaza.

Some of these foes with the feathered headdress were slaughtered by Samson's deft use of a donkey's jawbone or were crushed in his suicide. Their champion Goliath was vanquished by a remarkable shepherd boy's slingshot, and the rest of their army presumably was annihilated when David killed his "ten thousands." Yet, like a metastasizing cancer, the Philistines reappeared to decapitate King Saul and kill his son Jonathan, surviving to outlast the northern tribes of Israel and remain a painful thorn in the side of Judah. Not until its conquest by Nebuchadnezzar of Babylon was Philistia terminated, and even now its name lives on in the terms *Palestine* and *Palestinian*.

Just who were these fierce rivals of the Hebrews for nearly six hundred years, where did they come from, and how did they live? We cannot find the answers to our questions in the writings of Philistine historians, since apparently there were none or their works have perished. And yet answers there are, some of which have just come to light in the past decade.

In rich, intriguing detail, Neal Bierling responds to such queries regarding the Philistines by using three main sources of information: the Old Testament, the secular ancient histories of Egypt, Syria, and Mesopotamia, and—above all—archaeology. Bierling is no stranger to the spade. In addition to his work at other digs in Israel, he has visited or worked for a decade at Tel Miqne, the site of ancient Ekron, one of the five major Philistine cities.

The good earth has had its share of surprises here for Bierling—and for the entire scholarly world. Ekron, for example, not only survived its struggles with the Hebrews, but reached its heyday *under the Assyrians,* when it became a boom town for olive oil production in the Eastern Mediterranean before succumbing to the Babylonians. Even the armchair archaeologist will be stirred as he discovers, with Bierling, the layer of charred rubble at Ekron that all but shouted Nebuchadnezzar's fiery conquest of the city in the early 600s B.C.

This book is a dramatic example of how external sources and archaeology can reconstruct the history of a distinct civilization in the *total absence* of any internal written sources from that civilization. Until now, very little Philistine epigraphy has been discovered, and what has survived has not yet been translated. A similar problem exists with regard to Minoan Crete and Trojan Anatolia within ancient Greek history and Etruscan Italy in Roman history. The most stunning surprise of all in these pages is this: all four of these untranslated ancient cultures appear to have common roots in the Aegean world! Priam, Hector, and Achilles in Homer's *Iliad* have connections, however remote, with the Philistine Delilah, Goliath, and Achish in the Old Testament.

More than one scholar has concluded that when Philistine inscriptions finally *are* decoded, they may well turn out to be Mycenaean Greek in Philistine lettering, much as Minoan Linear B turned out to be Mycenaean Greek in Cretan lettering. The reasoning behind so apparently sensational a claim is this: the most reliable ethnic taproot of the Philistines is among the "Sea Peoples" of the Greek and Anatolian world who contributed to the turbulent 1200s B.C. through expeditions of plunder, conquest, and colonization across the Eastern Mediterranean. Both late Mycenaeans and proto-Philistines joined in this game of "musical realms," using the islands of Crete and Cyprus as staging areas or bridges. The Philistines, Bierling concludes, "were either Mycenaean Greeks (which may include Cretans) or western Anatolians who . . . fled the collapse of their society that is exemplified in the *Iliad* and the *Odyssey*" (p. 120). The Philistines then attacked Egypt, but were driven out by Pharaoh Ramesses III, who claims to have resettled them along the Mediterranean coast in Palestine.

This fascinating connection with ancient classical history is only one example of the brilliant insights Bierling delivers in these pages. After piecing together the provenance of the Philistines, he goes on to a careful interweaving of Israelite and Philistine history based on a biblical chronology, illuminating his research with the clear, unim-

10

peachable light of archaeology. All Philistine sites except Gaza and Gath have delivered a treasury of new information through their strata and artifacts, many of which were uncovered only months ago.

For a fresh appreciation of what ancient Hebrews had to face from transplanted Aegean-Anatolian sorts who had the technological advantage of iron for their tools and weapons, Neal Bierling's study—well-documented by the best efforts in current scholarship—must become standard reading.

Paul L. Maier
Western Michigan University
August 1, 1991

Preface

I first went to Tel Miqne-Ekron during the summer of 1981. My initial visit to the site was a short one, which, curiously, left me more disappointed than filled with excitement and wonder.

That summer I had been working as a supervisor at Tel Lachish at the suggestion of the directors of the Ekron dig, Dr. Sy Gitin of the Albright Institute in Jerusalem and Dr. Trude Dothan of Hebrew University. Neither of these two directors had yet spent a complete

Site supervisors (left to right) Neal Bierling, Ann Killebrew, Trude Dothan, and Sy Gitin at Camp Dorot.

13

The author, an assistant field supervisor, at the site.

summer season at the Tel Miqne-Ekron dig and wouldn't be doing so until 1984. However, during the spring of 1981, they had opened up a couple of squares for exploratory purposes in a cooperative effort with students from Brandeis University. At the time Dr. Gitin had suggested to me that working at the Tel Lachish dig would give me excellent exposure to the Israeli style of excavating which would in part be used at Tel Miqne-Ekron.[1]

One of my fellow staff members at Lachish, Julie Krieger, had been with the Brandeis students during their three weeks that spring at Tel Miqne. I was eager to see the site, and after a little prodding, Julie agreed that we could rent a car and drive to Kibbutz Revadim. She had stayed there while digging at Tel Miqne-Ekron, and I also would be doing so during my summers in Israel. She introduced me to Natan Aidlin, a member of the kibbutz and a coordinator of the spring dig. He took us to a bomb shelter turned into an archaeological museum, which was filled with artifacts already taken from the site.

14

Seeing the artifacts housed there piqued my curiosity even more. We drove through cotton fields, and in the distance I saw what looked like ramparts—a huge fortification wall. What a magnificent site, I thought. This was going to be infinitely better than reading about it.

"Is that it?" I asked.

"No," was Julie's laughing response. "That's a water reservoir."

That was also about as far as we could go in the car. There were no roads through the cotton field out to the site, and the irrigation of the field had left the tractor track sloppy, almost too difficult to walk through. But through the cotton field we did walk.

"There it is," Julie said finally. She looked at me with a wry grin.

"Where?" I asked.

"There," she pointed out, "that low rise with the burnt slope."

"That?" I said.

My response dripped disappointment. I had worked at Tel Lachish and at Tell Gezer, both of which have impressive mounds from which one can look down and imagine the ancient highways traveled by merchants and occasionally by unpredictable enemy armies intending their assaults against townspeople. In contrast to the mounds of Gezer and Lachish, this mound was scarcely distinguishable from the surrounding hills.

Serious digging began during the summer of 1984. The numerous sherds of Philistine pottery we soon were finding obliged me to smile at my simple and wrongheaded disappointment. My reaction to the less than imposing mound was far less material than my becoming acquainted with the pottery, which was unique and plentiful. All I needed to do was stub my toe, and there in the ground I'd find another distinctive piece to pick up.

For the archaeologist, the researcher, the student who can't resist wanting to know the biblical Philistines more intimately, Tel Miqne-Ekron is an unbelievably exciting dig—an unbelievably exciting dig in a mound scarcely distinguishable from the surrounding hills.

Acknowledgments

This book would not have been possible without the help and encouragement of numerous people. The project began while I was a graduate student at the University of Michigan, where Dr. George Mendenhall was my mentor.

The two most important people responsible for the completion of this book were my brother, Dr. Henry Bierling, who helped me get the mass of archaeological material into a publishable form for Baker Book House, and my wife, Dr. Marilyn (Joling) Bierling, who spent countless hours reading and critiquing the manuscript.

Special thanks go to two of my former professors at Calvin College and Seminary, Leonard Sweetman and Bastiaan Van Elderen, who kindly consented to read and critique the entire manuscript. Two colleagues from the field, Joe Seger of Mississippi State and Oded Borowski of Emory University, read the sections in connection with Tells Gezer and Halif and made important corrections and comments. Many thanks are also in order to a kindred spirit, Paul Maier from Western Michigan University, who kindly consented to write the foreword for this book and also provided numerous suggestions to improve the manuscript. Kudos to the students scattered near and far who helped out in the summer and made the sweaty work in the field more than endurable.

Of course, the book would not have been possible without the help of the directors of Tel Miqne-Ekron, Trude Dothan of Hebrew University and Sy Gitin of the Albright Institute, both in Jerusalem. Being able to work at the Philistine site of Tel Miqne-Ekron has been a dream come true. The pleasant experiences could not have happened without the cooperation of Kibbutz Revadim and all the wonderful people there. A special thanks should be given to Revadim's Gideon Münz

17

and Natan Aidlin. Thanks also to the Endowment for Biblical Research foundation, whose grant for the summer of 1990 in Israel enabled me to finish the research for this project.

Last, but not least, I must thank my children, Joel Michael, Rachel Noelle, and Sara Michelle, who have been able to accompany me to Israel twice. They finally were able to experience firsthand what kept drawing their dad away not only during the summer months but during the evenings of the school year as well in order to work on "the book."

On a sober note, a few days after I turned in my completed manuscript to Baker Book House, my older sister's life was suddenly completed. But through the pain I could hear her say, "It's okay, little brother; everything will be okay."

Introduction

Thus says the LORD:
    For three transgressions of Gaza,
    and for four, I will not revoke the punishment. . . .
    I will cut off the inhabitants from Ashdod,
    and the one who holds the scepter from Ashkelon;
    I will turn my hand against Ekron,
    and the remnant of the Philistines shall perish,
    says the Lord GOD.
[Amos 1:6–8]

The latter prophetical books from Amos through Zechariah are rife with similar condemnations of the Philistines. This preponderance of negative pronouncements is explained by the events in the earlier prophetical books of Joshua through Kings, where the details of biblical history are found.

In large part due to the current excavations at Tel Miqne-Ekron thirty miles west of Jerusalem, a more complete picture of who these Philistines were is becoming available. The excavations at Tel Miqne-Ekron, along with the information from other recent excavations, not only can help us understand why these people were nearly always seen in a negative light in the Old Testament but also can provide us clearer insight into their cultural and physical world. Thus, we can better understand their social and religious life in contrast to the social and religious life of God's chosen people, the Israelites. To understand this difference is to see what set the Israelites apart from the Philistines and see why the latter biblical prophets were so adamant in their pronouncements.

Tel Miqne-Ekron, a rich source of biblical-era Philistine artifacts.

Prior to the excavations at Tel Miqne-Ekron, which began in 1981, material data on the Philistines were sparse at best. Of the five major Philistine cities mentioned in the Bible (Ashdod, Ashkelon, Ekron, Gath, and Gaza) only one, Ashdod, had been extensively excavated. The Ashdod dig has yielded excellent material finds from the Philistines, though its Philistine phase is only one of several strata being excavated. Gaza, part of the Gaza Strip, is so densely populated today that excavation there is all but impossible. Gath (Tell es-Safi) has not been excavated since late in the nineteenth century. Ashkelon is presently being excavated, but it has so many occupational strata besides the Philistine ones that it will be some time before a workable mass of data is available for interpretative work. (Occupational strata, in contrast to strata containing only soil and rocks from erosion, are permeated with the debris and artifacts of human activity.)

Tel Miqne-Ekron, a fifty-acre site, is one of the largest archaeological sites from the biblical era. It is today quickly becoming the richest field of all the biblical-era Philistine excavations. The soil there is filled with Philistine pottery. Stub your toe, and chances are you will uncover a piece of that pottery. What makes Tel Miqne-Ekron particularly exciting is that its occupational strata are primarily those of the Philistine period. The more than one hundred olive oil presses that the current excavation has already uncovered are all presses from the Philistines. No other site in the Near East has presented archaeologists with such a plethora of oil presses. Philistine Ekron in

Highway sign
identifying
Tel Miqne-Ekron.

the seventh century B.C. must have been one of the largest centers of olive oil production in its day. But more importantly, in that same stratum, in conjunction with the oil presses and sometimes in the same room, four-horned "Israelite" altars have also been found.

Finding these two kinds of artifacts together, one totally secular and the other always thought of as religious in nature, sheds light on the ancient Near Eastern process of oil production. It also helps us understand Amos's indictment of God's people in chapter 6:4–7 where he refers to a pagan ritual and condemns the impious luxury of self-anointing and using "the finest oils."

Clearly, the Tel Miqne-Ekron excavations and others of the recent past have yielded the best insights to date into the world of the biblical Philistines. But even more compelling is the realization that these insights also give us a better understanding of the social and religious life of God's people as presented to us in Amos and elsewhere in the Old Testament. The aim of this book is to acquaint the armchair archaeologist with the archaeological evidence to date on Israel's neighbors, the Philistines, and to illustrate how this evidence illuminates the biblical world of Joshua and those who followed him.

1

The Philistines in Scripture

Before looking to the data collected in the various excavations of the last few years at Philistine sites, a brief review of the biblical presentation of the Philistines is in order. From the days of Joshua to those of Zechariah the prophet, the Philistines were generally viewed by the Israelites as the enemy. There are some exceptions to this portrayal, but these exceptions frequently haven't been widely recognized because of the several different names biblical writers have used in their references to the people of Philistia.[1]

To begin then, what did the Old Testament writers mean when they wrote the word *Philistine?* By way of comparison, remember that during the Exodus, the tribes of Israel were joined by non-Israelites, or "aliens" (Exod. 12:38; Num. 11:4; Josh. 8:35). This entire aggregate of people, Israelites and non-Israelites, became known as Israel. At a later time, when David was fleeing from Saul, he too was joined by non-Israelites (1 Sam. 26:6). In 1 Samuel 29:3, David and his entire company nonetheless are called Hebrews. Similarly, throughout the Old Testament the word *Philistine* is invariably used in its sociopolitical sense rather than with an ethnic or a linguistic meaning.[2]

It is likely that the "Sea Peoples" of the Egyptian records are the Philistines mentioned in the Bible. They had settled along the coast south of the Mount Carmel range and had formed a new federation of five chief city-states: Gaza, Ashkelon, Ashdod, Gath, and Ekron. This federation took on the name of its dominant group, the Philistines, and that name lives on today in the place name Palestine.

The earliest uses of the word *Philistine* in the Bible are in Genesis 21 and 26. In Genesis 21 Abimelech and the captain of his host, Phicol, left the land they had shared with Abraham and "returned to the land of the Philistines." In chapter 26, Isaac, due to the duress of a famine, traveled to "Abimelech king of the Philistines."

It is possible the use of the name Philistines in these chapters of Genesis indicates an early wave of raiders who had come by the sea and settled in the area. It is also possible that a copyist some centuries after the writing of the original chapter added or substituted a word he himself had grown accustomed to using with reference to the territory.

Abimelech, whose name is Semitic, was king of the Philistines. His captain, Phicol, had a non-Semitic name. Both are central characters in these early stories. Perhaps Phicol was a foreigner and the commander of a foreign mercenary troop. Clearly, the Bible leaves many questions that it raises unanswered, and questions about the backgrounds of these men also remain. In any event, there were centuries between the Philistines in the stories of Abraham's day and the Philistines with whom the descendants of Joshua were embroiled.

In Exodus 13:17 God did not allow the Israelites, as they left Egypt, to go to the Promised Land "by way of the land of the Philistines, although that was nearer." In Exodus 23:31 God, at Mount Sinai, stated: "I will set your borders from the Red Sea to the sea of the Philistines." In Joshua 13:1–2, with the Israelites now in Palestine, we read, "Now Joshua was old and advanced in years; and the LORD said to him, 'You are old and advanced in years, and very much of the land still remains to be possessed. This is the land that still remains: all the regions of the Philistines. . . . '" These indications in the Bible, when taken together with Egyptian historical records of the thirteenth to twelfth centuries B.C., provide a specific starting date for Israel's history of conflict with the Philistines.

The biblical text does not record that Joshua himself directly battled the Philistines. In Joshua 13 and in the succeeding passages, however, we read that the Philistines are present on the coastal plain and are perceived as a threat that needs to be driven out. The five chief cities of the Philistines are cited as cities yet to be captured. They are identified as part of Israel's tribal inheritance. The allotment of land for Judah is described in chapter 15. Verses 10–12 mention Timnah (where Samson's wife came from) and Ekron. Verse 31 mentions Ziklag as part of Judah's southern border, the city later given to David by Achish, king of Philistine Gath. Verses 45–47 mention that Ekron, Ashdod, and Gaza, down to the Mediterranean Sea, were all to belong to Judah, though in fact the territory was never successfully held and the children of Judah have had to share the land "to this day."

In Joshua 19:1–9, the territory that is to be Simeon's is described. Ziklag is included here as well. In chapter 19:43, Timnah and Ekron are again mentioned, though this time as belonging to the tribe of Dan. Because the sons of Dan "had difficulty taking possession of their territory" (19:47 NIV), they later left this their allotted tribal land and moved to an area north of the Sea of Galilee, there capturing Laish and renaming it Dan (Josh. 19:47; Judg. 18:29). This move probably occurred sometime after the Samson stories described in Judges 18 and following.

Judges 1:18 says of the Philistines and their cities: "Judah took Gaza with its territory, Ashkelon with its territory, and Ekron with its territory." Although a capture of these cities occurred, their occupation was problematic, as the following verse reveals: "but [Judah] could not drive out the inhabitants of the plain, because they had chariots of iron." It seems that Israel was unable to hold on to these Philistine territories for any length of time.

Judges 4 and 5 record the well-known battle of Deborah against Jabin, king of Hazor, which is in northern Israel. Perhaps most intriguing with regard to this piece of history is the question that also may serve as an index to the life and times of that era: Who was this general of Jabin called Sisera? Who was this man known even today for his iron chariots? Linguists tell us that Sisera is neither a Hebrew nor a Canaanite name. It is suggested he might have been one of the Sea Peoples of whom the Philistines were a part. We do know that some of the Sea Peoples had settled along the coast north of the Mount Carmel range (M. Dothan 1989, 63). In his iron chariots, Sisera at least possessed their technology. Additionally, he is said to have been from Harosheth Haggoyim, which means Harosheth of the Gentiles. This is believed to have been somewhere in the Sharon Plain, near where he gathered his forces to do battle with the Israelites and the place to which his surviving charioteers fled in terror after the battle.[3]

In Judges 10, as background to the Jephthah story, the Philistines are mentioned again, though they and their gods are not the center of consideration. The writer of Judges here lists the enemies to whom the Lord delivered the Israelites for a period of eighteen years, because they had fallen away from serving him, because they had "served the Baals and the Ashtaroth, the gods of Syria, the gods of Sidon, the gods of Moab, the gods of the Ammonites, and the gods of the Philistines" (10:6 RSV). Though the Ammonites were Jephthah's direct enemy according to the story, verse 7 reads: "And the anger of the LORD was kindled against Israel, and he sold them into the hand of the Philistines, and into the hand of the Ammonites" (RSV).

In Judges 13, the story of the Philistines is picked up again in the Samson saga. Placed in the time prior to the move of the tribe of Dan north of the Sea of Galilee (Judg. 18), the story shows Samson living in proximity to the Philistines and able to move freely among them (Judg. 14:1, 5; 16:1). Very likely this freedom of movement was possible because the Hebrews were subjects of the Philistines (14:4; 15:11). For some reason, not all five of the chief Philistine cities are mentioned in this account. Even Ekron, the city closest to Timnah, is not named directly. However, Delilah is said to have been from the valley of Sorek (Judg. 16:4). The scenes with her may have occurred near or in Ekron, which is in this valley. In addition, the Philistine lords, presumably including the lord of Ekron, did come to Delilah, and therefore Ekron would have been involved. Ashkelon lost thirty of its young men at the end of Samson's wedding party in Timnah, and Gaza lost its gates to Samson after he was locked inside. The story concludes with Samson asking the Lord God, "Let me die with the Philistines" (16:30), and Samson then kills more Philistines in his death than he had slain during his lifetime. With the demise of Samson, the Philistines exited from the biblical picture until the Samuel stories.

In 1 Samuel 4 the Philistines captured the ark of the covenant in the second of two consecutive battles with the Israelites. "So the Philistines fought; Israel was defeated, and they fled, everyone to his home. There was a very great slaughter, for there fell of Israel thirty thousand foot soldiers" (4:10). Israel's ark of the covenant went on a seven-month tour of Philistine cities. The five chief cities of the Philistines or their rulers are mentioned here and in following chapters, as are the numerous encounters that Samuel and Saul had with the Philistines. These struggles led to David's encounter with Goliath, recorded in 1 Samuel 17. After the death of Goliath, the

Philistines were chased "as far as Gath and the gates of Ekron" (v. 52).

All but three of the remaining chapters in 1 Samuel contain references to the Philistines and detail their encounters with Saul, Jonathan, and David. We read how David eventually sought refuge with the Philistine Achish, ruler of Gath, and evidently swore loyalty to him. The city of Ziklag was given to David as a reward for this loyalty. From this city fortress, David made his many forays against the enemies of Israel, the Philistines in particular, and in all of these ventures he left no survivors who might report back to Achish. Other Philistine rulers, however, did not trust David, and in preparation for their battle against Saul sent David back to Ziklag. Upon his return there, he found that his Philistine city had been sacked by the Amalekites, who had also taken his wives and children captive.

Second Samuel contains few references to the Philistines. These report David's final battles against them in his efforts to subjugate the traditional enemies of his people.

First Chronicles provides some additional detail. First Chronicles 11:15–19 records the story of a Philistine garrison at Bethlehem at a time when David, fleeing from Saul, was out in the wilderness. David longed for water from his hometown well, the well at Bethlehem's gate, and three of his warriors risked their lives by breaking through the Philistine camp in order to get some of that water. We read in later chapters that after David was anointed king over all Israel the Philistines attacked him, evidently fearing his new independence. David defeated them, and the Chronicler adds, "and at David's command they [the captured Philistine gods] were burned." While capturing Gath and Gezer, David fought and killed their giants, some of whom were reported to have six fingers and toes (1 Chron. 14:8–17; 18:1; 20:4–8).

But 1 Chronicles also allows a view of the Philistines often overlooked. The Cherethites, Pelethites, Gittites, and Carites were all somehow part of the Philistine federation. Nonetheless, they formed David's personal bodyguard, the bodyguard that remained loyal to him even when almost all others had deserted him for various reasons. In 2 Samuel 15:18ff., when Absalom forced his father to flee from Jerusalem, this bodyguard fled with David. Some one hundred years later, this same royal bodyguard, in loyalty to King David's family, helped install the seven-year-old Joash on David's throne in Jerusalem in place of King Ahab's daughter, Athaliah (2 Kings 11).[4]

27

The references to the Philistines in 1 and 2 Kings, 2 Chronicles, and several of the prophetical books covering the period of the kings after David are few in number. First Kings 8:9 and 2 Chronicles 5:10 may contain the first references in this period, although they are indirect. They concern Solomon and his moving the ark of the covenant into the great temple he constructed in Jerusalem. Both verses mention that by then the ark contained only the two stone tablets. In mentioning what the ark contained the writers obliquely remind their audience of the missing articles—the golden container of manna and Aaron's staff. In this way, they subtly remind readers of the Israelites' long, troubled history with the Philistines who had captured this ark in the days of Eli and Samuel.

In these passing sentences, the writers might also be reminding their audience why the people of Israel in that day intuitively despised the Philistines.[5] Not only had these pestilent neighbors killed their judge Samson, but also during those final days of the judges they had captured the ark of the covenant and may have either kept or destroyed the golden pot of manna and Aaron's staff—the artifactual reminders of how the Lord God provided for his people while they wandered through the wilderness. To be reminded of this much was to remember additionally that it was also the Philistines who in effect killed their first king, Saul, and desecrated his body on the walls of Beth-shean.

The specific references to the Philistines in the books of the Kings show that the writers had learned to recognize a separate Philistine territory. At times this territory was under the control of Israel or Judah, and at times it was seen as an obviously independent region (1 Kings 4:21; 15:27; 2 Kings 8:2–3). Solomon ruled at least to the borders of Philistia (2 Chron. 9:26), but, some sixty years later (c. 870 B.C.), we see the Philistines listed as one of the groups bearing tribute to King Jehoshaphat of Judah (2 Chron. 17:11). Of singular interest is the passage in 2 Kings 1:2–17, where King Ahab's successor, Ahaziah, a contemporary of Jehoshaphat of Judah, sent men to the Philistine city of Ekron to consult the god Baal-zebub. Ahaziah was grievously ill and wished to ask of the Philistine god whether he would recover. This passage is significant because it illustrates the influence of the Philistines in Israel at that time and because it demonstrates the validity of the Lord, Israel's God, against a powerless and unavailing Philistine god, Baal-zebub. (This will be discussed further in chapter 6.)

In 2 Chronicles 21 we read that Jehoshaphat's son, Jehoram of Judah (849–843 B.C.), the king who married Athaliah, King Ahab's and Queen Jezebel's daughter, had difficulties with numerous enemies during his reign. Among the enemies that the Lord raised up against him were the Philistines (21:16). Some fifty years later, during the eighth century B.C., King Uzziah of Judah was able to defeat the Philistines of Gath and Ashdod (2 Chron. 26:6–7), and Gath is not mentioned again in biblical history after 2 Chronicles 26. King Uzziah (783–742) reigned during the period of the prophet Amos, circa 750 B.C., whose stark and memorable prophecy warrants a more thorough discussion in a later chapter (see pp. 194–98).

During the reign of Uzziah's grandson, the wicked Ahaz (735–715), the Philistines were able to capture several towns of Judah (2 Chron. 28:18–19). The writer of the Chronicles makes dramatically clear that the Lord allowed this to happen as the result of Ahaz's wickedness: "And the Philistines had made raids on the cities in the Shephelah and the Negeb of Judah, and had taken Bethshemesh, Aijalon, Gederoth, Soco with its villages, Timnah with its villages, and Gimzo with its villages; and they settled there. For the LORD brought Judah low because of King Ahaz of Israel. . . ."

These were the days of Isaiah, who uttered several messianic messages during this tempestuous reign (e.g., Isa. 7:14). In 2:6, Isaiah presents a negative portrait of the Philistines when he refers to "soothsayers like the Philistines." In 9:12, after we encounter the well-known messianic passage "For to us a child is born, to us a son is given" (v. 6 RSV), Isaiah emphasizes that the Lord has used the Philistines to punish Israel for its wickedness. There is another shift in chapter 11. Here Isaiah states that both Israel and Judah together with the Messiah will "swoop down on the backs of the Philistines in the west" (11:14). In 14:28–32, a message to the Philistines is specifically dated to the year King Ahaz died, circa 715 B.C.: "Wail, O gate; cry, O city; melt in fear, O Philistia, all of you! For smoke comes out of the north, and there is no straggler in its ranks" (Isa. 14:31).

The final references to the Philistines in Chronicles concern Judah's King Ahaz. Ahaz is followed by the good king, Hezekiah, circa 700 B.C., and in 2 Kings 18:8 we read that Hezekiah was able to defeat the "Philistines as far as Gaza and its territory." (See chapter 7 for further discussion.) This is the latest obvious mention of the Philistines in the Old Testament history of the kingdoms.

The Book of Jeremiah, covering the final years of Judah's existence as an independent nation, circa 600 B.C., becomes our next focus. In a descriptive passage detailing the wrath of the Lord, Jeremiah 25:17ff., the Philistines and their cities Ashkelon, Gaza, Ekron, and Ashdod are mentioned in the catalogue of peoples destined for annihilation. Chapter 47 describes specifically the manner in which destruction will come to the Philistines. Perhaps this chapter in Jeremiah underscores the event that occurred during the reign of King Josiah, whose death is described in both 2 Kings 23 and 2 Chronicles 35. An Egyptian army led by Pharaoh Neco was enroute to wage war against Carchemish to the north in an effort to aid Assyria against the rising power of Babylon. Josiah not only was unsuccessful in his efforts to stop Neco, but also was fatally wounded by Egyptian archers. His death prefigures the loss of independence that Judah was about to suffer. Jeremiah is reported by the writer of the Chronicles to have composed a lament for Josiah (2 Chron. 35:25) and to have prophesied the destruction of Philistia by Babylon (Jer. 47).

The writings of Zephaniah and Ezekiel could only have been produced during this time of despair so poignantly introduced in the lamentations of Jeremiah. Judah and Jerusalem were going to be destroyed by the Babylonian king Nebuchadnezzar. Ezekiel in his complaint explains that because the Philistines had sought the destruction of Judah, they would be destroyed as well. Zephaniah, prophesying during the days of Josiah (ca. 620 B.C.), corroborates this prophecy of Ezekiel, saying that the Philistine cities would be destroyed and their lands would become the pasture land for the remnant of Judah: "For Gaza shall be deserted, and Ashkelon shall become a desolation; Ashdod's people shall be driven out at noon, and Ekron shall be uprooted. Ah, inhabitants of the seacoast, you nation of the Cherethites! The word of the LORD is against you, O Canaan, land of the Philistines; and I will destroy you until no inhabitant is left. And you, O seacoast, shall be pastures, meadows for shepherds and folds for flocks" (Zeph. 2:4–6).

The final reference to the Philistines in the Old Testament is found in the writing of Zechariah, a prophet who lived and worked circa 520 B.C. It is likely that he was a contemporary of the prophet Haggai. In chapter 9 of Zechariah's work, the destruction of the remaining Philistine cities is graphically and matter-of-factly foretold. Zechariah's words summarize what had become the dominant biblical sensibility regarding the Philistines:

The word of the LORD is against the land of Hadrach and will rest upon Damascus. For to the LORD belongs the capital of Aram, as do all the tribes of Israel; Hamath also, which borders on it, Tyre and Sidon, though they are very wise. Tyre has built itself a rampart, and heaped up silver like dust, and gold like the dirt of the streets. But now, the Lord will strip it of its possessions and hurl its wealth into the sea, and it shall be devoured by fire.

Ashkelon shall see it and be afraid; Gaza too, and shall writhe in anguish; Ekron also, because its hopes are withered. The king shall perish from Gaza; Ashkelon shall be uninhabited; a mongrel people shall settle in Ashdod, and I will make an end of the pride of Philistia. I will take away its blood from its mouth, and its abominations from between its teeth; it too shall be a remnant for our God; it shall be like a clan in Judah, and Ekron shall be like the Jebusites. [Zech. 9:1-7]

From this brief outline of the Old Testament use of the word *Philistine* from the thirteenth to the sixth centuries B.C. we turn to a synopsis of the archaeological record at Tel Miqne-Ekron which covers roughly the same period. After a discussion of the origins of the Philistines (chap. 3), I will examine how the archaeological record of various Philistine sites sheds light on and meshes with the biblical record.

⚜2⚜

Ekron: The Archaeological Record

A day or so before we began the actual excavating at the Tel Miqne-Ekron site in June 1984, the entire staff walked out to the highway that runs from Ashkelon to Jerusalem to place signs marking the dig. The signs were scarcely in place before we all realized the comedy of our effort. Our signs were small, a mere fifteen inches by six inches. There was no way they would be seen by travelers or even by colleagues looking for the excavations as they cruised past at highway speeds.

This situation reflected an earlier experience in 1980 when directors Sy Gitin and Trude Dothan were in the field studying maps, trying to figure out precisely where Tel Miqne-Ekron was. The archaeological "signs" were small, too, and they had almost missed them. The area where the tell was supposed to be was a logistical base for the farmers of a kibbutz. The mound they had found and were standing on, a mere seven meters above the plain planted with cotton, seemed too unimpressive to warrant consideration. But that mound was then and is now the site believed to be the biblical Ekron.[1]

Tel Miqne-Ekron was originally surveyed in April 1924 by William Foxwell Albright, who is often referred to as the father of American biblical archaeology. In Arabic the site is called Khirbet

33

(ruins of) el-Muqanna' and bears the name of the stream that flows immediately by it. Albright noted that the debris layer was not particularly deep and that he found no remains of a Bronze Age settlement. He did remark on the numerous sherds of Philistine pottery found that dated from the early Iron Age I (twelfth century B.C.). On the basis of these sherds he also came to believe that the site was abandoned after the Persian period, circa fourth century B.C. He found physical evidence for ruins of a fortification system and thought that with everything considered, including biblical and extrabiblical sources, this site had to be Eltekeh, a tribal town of Dan which later gained prominence as the location for a major battle between Assyria and Egypt that occurred shortly after the fall of the ten northern tribes of Israel. Albright had already identified another site, Qatra, as that of the biblical Ekron. The map on page 35 shows where Qatra is located and where Eltekeh is now believed to have been.

Albright's site identification remained in place for more than three decades. In 1953, however, some scholars began to question his conclusion that Qatra was Ekron. In 1957 Joseph Naveh conducted an extensive survey of Khirbet el-Muqanna' for Israel's Department of Antiquities (Naveh 1958). Naveh considered the identical evidence that Albright had considered, both the biblical and nonbiblical records, including the works of the early church father Eusebius. He also examined all the extant archaeological data. He concluded, contrary to Albright, that Muqanna' was Ekron.

In part, Naveh based his opinion on the following information: 1) the large quantity of Philistine pottery at Muqanna'; 2) the large size of the Muqanna' site, a size that corresponds with the information that Ekron, having been one of the chief Philistine cities, likely covered forty or more acres (compared with the thirteen acres of Jericho, the eighteen acres of Lachish, the thirteen acres of Megiddo, and the twelve acres of David's Jerusalem); 3) the relative insignificance of Eltekeh according to the extant historical data; and 4) the stories of the return of the ark of the covenant and of the Israelites' pursuit of the Philistines after David killed Goliath, both of which fit the Muqanna' location better than that of Eltekeh. Naveh's studied conclusions left Albright unconvinced, however.

Until 1981 and 1982, when some of the exploratory squares at Tel Miqne-Ekron were first excavated by the dig's directors in their joint effort with Brandeis University students, it had been thought that there was no Bronze Age settlement (pre-1200 B.C.) at this site. Dr.

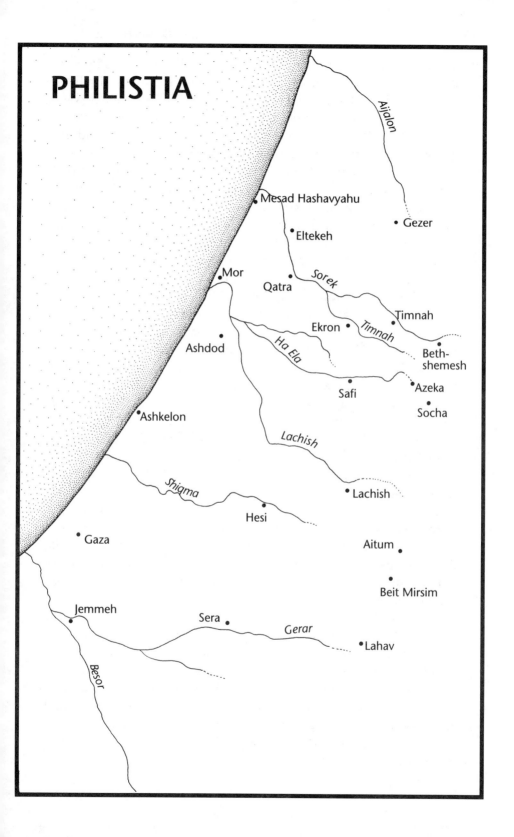

PHILISTIA

Aijalon

Mesad Hashavyahu

• Gezer

• Eltekeh

Mor

Sorek

Qatra

Timnah

Ekron

Timnah

Ashdod

Ha Ela

Beth-
shemesh

Azeka

Safi

Socha

Ashkelon

Lachish

Shiqma

Lachish

Hesi

Gaza

Aitum

Beit Mirsim

Jemmeh

Sera

Gerar

Lahav

Besor

Trude Dothan, in her major work on the Philistines, stated the standard opinion: "Khirbet Muqanna' was founded by the Philistines and existed until the Persian period. Like Tell Qasile, it was an entirely new settlement, not one built over an earlier Canaanite city" (1982a, 88). Both of the exploratory sessions in 1981 and 1982 uncovered quantities of sherds from the earlier Bronze ages, but all of the sherds were found in fills and not in the clear remains of buildings. Even as late as August 1982, after the second exploratory session conducted earlier during that spring, Dr. Dothan still believed that, in spite of the Bronze Age sherds, which suggested a constant occupation at the site, the earliest architectural evidence dated to the twelfth century B.C. (T. Dothan and Gitin 1982).

Not until the archaeological work done during the summer session of 1984 was it discovered that the Tel Miqne-Ekron mound includes a Canaanite city razed by an invading people who had come by way of the sea. These invaders were the Philistines. That find was only one of the striking discoveries made that summer.

This discovery also provides an excellent example of what the reader must remember when working with archaeological data. Each new season of excavation may mean that the conclusions of the previous seasons might need to be revised. It is now apparent that the archaeological record of Ekron to date begins with the fifteenth/fourteenth century B.C. and concludes with the seventh century B.C. This time period closely parallels the time period of the biblical references made to the Philistines.

What drew the original inhabitants to settle the area at Tel Miqne-Ekron? Water. In this generally arid land a convenient water source becomes a comfortable invitation to stay, and the ancient Canaanites did find a perennial stream flowing here. Today this stream is called the Nahal (stream) Timnah; it still flows into the Nahal Sorek, as it has for centuries (see map, p. 35).

A second feature the ancient people looked for in their building sites was high ground. The high ground in this area was generally unsuited to farming but was surrounded by good farming land. Building their settlements on the high ground offered these people a convenient overview of their fields and, more importantly, a defensive advantage in the event of possible attack from passing marauders. Invariably these high-ground settlements made defensive measures more viable and therefore were sites eagerly sought out by the original inhabitants of the area.

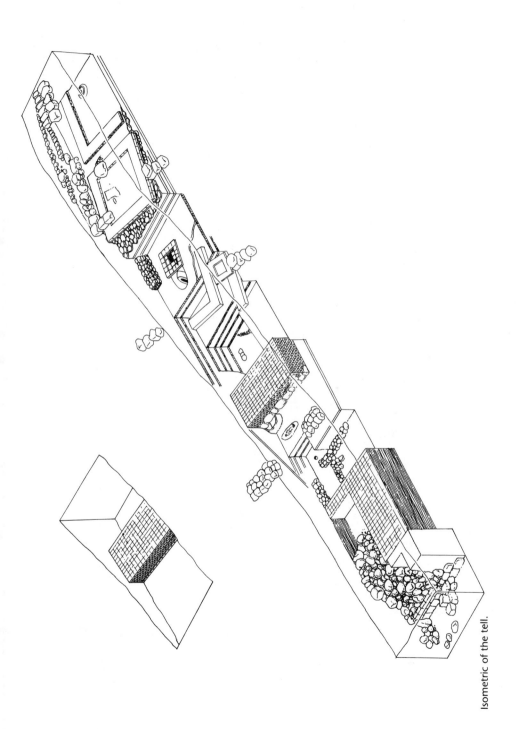

Isometric of the tell.

A third feature that attracted settlers to Ekron was its location at the junctions of ancient highways. Because it was located along the Via Maris, a major north-south highway connecting Egypt with Mesopotamia, and along the east-west highways connecting Ashdod to Gezer and connecting to Beth-shemesh along the Nahal Sorek, Ekron grew quickly in importance. A city located so strategically along the ancient interchange of highways could not long remain obscure.

Though the Tel Miqne-Ekron mound today rises no more than seven meters above the plain, from it the important Old Testament site of Gezer, a short distance to the northeast, can be seen clearly. Tell es-Safi, very likely the site of Philistine Gath, is visible to the south. The coastal plain, with the Mediterranean Sea just out of sight, stretches as a flat expanse to the west, and the foothills, or Shephelah, rise dramatically to the east. Ekron, then, is located on the eastern edge of the coastal plain which in antiquity separated Philistia from Judah. Archaeologists have determined that the mound was some four meters higher prior to the sixth century B.C. During the past twenty-five centuries not only has soil eroded off the top of the mound, but alluvial soil coming down the Nahal Timnah has been deposited throughout the surrounding area.

Current excavations indicate that the original Canaanite inhabitants were already at the site in the fifteenth/fourteenth century B.C., when the Israelites were still in Egypt. During the Late Bronze II period (1400–1200 B.C.), this original settlement and perhaps a second one may have been unwalled. Excavation rooms have yielded vessels and installations indicating both domestic and industrial activity. A burial site containing artifacts dating to this early period was uncovered at the edge of the mound. Interestingly, many of the artifacts uncovered have their origins in other lands: the Aegean, Cyprus, Anatolia (Turkey), and Egypt. These finds corroborate the international flavor that even the biblical Joseph stories dating from the same period give glimpses of.

One criterion marking the transition from the Late Bronze Age to the Iron Age has always been the cessation of imports from the Aegean and Cyprus into Canaan. The international mixture of artifacts found in the Late Bronze layer of earth at Tel Miqne is not present in the next layer, signaling the end of the Late Bronze Age there.

It was during the following Iron I period (1200–1000 B.C.), however, with the arrival of the Philistines, that Ekron became a settlement of note, a place name on ancient maps, and a reference in

Mycenaean IIIB imported krater (fourteenth century B.C.) found in a tomb at Tel Dan.

ancient historical texts. This was the period of Joshua, the judges, and those peoples caught up in the conflicts reported in the 1 Samuel stories.

This was also the period when a wall was constructed directly around the original Canaanite settlement. This wall, nearly eleven feet thick, completely surrounded the fifty-acre site. By comparison, the Jebusite city of Jerusalem, which was contemporary to the city of Ekron and was later captured by King David, walled in approximately twelve acres circa 1200 B.C. A second significant archaeological discovery dating to this period was the pottery found at Ekron; it proved to be a new type called Mycenaean IIIC:1b.

The wave of destruction that swept through Greece at the end of the thirteenth century B.C. ended the import into Cyprus and Canaan of the grand Greek pottery referred to as Mycenaean IIIB. This pottery is so beautiful that Amihai Mazar mentions that pieces of it were "probably traded as objects of art and precious tableware" during the Late Bronze Age (1990, 263). The new type of pottery, IIIC:1b, is similar in style and construction to the old imported Mycenaean IIIB pottery, thus reflecting the same traditions and skills. But it differs most importantly in that it was made locally, a fact determined by submitting sherds to neutron activation analysis.

This analysis provides a chemical "fingerprint" of the sherds' composition, and this "fingerprint" can be compared with the chemical "fingerprint" of sherds' from other sites (Gunneweg et al. 1986, 15). The pottery is referred to broadly as Mycenaean IIIC, and the *1b* refers specifically to the subdivision of it found on Cyprus and the Philistine coast. Most archaeologists on Cyprus do associate this IIIC:1b pottery with Achaean (Greek) refugees fleeing to Cyprus from the destruction of the Mycenaean centers in Greece.

At Ashdod and Ekron, the two chief Philistine sites where stratigraphic excavation has occurred, this new pottery was found directly above the Late Bronze layer. The pottery is identical in style and decor to that excavated on Cyprus, but it was locally made; therefore, at both sites it is called Mycenaean IIIC:1b. It will be developed in chapter 3 that the "Achaean" refugees on Cyprus were the ancestors of the "Philistines" in what came to be called Philistia in Canaan (A. Mazar 1990, 307–8).

The numerous Mycenaean IIIC:1b fragments from the small bowls and kraters (larger bowls) are typically painted with geometric patterns and bands in shades of dark brown to red. Some are decorated with bird or fish motifs as well. The excavated areas at Ekron include an industrial area, where kilns and furnaces that may have been used to make this pottery have also been found.

The new fortifications at Tel Miqne-Ekron, the cessation of Mycenaean IIIB pottery imports, the new style in pottery, the kilns, and other new architectural features all point to the arrival of the Sea Peoples, of whom the Philistines were a part, during the first third of the twelfth century B.C. At some point still in the first half of the twelfth century an unmistakable new form of pottery appeared, the classic Philistine pottery.

I remember the transition being revealed during excavation as a gradual but clear change from Mycenaean IIIC:1b to the later Philistine pottery. As we uncovered different levels and dug in different areas, we were able to predict precisely when we would be finding the different styles and at what depth. The classic Philistine pottery is called "bichrome" (two-color) ware. This attractive pottery, again locally made and definitely related to its predecessor, is distinctive with its white slip (background) and its red and black decorations in the forms of birds, fish, or metopes containing geometric shapes. Most of the forms of the vessels are Mycenaean in origin, as are the designs on the vessels. There is some evidence of borrowing from the Cypriots, Egyptians, and Canaanites, and it is with this pot-

Mycenaean IIIC:1b monochrome sherds from the first third of the twelfth century B.C.

tery that Trude Dothan believes we can associate the first historical mention of the Philistines in the twelfth-century Egyptian records of Pharaoh Ramesses III.[2]

Ekron peaked as a political and geographical center during the eleventh century B.C. This was the century during which David grew from of his obscure youthful activities to become Israel's second and most important king. The ruins of Ekron reveal a well-planned settlement of buildings from this period, and perhaps even a governor's residence or temple complex. This is also the layer where a great deal of evidence of the cultic practices at Ekron surfaces. Rooms and implements most likely used in divining the will of the gods were recovered. Some of these artifacts may be traced back into the twelfth century, but clearly most date to the eleventh century. The quality of the distinctive Philistine artifacts deteriorated toward the end of that century, which is to say that, based on the evidence of the artifacts, the Philistines seem by that time to have adopted a great deal of Egyptian and Phoenician influence in their ceramics. Unlike the colorful pottery of the earlier years, many of the specimens found from the late eleventh century B.C. have a red slip.

Sometime around 1000 B.C. the city was attacked. The directors of the excavation, using biblical and Egyptian records, have con-

Twelfth-century B.C. Philistine bichrome pottery from Ashdod.

cluded that the attack was committed by either David or the Egyptians. For a couple of summers in the mid-1980s, the archaeologists on site talked about the tenth through eighth centuries B.C. as "missing," due to a lack of material remains dating to this period. Presently, it is believed that after the attack by either David or the Egyptians, Ekron was largely abandoned.

The fifty-acre site likely had been reduced to little more than ten inhabited acres; the large, fortified urban center apparently had become a small, unfortified settlement. Occupation evidence during this time can be found only on the acropolis of the tell. For the next 270 years, to about 700 B.C., there appears to have been little change. It was during this time, circa 850 B.C. when Ekron covered only ten acres, that King Ahab's son Ahaziah challenged the prophet Elijah by attempting to consult Baal-zebub, the god of Ekron, about a personal injury (2 Kings 1).

An interesting development occurred during the summer dig of 1984 in the acropolis section of the tell. Directors Trude Dothan and Sy Gitin, encouraged aggressively by staff geoarchaeologist Arlene Rosen, wanted to examine the ground directly below and to the side of the mound to determine what the eroded soil from the past contained. A backhoe was brought in and positioned in the cotton field below and about thirty meters east of the current probes. It wasn't long before the backhoe struck a huge section of finely cut ashlar masonry. The walls of the trench made by the backhoe were trimmed, and Dothan and Gitin began their work determining to which period this unexpectedly discovered wall several meters below the tell belonged.

At first it was postulated to be a Late Bronze fortification belonging to the Canaanites who had inhabited the site prior to the Philistines. A difficulty with this theory may be that no other Palestinian sites dating to this period, circa 1200 B.C., have been found with Late Bronze fortification walls. The excavation summary report prepared that fall stated tentatively that this was a Middle Bronze wall of the first half of the second millennium B.C. (T. Dothan and Gitin 1985, 68).

Digging sessions of 1985 and 1986 saw this area extensively excavated. But during the 1986 session the archaeologists encountered a major physical difficulty. The wadi, Nahal Timnah, just yards away from the tell (see map, p. 35), was affecting the digging. The deeper the archaeologists dug, the wetter the soil became, and finally they encountered mainly water. Bilge pumps were started up, but the water seeped in as fast as it could be pumped out. The ashlar masonry threatened to slide down into the trenches, endangering the workers. Digging had to be halted before the base of the wall was reached.

Nonetheless, as indicated in the photo on page 172, a seven-meter-tall mudbrick tower faced with large blocks of ashlar masonry was uncovered. In addition, there was sufficient evidence to suggest that the tower and the wall dated to the "missing" tenth century B.C. The settlement of Ekron had evidently continued in this upper acropolis corner of the mound. Apparently, the water table of 1986 was significantly higher than the water table of the tenth century B.C. Subsequent excavating during the following summers has brought to light the perimeters of this tenth-century B.C., ten-acre city and the discovery that in antiquity this site was at least four meters higher than it is at present.

Whether Ekron was destroyed by King David or by the Egyptians, it afterward remained a settlement covering considerably less than its previous fifty acres. Nothing there changed much physically or archaeologically through most of the eighth century B.C., to the time when Israel fell victim to the Assyrian invasions.

Olive press room as it might have looked when Ekron was known as a production center for olive oil.

The Old Testament records predictions by the prophets of the impending fall of Israel to the Assyrians and the travail that was to be suffered by Judah, as well as repeated reminders that the Philistines too would become subject to Assyria. Surprisingly, the artifacts found in the tell dating to the end of the eighth century B.C. indicate that being subject to the Assyrians meant growth and prosperity for the inhabitants of Ekron. The city grew beyond its former size of fifty acres and again was found to have a huge surrounding defensive wall. Remains of this wall have been discovered in several parts of the tell.

The end of the eighth century through the seventh century B.C. was the period during which Ekron developed its reputation as a producer of olive oil. Twentieth-century engineers have estimated, based on the number of installations uncovered, that Ekron's olive oil production could have been upwards of one thousand tons, or 290,000 gallons in a season. This would equal 20 percent of Israel's olive oil production for export today (Gitin 1990, 39).

The seventh-century B.C. city that lies just a few inches beneath the excavator's spade is the Ekron cited in the Assyrian texts, in Kings and Chronicles, and in the writings of Amos, Jeremiah, and Zephaniah. The combined evidence of the contemporary literature and especially the Assyrian texts, the more than one hundred olive oil installations already uncovered at the site, and the hundreds of textile loom weights found demonstrates incontestably that Ekron prospered under the rule of the Assyrian empire. These Assyrians remained in control of Philistia until approximately 630 B.C.

Interestingly, thirteen four-horned altars have also been uncovered at the site thus far. Typologically, it has been hypothesized that these altars were made by Israelite craftsmen. We shall see that the discovery of these altars is a physical reminder of the prophesies of Jeremiah and Zephaniah predicting the fate of Philistia and Judah.

Historical writings contemporary to Amos and other latter prophets give evidence that Egypt was partially in control of this area until the Babylonian king Nebuchadnezzar swept through—perhaps involved in destroying Ekron himself. Zechariah's last words against Philistia, specifically mentioning Ekron in 9:5–7, appear to be the final written reference to the city found in the biblical texts. What follows in the literature is a conspicuous silence which may very well reflect what excavation of the site has made obvious: the city was for the most part abandoned at the end of the seventh century B.C. and remained largely uninhabited. Except for oblique references in the

Four-horned altar uncovered at Ekron.

literature of Roman and Byzantine times, Ekron and the Philistines disappeared twenty-five hundred years ago. They have gone the way of the Jebusites of Jerusalem, as predicted in the writings of Zephaniah and Zechariah. To where, only God knows.

> Seek the LORD, all you humble of the land,
>   who do his commands;
> seek righteousness, seek humility;
>   perhaps you may be hidden on the day of the LORD's wrath.
> For Gaza shall be deserted,
>   and Ashkelon shall become a desolation;
> Ashdod's people shall be driven out at noon,
>   and Ekron shall be uprooted.
> [Zeph. 2:3–4]

> . . . and I will make an end of the pride of Philistia.
>   I will take away its blood from its mouth,
> and its abominations from between its teeth;
>   it too shall be a remnant for our God;
>   it shall be like a clan in Judah,
>   and Ekron shall be like the Jebusites.
> [Zech. 9:6b–7]

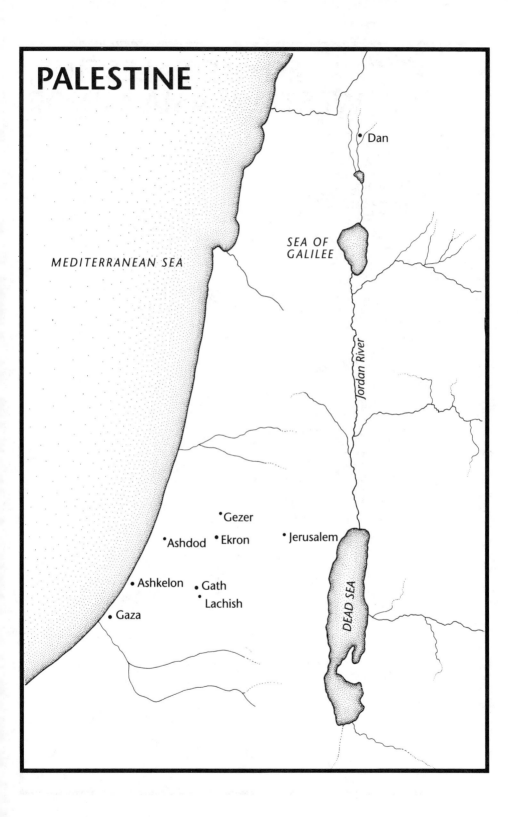

PALESTINE

MEDITERRANEAN SEA

SEA OF GALILEE

Jordan River

• Dan

• Gezer

• Ashdod • Ekron

• Jerusalem

• Ashkelon • Gath

• Lachish

• Gaza

DEAD SEA

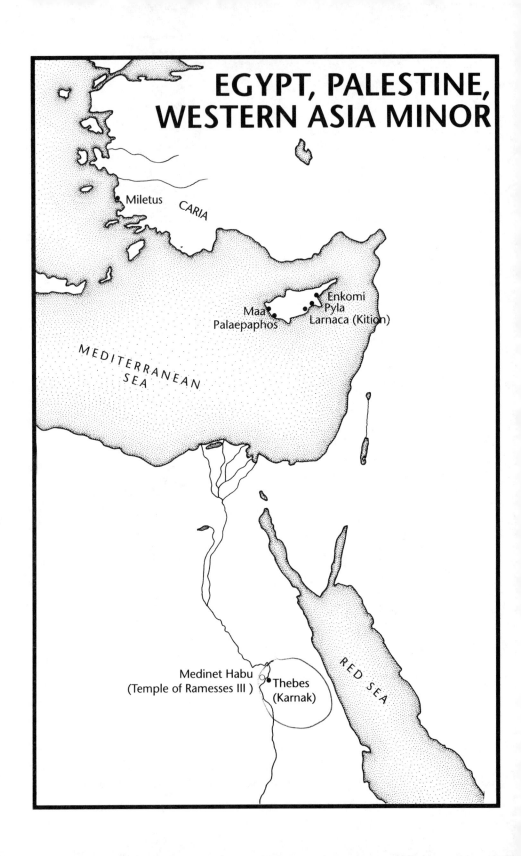

EGYPT, PALESTINE, WESTERN ASIA MINOR

Miletus

CARIA

Enkomi
Pyla
Maa
Palaepaphos
Larnaca (Kition)

MEDITERRANEAN
SEA

RED SEA

Medinet Habu
(Temple of Ramesses III)
Thebes
(Karnak)

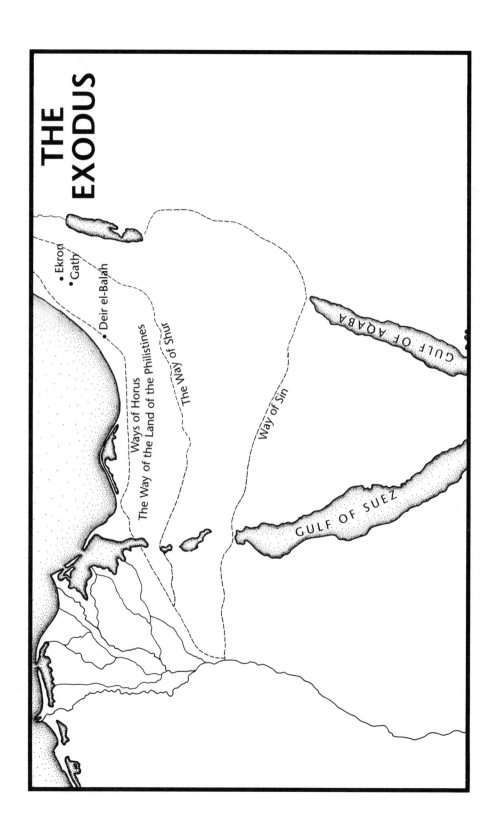

THE
EXODUS

Ekron
Gath
Deir el-Balah

Ways of Horus
The Way of the Land of the Philistines
The Way of Shur

Way of Sin

GULF OF AQABA

GULF OF SUEZ

3

The Origins of the Philistines

Attacks on Egypt[1]

Most of the biblical stories that mention the Philistines are found in the Old Testament books of Judges and 1 Samuel. Who were these enigmatic people? Where did they come from? Were the biblical Philistines related to the Sea People invaders mentioned in the Egyptian histories of the period? Some Egyptian court records of the twelfth century B.C. mention the Philistines specifically as part of a group of invaders from the sea who were repulsed and then were settled in Canaan. Were the Egyptians referring to the same people we read about in Judges and 1 Samuel?

These questions will be addressed by first examining the Egyptian records concerning the Sea People invaders to see if we can determine from them the origins of the Philistines. After having done so, we will look at the intriguing plague account in 1 Samuel 5 and 6 and compare it with a parallel account in the *Iliad*, book 1. The ritual ascribed to the Philistines in the 1 Samuel account may provide another clue to their origins. In addition, our investigation will lead us to the Aegean, to Anatolia, to Egypt, and to Cyprus to examine ancient Near Eastern literature and archaeological remains.

According to the Egyptians, the Philistines were just one tribe of a confederation of tribes who invaded Egypt and settled on the coastal plain south of Mount Carmel. They evidently became the dominant group in this confederation, because the writers of the Old Testament seem to use the word *Philistine* as a generic term to describe all the people who were moving onto the coastal plain at the time that the Israelites were carving a niche for themselves in the hill country of Canaan under Joshua and the succeeding judges.

The Egyptians tell of two great movements against them of people scholars have dubbed "the Sea Peoples." The Egyptians themselves do not use the phrase *Sea Peoples*, however, nor do they have a single generic name for all of the invaders, as found in the Bible. Instead, they refer to the invaders as "foreigners from the sea" coming from the "northern countries" or "their islands" beyond the sea, that is, the Mediterranean. The first invasion, recorded at Karnak in Upper Egypt, was in the fifth year of Pharaoh Merneptah, during the final third of the thirteenth century B.C. (See pp. 90–91 for an explanation of this dating.) The Karnak record lists five specific groups as part of that invasion (Barnett 1975, 366–69):

	Other spelling/ pronunciation
1. A-qi-ya-wa-sa/ A-qi-wa-sa/ Ekwesh ('-k-w'-s')	
2. Ta-ru-sa (Tw-rw-s'/ Tw-ry-s')	Tursha
3. Rw-ku (Rw-kw)	
4. Sa-ra-d-n/ Sa-ar-di-na (S'-r'd-n)	Sherden
5. Sa-k(a)-ru-su (s'-r'-rw-s')	Sheklesh

Not all scholars agree about the relationships that exist between these names and known sociopolitical groups or places, but let us focus on the more popular, probable, and accepted associations. The first name is generally linked to the Homeric Achaeans, the second to the Trojans, the third to the Lukka/Lycians of southwest Anatolia, the fourth to settlers from Sardis in western Anatolia who moved to the area of Akko north of Mount Carmel and eventually to Sardinia in Italy, and the fifth to the Sheklesh who may have moved later to Sicily. This Karnak list does not include the Philistines, who are named some forty years later in a record of a second attack on Egypt.[2]

This second attack of the Sea Peoples by land and sea occurred during the reign of Pharaoh Ramesses III, years five and eight, around 1175 B.C. The battle scenes and names of the invaders are recorded at Medinet Habu, near Thebes in Upper Egypt (Pritchard 1969, hereafter *ANET*, 262):

		Other spelling/ pronunciation
1.	Pe-ra-sa-ta/ Peleset (Pw-r-s-ty)	Philistine
2.	Tjikar (T-k-k[-r])	Tjekker
3.	Sa-k(a)-ru-su	Sheklesh
4.	Danuna (D-y-n-yw-n)	Danaoi
5.	Wasasa (W-s-s)	Weshesh

The first on the list are the Philistines; the second are the Tjekker, who may have settled on Cyprus at the end of the thirteenth century B.C. and who later settled in Dor, south of Mount Carmel on the Palestinian coast, according to a late twelfth- and an eleventh-century B.C. Egyptian document; the third are also in the Merneptah list and are the only ones to be mentioned in two records; the fourth are the Homeric Danaans; and the fifth possibly are Carians of western Anatolia.[3] All the Sea Peoples, according to Albright, came from the Aegean orbit (1975, 508). At Medinet Habu the Philistines and the names of the other Sea Peoples occur together, probably because the Egyptians knew them to be related geographically. The following words on the walls at Medinet Habu attest to the Sea People alliance:

> . . . The foreign countries made a *conspiracy* in their islands. All at once the lands were removed and scattered in the fray. No land could stand before their arms, from Hatti, Kode, Carchemish, Arzawa, and Alashiya on. . . . They were coming forward toward Egypt, while the flame was prepared before them. Their confederation was the Philistines, Tjeker, Shekelesh, Denye(n), and Weshesh, lands united. They laid their hands upon the lands as far as the circuit of the earth, their hearts confident and trusting: "Our plans will succeed!" [*ANET*, 262]

The reliefs on the temple walls at Medinet Habu give us excellent portrayals of civilian and combatant dress, weaponry, ships, chariots, wagons to move people and supplies, and military tactics. This

Drawing of a relief showing Ramesses III battling the land forces of the Sea Peoples.

Detail of an ox-drawn cart from the relief.

Detail of a chariot.

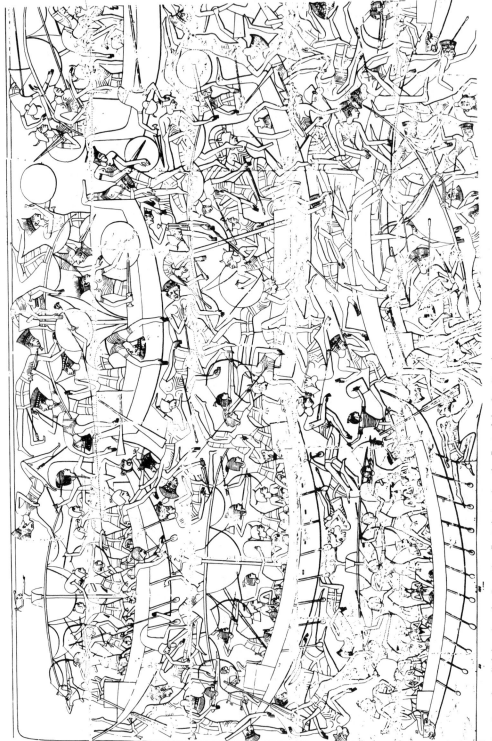

Drawing of a relief showing the Egyptian fleet destroying the fleet of the Sea Peoples.

Detail of an ox cart.

Ramesses III presents captives of the Sea Peoples to Amuon and Mut (here and p. 58, top).

Ramesses III presenting Libyan and Sea People captives to the Theban Triad.

depiction of the Sea Peoples has much in common with descriptions of the Aegean peoples from other sources.[4] For example, the Philistines at Medinet Habu are pictured wearing "feathered head-dresses" very similar to those pictured on the Phaistos Disk, a round, baked clay disk discovered on Crete at Phaistos and dated to the Middle Minoan IIIB period, circa 1600 B.C. The disk was found with a tablet inscribed with Linear A, which is the earliest form of writing found on Crete and is not yet deciphered. The clay and firing of the disk are not similar to what is generally found on Crete; it is possibly an import from Caria or Lycia in southwest Anatolia (Barnett 1975, 362–63; Pendlebury 1965, 170).

The Phaistos Disk, which depicts Lycian or Carian warriors with feathered helmets similar to those worn by the Philistines.

The feathered headdresses, according to Herodotus and a late Assyrian text, are typical of Caria and Lycia during the Bronze Age. Later, the same style of headdress is also worn by "Ionian and Karian warriors in an Assyrian relief, and by a Lycian contingent in Xerxes' fleet" (Burn 1930, 143). Herodotus states that "the Greeks are indebted to them [Carians] for three inventions: fitting crests on helmets, putting devices on shields, and making shields with handles" (Rieu 1954, 82). The *Iliad*, however, does not describe a feathered helmet similar to that of the Sea Peoples, though it describes various other types of helmets.

The feathered headdress also appears on a ceramic, anthropoid coffin uncovered at Beth-shean in Israel. The coffin may date to approximately 1040 B.C., roughly the time of King Saul's reign and his death in the area by Philistine hands (T. Dothan 1982a, 274–76). According to 1 Samuel 31:10, Saul's body was hung by the Philistines at Beth-

Anthropoid coffin found at Beth-shean; the feathered headdress resembles those of the Sea Peoples.

shean. Anthropoid coffins have been found at other sites associated with Egyptian rule in both Egypt and Canaan. In addition, feathered headdresses appear on Sea People warriors pictured on a twelfth-century ivory game box and on a conical seal from Cyprus. The distinctive feathered headdress clearly seems to belong to the Sea Peoples, the Philistines in particular.

In addition to showing feathered headdresses, the Phaistos Disk links Crete and Anatolia in other ways. The disk also pictures beehive-type structures (probably huts), which have features similar to those of Lycian architecture in southwest Anatolia. As well as mentioning the huts, Pendlebury cites the type of bow pictured on the disk as having an Asiatic origin (1965, 170). He believes that Anatolia played an important role on Crete in both the Early Minoan (before 2000 B.C.) and Middle Minoan (ca. 1800 B.C.) periods (1965, 53, 121–22). Nearly five hundred years separate the Phaistos Disk and the Egyptian reliefs at Medinet Habu (T. Dothan 1982a, 13), pointing to long-standing ties between Crete and Anatolia.

Other arms pictured at Medinet Habu, such as long, tapered swords, spears, javelins, shields, and corselets, are similar to those described in the *Iliad* (Wainwright 1956, 203). "It will be noted that in spite of differences in detail, the general resemblance of the Achaean equipment to that of the Shardena and Pulesati [Philistines] is marked" (Lorimer 1950, 201). Further, the ships of the Sea Peoples at Medinet Habu and on the Phaistos Disk are similar to those shown on a Mycenaean Greek vase found on Skyros, an island in the Aegean between Athens and Anatolia (Raban and Stieglitz 1991, 38–39; T. Dothan 1982a, 7, 11; Barnett 1975, 373). The kilts worn by the Philistines at Medinet Habu also have Anatolian affinities: "such a tasselled kilt is worn by a Southern Anatolian god on a stele from near Cagdin" (Barnett 1975, 372). In addition, the chariots of the Sea Peoples contain three men with spears, following the Hittite, rather than the Egyptian custom of only two men with bows. Also, the wagons and hump oxen of the Sea Peoples pictured on the reliefs are strictly Anatolian (T. Dothan 1982a, 5–13; A. Mazar 1990, 302–6; Sandars 1978, 121–31; Yadin 1963, 2:249–51).

The scholars referred to above make numerous other comparisons between the Sea Peoples pictured on the Medinet Habu reliefs and the Greeks from the Mycenaean and Anatolian world. These comparisons of modes of dress, weapons, and means of travel cannot be considered as conclusive evidence that the Sea Peoples, of which the Philistines were a part, were from the Aegean and from Anatolia, since these various modes could have been adopted through travel and trade. However, any study of these characteristics will reveal that the Sea People, including the Philistines, have much in common with the Mycenaean world and with Anatolia, especially the west and southwest sector.

As Ramesses III prepared for battle, according to the reliefs at Medinet Habu, he stated, "the Peleset (Pw-[r']-s'-t) are hung up, [—] in their towns . . ." (Breasted 1906, 4:41). It would appear that some of the Peleset/Philistines were in Palestine even before Ramesses III defeated them. Perhaps some of the Sea Peoples had settled at a few sites in Canaan as conquerors or as Egyptian mercenaries, and due to a problem with them, Ramesses III put down their towns (Albright 1975, 511; Stiebing 1980, 14). It is possible that there was a pre-Ramesses III settlement of Sea Peoples at Ekron, according to T. Dothan, but not at Ashkelon, according to Stager (see pp. 97–101). Ramesses III used his warships, troops, and chariotry to overpower the invasion on both land and sea:

Those who reached my frontier, their seed is not, their heart and their soul are finished forever and ever. Those who came forward together on the sea, the full flame was in front of them. . . . They were dragged in, enclosed, and prostrated on the beach, killed, and made into heaps. . . . [*ANET*, 262–63]

. . . The northern countries quivered in their bodies, the Philistines, Tjekk[er, and . . .]. They cut off their (own) land and were coming . . . on land; another (group) was on the sea. [*ANET*, 263]

Ramesses III boasted that he not only defeated the Peoples of the Sea, but also forced them to settle in citadels in what today we call Palestine or Israel (see also B. Wood 1991, 44–52, 89–90).

I extended all the frontiers of Egypt and overthrew those who had attacked them from their (lxxvi 7) lands. I slew the Denyen in their islands, while the Tjeker and the Philistines were made ashes. The Sherden and the Weshesh of the Sea were made nonexistent, captured all together and brought in captivity to Egypt like the sands of the shore. I settled them in strongholds, bound in my name. Their military classes were as numerous as hundred-thousands. I assigned portions for them all with clothing and provisions from the treasuries and granaries every year. [*ANET*, 262]

Ramesses even recorded that the vanquished Peleset/Philistines said to him, "Give us the breath for our nostrils thou King, son of Amon" (Sandars 1978, 132). That is to say that, according to Ramesses, the Philistines recognized him as a god, for the gods give life, give breath.

The reign of Ramesses III at the beginning of the twelfth century coincided with the period of the judges in the Bible. Ramesses boasted that he settled the Peoples of the Sea in Palestine, and their presence there is also noted in another Egyptian document, the Onomasticon of Amenope, which dates to the end of the twelfth century. This document lists the Sea Peoples living in Canaan within the Egyptian sphere of influence: the Sherden, the Tjekker, and the Philistines. It also mentions the Philistine cities on the coast: Ashkelon, Ashdod, and Gaza. These cities were on the Egyptian line of defense, according to the Egyptian record. As will be detailed in later chapters, the material culture of the Philistines at Ashdod, Ekron, and other sites clearly displays Egyptian influence, corroborating the written evidence (A. Mazar 1990, 305; T. Dothan 1982a, 3–4; 1982b, 26).

Two earlier lists, which have not yet been mentioned, are also significant to our study: first, the list from Pharaoh Ramesses II of the

Hittite allies that fought against him and, second, the Hittite list of the Assuwa League of allies (in western Anatolia) who struggled against them.

Pharaoh Ramesses II fought against the Hittite king Hattusili III at Kadesh of the Orontes in northern Syria around 1285 B.C. He recorded the names of the Hittite allies who opposed him; among them are the following: 1) Pi-da-sa, 2) Da-ar-d(a)-an-ya, 3) Ma-sa, 4) Qa-r(a)-qi-sa, 5) Ru-ka, and 6) Arzawa. The first name has been associated with Pedasos in Mysia of the Troad south of Troy, the second with the Dardanoi of the Troad, the third with southwest Anatolia, the fourth with Caria, the fifth with Lukka/Lycia, and the sixth with Arzawa in western Anatolia (Barnett 1975, 359–62; Breasted 1906, 3:123ff.; Gardiner 1961, 262ff.).

The Assuwa League was defeated by the Hittites around 1250 B.C. It had been formed to fight against the collapsing Hittite empire. The list of its members contains the names of twenty-two allies from western Anatolia. Three of these names are immediately familiar: Luqqa (Lycia), Ta-ru-i-sa (Troy), and Karkija (Caria). Also mentioned are Wilusiya (Ilios) and Warsiya (Lycia) (Albright 1950, 169; Gurney 1952, 56–58; Stubbings 1975, 349–50). A few years after the defeat of the Assuwa League by the Hittite king Tudhaliya IV, Lycia, Caria, and possibly a few others showed up among the Trojan allies fighting against the Achaeans, according to the *Iliad*.

There is some disagreement among scholars about the identities of the members of the Assuwa League. Garstang and Gurney agree that Wilusiya is probably Ilios (Troy) and that Warsiya may be associated with Lukka (Lycia). However, they do not equate Luqqa with Lukka (Lycia), for that would put the Assuwa League both north and south of Arzawa, in west central Anatolia. For them, the Assuwa League was strictly in northwest Anatolia, stretching north of Arzawa to the Troad (1959, 105–7). It should also be noted that Homer in the *Iliad* seems to refer to two Lycias. In book 2.876–77 and book 5.479, Sarpedon is a leader of the Lycians from "distant Lycia" by the river Xanthus in southwest Anatolia. Pandarus is another leader of Lycians, but they are from the region of the Anatolian Mount Ida near Troy (2.824ff. and 5.105, Rieu 1950, 61, 95). Lycians are also mentioned in the royal Egyptian Amarna letters of the fourteenth century B.C. as raiders of Alashiya (Cyprus or parts of it) and Egypt; the king of Alashiya is said to have sent out ships to watch for their approach.

List	Name	Identification	Possible Locale	
Ramesses II ca. 1285 B.C.	Pi-da-sa	Padasian	Western Anatolia	
	Da-ar-d(a)-an-ya	Dardanian		
	Ma-sa	SW Anatolian		
	Qa-r (a)-qi-sa	Carian		
	Ru-ka	Lycian		
	Arzawa			
Assuwa League ca. 1250 B.C.	Lukka	Lycian	Western Anatolia	
	Wilusiya	Ilian		
	Karkija	Carian		
	Warsiya	Lycian		
	Ta-ru-i-sa	Trojan		Achaeans/ Danaans against Troy and allies ca. 1225 B.C.
			Western Anatolia	Dardanian Lycian Phrgian Pelasgian Mysian Carian Maionian
Merneptah ca. 1215 B.C.	A-qi-wa-sa			
	A-qi-wa-sa			
	Ta-ru-sa			
	Rw-ku			
	Sa-ar-di-na	Achaean		
	Sa-ra-d-n			
	Sa-k (a)-ru-su	Trojan Lycian	Aegean and Western Anatolia	
Ramesses III ca. 1175 B.C.	Sa-k (a)-ru-su	Sherden		
	Pe-ra-sa-ta			
	Peleset	Sheklesh		
	Tjikar			
	Tjikal	Sheklesh Philistine		
	Danuna			
	Wasasa	Tjekker	Aegean and Anatolia	
		Danaan Carian		

The chart on page 64 demonstrates how names on the Egyptian and Hittite lists just described compare with the Trojan and the Achaean groups and allies named in the *Iliad*. Note especially the similarities between the names of the Sea Peoples, on Ramesses III's and Merneptah's lists, and of the allies of the Trojans. Most Near Eastern scholars agree that the Sea Peoples came from the Aegean-Anatolian orbit (Stiebing 1980, 14). As can be seen from the list of Ramesses III, the Egyptians considered the Philistines to be one of these invading Sea Peoples. It appears then that the Philistines can be associated with the Trojans of western Anatolia and with the Achaeans. The best areas to search for the specific point of origin of the Philistines seem to be western Anatolia, Crete, and the Greek peninsula in the locale of Athens and Mycenae.

The Near East of the thirteenth and twelfth centuries B.C. witnessed the decline and near collapse of the Egyptian and Hittite empires. The Aegean world was also in turmoil. Countless cities besides Troy were sacked, and the Sea Peoples migrated as a result of the economic, environmental, social, and political upheaval in the Aegean at this time (Stiebing 1980, 15). Greek writers such as Aeschylus, Euripides, Herodotus, and Thucydides spoke along with Homer of the revolutions and ferment of the thirteenth century B.C., which, as we have seen, seem to have provided the momentum for the Sea Peoples' attacks on Egypt.

> The late return of the Greeks from Troy caused many revolutions, and factions ensued almost everywhere; and it was the citizens thus driven into exile who founded the cities. [He cites examples in Greece, Ionia, the islands, and Italy] . . . many years had to elapse before Greece could attain to a durable tranquillity undisturbed by *migrations* [emphasis mine]. . . . All these places were founded subsequent to the war with Troy. [Thuc. 1.12 (Livingstone 1972, 40)]

Locating the Biblical Caphtor[5]

Are there passages in the Bible which contribute to the search for the origins of the Philistines? Origins of peoples is not a focus of the Bible, but Genesis 10 with its "Table of Nations" is a unique document and gives us a starting point. The Philistines are named and linked in verses 13 and 14 to Egypt and a place called Caphtor: "Mizraim [Egypt] begot . . . the Pathrusim, the Casluhim, and the Caphtorim, from whom the Philistines descended" (Speiser 1964, 64, 68–69; see also NRSV). The list linking Egypt to the

Caphtorim/Philistines might not indicate Philistine filial relationship with Egypt, but it could refer to a geographical relationship. The Israelites were familiar with the Philistines on the coastal plain to the west; therefore, this information was added to inform the reader that the Philistines, associated with the Egyptians, were originally from Caphtor.

The reason the Anchor Bible Commentary (Speiser 1964) and the New Revised Standard Version placed the phrase "from whom the Philistines descended" *after* the word *Caphtorim*, differing from the Revised Standard Version and the New International Version, is that both Jeremiah 47:4 and Amos 9:7 make it clear that the Philistines are from Caphtor (see also Bromiley 1979, hereafter *ISBE*, 1:610).

> Ah, Yahweh will destroy the Philistines,
> Last leavings of Caphtor's isle.
> [Jer. 47:4 (Bright 1980, (1980, 309)]

> Did I not bring Israel up from the land of Egypt,
> and the Philistines from Caphtor? . . .
> [Amos 9:7]

It is also interesting to note here that the Philistines are not listed with the pre-Israelite nations in Canaan in Abraham's time (Gen. 15:19–21). If the text reflects a tradition that goes back to the Mosaic period, this is logical to expect, since the Philistines were not "settled" by Pharaoh Ramesses III on the coast of southern Canaan before the time of Moses.

Therefore, if the Caphtorim were the ancestors of the Philistines (Stiebing 1980, 14) and the Philistines of Medinet Habu did not arrive in Canaan before the time of Ramesses III, then Deuteronomy 2:23 may also give us an approximate time for the coming of the Philistines into Canaan. There, Moses reviews the chronology of events after leaving Egypt and states, "As for the Avvim, who had lived in settlements in the vicinity of Gaza, the Caphtorim, who came from Caphtor, destroyed them and settled in their place." Moses does not use the term *Philistines*, though Joshua does. The southern coast of Canaan, including Gaza, is the territory Joshua associated with the Philistines. The passage from Deuteronomy 2 supports Joshua 13:2–3, which clarifies the boundaries of the Philistine territory yet to be conquered, territory which formerly belonged to the Avvites, who were Canaanite: "This is the land that remains: all the regions of the Philistines and Geshurites: from the

Shihor River on the east of Egypt to the territory of Ekron on the north, all of it counted as Canaanite (the territory of the five Philistine rulers in Gaza, Ashdod, Ashkelon, Gath and Ekron—that of the Avvites) . . . " (NIV).

Part of the same territory is also said to be home to the Cherethites or Cretans (1 Sam. 30:14 and Stiebing 1980, 14), who with the Pelethites became David's personal, professional Philistine military force. The Cherethites/Cretans and the Philistines are linked in Ezekiel 25:15–17 and in Zephaniah 2:4–7 in the prophecies against Philistia. The name Pelethite may be an adaptation of the name Philistine (*ISBE* 1:610; 3:736–37; Douglas 1962, 207–8); if so, then we have another link between Caphtor/Crete and the Philistines.

Let us look further at the Cherethites, who composed part of David's bodyguard. First Samuel 30:14 speaks of the "Negeb of the Cherethites/Cretans." It is easy to see from the Hebrew why scholars equate Cherethite with Cretan. Cherethite is *kereti*. Hebrew script is consonantal, and notice that *kereti* has the same consonants as in the name Crete (McCarter 1980, 435; Albright 1975, 512; Stiebing 1989, 175–76). One biblical reference to the Cherethites though, 2 Samuel 20:23, reads *kari* rather than *kereti*; therefore, this reference could be translated as *Carians* rather than *Cherethites*. However, it may be concluded that at least some of the Philistines/Sea Peoples came from Crete.

As we have seen, the coastal area of Canaan became home to Caphtorites, Cherethites (Cretans), Pelethites, Carians, and others (Gittites of Gath, for example, who will be discussed later). Somehow the Philistines, who appeared in the Egyptian records early in the twelfth century, seem to have absorbed the others and become the dominant force, since the Bible refers primarily to Philistines (Albright 1975, 511). A similar example of a mixture of peoples being called by one name comes out of the exodus from Egypt, when Israel was joined by "rabble" (Num. 11:4), making it a "mixed crowd" (Exod. 12:38) with "aliens" (Josh. 8:35). The entire group came to be called Israel or the Israelites, since the descendants of Jacob were dominant. This, I believe, is true for the Philistines as well.

Most biblical scholars agree that the location for Caphtor is the island of Crete and its environs.[6] During the first half of the second millennium B.C., Crete evidently controlled much of the Aegean and its coastline, which included western Anatolia, and traded throughout the region. During parts of the second half of this millennium, the Late Bronze Age, Crete was controlled by the Mycenaean Greeks of mainland Greece; this lasted up to the thirteenth century B.C. when Knossos, the major city on Crete, was destroyed, as were numerous cities in the Aegean. The Mycenaean Greeks not only controlled or traded with Crete and western Anatolia, but also had extensive trade with the entire eastern Mediterranean, including the area along the coast south of Mount Carmel, which came to be known as Philistia by the twelfth century B.C.

On the northern coast of Canaan opposite the island of Cyprus lie the ruins of Ugarit, a city-state destroyed about the time that the Sea Peoples were moving through the area towards Egypt. From these ruins a text was found speaking of a ship from "Kapturi." Another text from Ugarit speaks of a place called "Kptr," but no specific location is given in either case. However, Egyptian records of the Late Bronze Age speak clearly of four localities on Crete or "Keftiu" (Kftyw), which could also be translated "Caphtor" in the Egyptian language (T. Dothan 1982a, 13, 21, and footnotes; Stiebing 1989, 175). There is almost universal agreement that the Egyptian "Kftyw" refers to Crete (Macqueen 1986, 162 n. 30).[7] We have noted that the Bible says the Philistines came from Caphtor, which, when examined with other biblical passages, appears to be Crete. It would be reasonable to conclude that extrabiblical sources, too, seem to equate Caphtor with Crete.

No doubt, as the Bible states, some of the Philistines had their origins in Caphtor/Crete. However, remember that in our examination of the Egyptian records for the Sea People invaders, during the reigns of Merneptah (ca. 1215 B.C.) and Ramesses III (ca. 1185 B.C.), we noted an Aegean—and especially a western Anatolian—origin for the invaders. In order to determine the heritage of the people the Bible refers to as the Philistines, I believe that we must expand the scope of our search beyond Crete to encompass the entire Aegean. With a further examination of biblical and extrabiblical material, I believe that we are even able to place part of this "Philistine" confederation on the Troad at the time of the Trojan War in the thirteenth century B.C.

A coalition of five city-states and their lords like that of the Philistines (Gaza, Ashkelon, Ashdod, Gath, and Ekron) was common to Bronze Age Greece, and such a coalition is evident in the *Iliad* (2.484ff., Lattimore 1951). The Bible uses the word *seranim* or its singular form *seren* twenty-one times for the lords or rulers of the five Philistine cities (e.g., 1 Sam. 5:8; 6:4, 16–18). This word appears to have been borrowed from the Philistines and may be related to the Greek word *tyranos* (tyrant) (T. Dothan 1982a, 18–19; A. Mazar 1990, 306; Achtemeier 1985, 790; *ISBE* 3:842; Buttrick 1962, 3:792). In reading the plague story of 1 Samuel 5 and 6, as well as the account of the Philistine lords disagreeing among themselves and telling Achish to send David back to Ziklag (1 Sam. 29), it becomes clear that no one lord had absolute power over military affairs. This is analogous to the situation in the *Iliad* where Agamemnon was the overlord of the kings of the other city-states, yet Achilles could oppose him vehemently with impunity (1.121–87, Rieu 1950; M. Wood 1986, 145).

The names Achish and Goliath are not Semitic, and parallels to these names may be found on Crete and in western Anatolia (Achtemeier 1985, 790; Buttrick 1962, 3:792; Albright 1975, 513). The biblical Achish may have had the same name as the Dardanian Anchises, the father of Aeneas from the Troad (Buttrick 1962, 3:792; T. Dothan 1982a, 22–23; Wainwright 1959, 77). The Dardanians were also on the list by Ramesses II of Hittite allies (see p. 64). Some sources, when discussing the origins of the Philistine names in the Bible, will mention the Luwian language. The Luwian language, according to extrabiblical material, was used in western Anatolia in the Late Bronze Age, the end of which witnessed the movement of the Sea Peoples (A. Mazar 1990, 306; Mendenhall 1973, 107; Barnett 1975, 440). Among the people who spoke Luwian were the Lukka/Lycians, mentioned in ancient lists (p. 64) as Hittite allies, as Trojan allies, and later as one group among the Sea Peoples who invaded Egypt (Barnett 1975, 440–41; Stiebing 1989, 176).

We presently possess few examples of Philistine writing, but some tablets, associated with Philistine pottery, were found at Deir Alla in the Jordan Valley. The script has not yet been deciphered, but it is believed by some scholars to be related to scripts used in the Aegean. They point specifically to a Cretan script called Linear A, which has a "purely phonetic syllabary, analogous to the Cypriot and in part to the *Carian* [emphasis mine]" (Albright 1975, 510; see also Stieglitz 1982a, 31 with picture, and Raban and Stieglitz 1991, 40).[8] George Mendenhall suggests that the tablets are closer to the western Anatolian language Luwian (1973, 161).[9]

The Phaistos Disk mentioned earlier was found on Crete but may have been an import from Caria in southwest Anatolia. Miletus, in Caria, may have been settled first by Cretans, then taken over by the Mycenaeans. According to the *Iliad*, Miletus was in Carian hands by the time of the Trojan War (2.867–68, Rieu 1950, 62; Cook 1975, 794–95; Huxley 1960, 13–14). The ties of the biblical Philistines to Crete and western Anatolia seem to be strong.

Further, the Cretans had definite associations with the allies of the Trojans (the Carians and the Lycians), and these allies were later among the Sea Peoples. Crete had also sent a contingent to Troy as an ally to the opposing Achaeans (*Iliad* 2.645–52, Lattimore 1951; Stubbings 1975, 349). There is even a legend that Troy was settled by Cretans.

The chart on page 64 demonstrates that some of the peoples listed were associated with one another for more than one hundred years, and this association included the Achaeans, who entered the scene along with the Sea Peoples. The "Philistines," as named in the Bible and discussed above, had more than just a passing acquaintance with Crete, the Troad, and western Anatolia; we must conclude that they originated in these regions.

An additional clue concerning the origins of the Sea Peoples may be available from an examination of rectangular chamber tombs at Tell el-Far‘ah in southern Israel (Waldbaum 1966, 332–40; T. Dothan 1982a, 260f., 294; A. Mazar 1990, 300, 326–27; B. Wood 1991, 51–52). This site is located about fourteen miles south of Gaza and around sixteen miles west of Beersheba on the trade route linking Egypt and Mesopotamia (Negev 1986, 137). Jane Waldbaum presents a case for relating these tombs to Mycenaean chamber tombs at Mycenae and other Mycenaean areas. There are two different series of tombs at Tell el-Far‘ah relevant to our study. The first is the group of tombs from cemetery 900, which is dated to the Late Bronze Age/Iron Age IA in the late thirteenth and early twelfth century B.C. The artifacts in these tombs date from the Ramesses II period down to Ramesses IV. Waldbaum ascribes the cemetery 900 tombs to an earlier wave of Sea Peoples who may have become Egyptian mercenaries stationed at Tell el-Far‘ah. This is possible, since the Sheklesh (Sa-k(a)-ru-su), mentioned both in the Merneptah and Ramesses III lists as invaders, were also mercenaries *on the side of* Ramesses III in his battle against the Sea People invaders. The Sheklesh already had been mercenaries for the Egyptians in the time of Ramesses II in the thirteenth century B.C. Waldbaum states that these rectangular chamber tombs "lend strong support to the theory that the Philistines had more than casual connections with Mycenaean civilizations" (1966, 332).[10]

The second series of tombs is in cemetery 500 and dates to the second half of the twelfth and into the eleventh century. Philistine grave goods are plentiful in these tombs, which also contain anthropoid coffins. The Aegean origin of those buried in the tombs is clear based on the tomb architecture and the artifacts (T. Dothan 1985, 171). Therefore, Waldbaum's study of the Tell el-Far'ah cemeteries also brings the Philistine origins into the Aegean orbit.

The Plague on the Philistines

It is known from Egyptian records that the attacks on the Egyptians by the Sea Peoples from the Aegean occurred during the second half of the thirteenth century and the first half of the twelfth century B.C. Again, in the Bible this is the period of the judges, which ends with Samuel in the eleventh century. Our examination of the Bible thus far has concentrated on specific verses and words which have helped answer our questions about who the Philistines were and where they came from. The Bible also contains a story which can be used to examine the relationship between the Philistines, the Aegean, and western Anatolia and even suggests that some of the Philistine forebears may have been Mycenaean Greeks present on the plains of Troy in that classic battle for Troy between the Achaeans and the Trojans in the second half of the thirteenth century B.C.

First Samuel 4–6 records the capture of the ark of the covenant by the Philistines due to the incorrect assumption on the part of the Israelites that taking the ark into battle guaranteed the presence of God on their side. The Lord God of Israel caused great consternation and death by means of a plague among the Philistines while the ark was in their hands, and so the Philistine lords joined together to plan how to return the ark to Israel. The ritual used by the Philistines to return the ark in 1 Samuel 6 has an older and parallel account in the *Iliad*, book 1, and to a lesser extent, is similar to a Hittite/Arzawan ritual. I believe that the similarities between the ritual used in the *Iliad*, book 1, and the ritual used later by the Philistines in 1 Samuel 6 provide us with evidence that some of the biblical Philistines were Achaean. It is logical to assume that the Sea Peoples, when they migrated from the Aegean and from western Anatolia and the plains of Ilium to Egypt and Palestine, carried with them the stories and rituals of their culture.

71

1 Samuel 5–6	The *Iliad,* book 1
1. The Philistines hold the ark of God, a trophy of war. (5:1ff.)	1. The Achaeans hold the daughter of Chryses, a priest of Apollo Smintheus. (lines 10ff.)
2. Yahweh sends a deadly plague upon the Philistines as a penalty. (5:6, 9, 11–12).	2. With his arrows Apollo inflicts a deadly plague on the Achaeans. (lines 10, 44ff.)
3. An assembly of the people and the Philistine chiefs is called in each city. (5:7–8, 10–11)	3. An assembly of the troops and chiefs is called. (lines 54ff.)
4. The Philistines call for the priests and diviners. (6:2)	4. The Achaeans call for a prophet or priest, or even an interpreter of dreams. (lines 62ff.)
5. They determine that the ark must be returned with "guilt offerings." (6:3ff.)	5. They determine that the daughter must be returned with "holy offerings." (lines 92ff.)
6. Gold models are made of the tumors and mice/rats. (6:4ff.)	6. Apollo is here called Smintheus, the mouse god. (line 39)
7. The oxen carrying the ark and the offerings are driven towards the land of the enemy. (6:7–12)	7. Oxen for the offering are placed on board ship because Chryses lives on an island. (lines 308–10)
8. The Philistine chiefs follow the ark. (6:12–16)	8. A chief and a select crew are chosen to accompany the daughter. (lines 141ff., 309ff.)
9. Upon arrival, the oxen are sacrificed. (6:14)	9. Upon arrival, the oxen are sacrificed. (lines 446ff.)

The parallel accounts are listed in the order they occur in their narratives.

Some biblical commentators see two separate afflictions recorded in the Samuel account: a plague of boils or tumors and a plague of mice or rats. The Philistines themselves may have seen two disconnected afflictions, not associating the rats with the tumors. However, since boils are a symptom of the bubonic plague and the plague is frequently carried by the fleas on rats, most authorities identify what is described in 1 Samuel as the bubonic plague, a malady endemic to the Near East during this Late Bronze/Iron period (Gaster and Frazer 1969, 452; Mendenhall 1973, 107). By making golden models of the rats and sending them away out of their cities with the ark, the Philistines were reacting to the plague from Yahweh with a practice standard in the worship of their own gods (Gaster and Frazer 1969, 452; Wainwright 1959, 77–78).

Absent from the *Iliad* account is the driving of the oxen on the road. However, even if this were part of their ritual, the Achaeans would have been prevented from carrying it out, since the priest of Apollo Smintheus, whom they had offended, lived on the island of Tenedos, off the coast of Anatolia southwest of Troy, and it was to this island that the girl had to be returned along with holy offerings. They did, however, put cattle for an offering on board the ship to Tenedos.

East of the Troad lived the Hittites who, during the Late Bronze Age, developed an empire that rivaled Egypt. Among the religious rituals that the Hittites used to rid themselves of the plague was one of driving animals down the road away from the community:

> These are the words of Uhha-muwas, the Arzawa man. If people are dying in the country and if some enemy god has caused that, I act as follows:
> They drive up one ram. . . . They drive the ram onto the road leading to the enemy and while doing so they speak as follows: "Whatever god of the enemy land has caused this plague—see! We have now driven up this crowned ram to pacify thee, O god! Just as the herd is strong, but keeps peace with the ram, do thou, the god who has caused this plague, keep peace with the Hatti [Hittite] land! In favor turn again toward the Hatti land!" They drive that one crowned ram toward the enemy. [*ANET*, 347]

In performing this ritual the Hittites followed the advice of an Arzawan priest. Arzawa was a political entity and was already a rival of the Hittites beginning early in the sixteenth century B.C. Arzawa continued to be a rival throughout the Late Bronze Age, obliging the Hittite kings to repeatedly campaign against it. At times Arzawa was independent, and we know from a fourteenth-century B.C. letter addressed to the king of Arzawa that an Arzawan daughter was given in marriage to the pharaoh of Egypt (Mercer 1939, 1:183–85).

Arzawa, south of Troy, apparently included the area where Ephesus is located (Macqueen 1986, 37–39; M. Wood 1986, 179–81) and was a neighbor of Caria and Lycia, one or the other of whom is mentioned in every list on the chart on page 64. It became an ally of its rival the Hittite empire against Egypt (Barnett 1975, 360). Because Arzawa, Lycia, and Caria used the same or similar Luwian dialects (Gurney 1952, 130; Albright 1975, 513),[11] the possibility exists that the ritual of the Arzawans (and Hittites) could also have been an accepted ritual of the Carians and the Lycians, who were allies of the Trojans and were among the Sea Peoples that invaded Egypt.

Now let us return to the "mouse god" of the *Iliad* on the island of Tenedos. Apollo has numerous epithets, but in the *Iliad*, book 1, he is called Smintheus, the mouse god. Smintheus shrines have been found only in the northwest sector of Anatolia, one of the possible places of origin for the Philistines. "The chief shrine was at Chyrsa on the coast of the Troad . . . in which temple mice were kept, and in which a mouse was carved at the foot of the statue of Apollo. There was also a temple dedicated to Apollo Smintheus on nearby Tenedos, and here as Smintheus he was the ruling divinity" (R. Miller 1939, 34–35; M. Wood 1986, 234 has similar information).

Apollo also had a temple on Chios, a large island south of Troy, and there were sites with Smintheus as part of their name on the Troad south of Troy (Cook 1974, 37–40) and on the island of Rhodes. The island of Chios is directly off the coast of Izmir/Smyrna near Mount Sipylus, which is the region where George Mendenhall matches the word *Philistine* (Peleset) with a Greek dedicatory inscription (Mendenhall 1974). The area around Mount Sipylus was probably part of Arzawa, with the Carians and Lycians to the south. The Greek geographer Strabo (late first century B.C. to early first century A.D.) quotes the Greek poet Kallinos, who claimed that Troy was colonized by Cretans. Smintheus may be a Cretan word, though it has also been identified as western Anatolian (Mysian) (Leaf 1923, 240; R. Miller 1939, 35; M. Wood 1986, 180). The *nth* sound of Smintheus, according to A. R. Burn, is characteristic of Cretan, Carian, and southern Aegean (1930, 89). Whether the movement of culture and language was from Crete to western Anatolia or vice versa cannot be determined, and places in both regions sharing similar names are common and widespread. For example, Mount Ida in the Troad shares its name with the sacred mountain in Crete. Thus, many ties have been demonstrated between the Troad and Crete.

Presently there is not much archaeological evidence for Late Bronze and early Iron Age (fourteenth-eleventh centuries B.C.) settlements in western Anatolia, especially in the southwest, in Lycia and Caria (Cook 1974, 37–40). Too little archaeology has been done in this large area, and of what has been done, little seems to have been dug below the layers of the Classical Age. Another problem in excavating Lycia and other places in western Anatolia is the silting up of rivers along the Anatolian coast. Ephesus, a little further north, is a prime example of an area being buried in silt. Currently, the archaeological evidence is somewhat inconclusive as to precisely which sites in western Anatolia the biblical Philistines might have come from, but hopefully more work can be done in Turkey to match the extensive excavations in Israel.

Apollo Smintheus was recognized in the *Iliad*, book 1, as being the sender of and the averter of the plague, and the mouse symbol was used to counteract the force of the plague. The Philistines saw the Lord God of Israel as the sender of and the averter of the plague, and they made the models of the mice and tumors to appease this god. G. A. Wainwright, using Strabo, mentions that the Tjekker, one of the Sea Peoples accompanying the Philistines in the attack on Egypt (see p. 64), were from the Troad, where Apollo Smintheus was revered (1959, 77–78). It is certain that the Tjekker settled just north of the biblical Philistines at Dor on the coast on the Plain of Sharon south of Mount Carmel (Wainwright 1959, 78; Negev 1986, 118; M. Dothan 1989, 64). Wainwright would like to link David's Philistine city, Ziklag (1 Sam. 27, 30), with the Tjekker name, Zakkal (1959, 78).

Another epithet for Apollo was the "Lycian god" (*Iliad* 4.101, Rieu 1950, 79), and his mother, Leto, was also considered to have been from Lycia of southwest Anatolia. Apollo and the Semitic god Dagon, whom the biblical Philistines adopted, were both associated with agriculture (more about Dagon in chap. 4; see also 1 Sam. 5). In any case, it is unlikely that the biblical Philistines were unaware of Apollo Smintheus.

The plague account in 1 Samuel 5–6 follows the plague account in the *Iliad*, book 1, very closely, and we have found no other account that is similar to them. It is improbable that the two arose independently of each other. Rather than being only the result of transference by means of trade, this resemblance between the two accounts is probably a result of direct cultural transmission through the migration of the Sea Peoples from the Aegean world to Palestine. Archaeological and textual data—including Greek legends—show that Cretan, Mycenaean, and western Anatolian history are tightly interwoven in the Late Bronze Age of the fifteenth-thirteenth centuries B.C. In spite of this evidence, the paucity of recent excavated sites in western Anatolia that go back to the Late Bronze Age makes it difficult to state unequivocally that the biblical Philistines came from western Anatolia.

One major exception to this lack of archaeological excavation in western Turkey is Troy. It is to this site I wish to go next. I believe that the Trojan War was indicative of the upheavals in the latter half of the thirteenth century B.C. that led to the movement of the Sea Peoples through western Anatolia, Cyprus, and the east coast of the Mediterranean, and down into Egypt, where they were repulsed to settle in Canaan, later referred to as Palestine. We also know from the lists on page 64 that some of the Trojans' allies during the Trojan War were Sea Peoples. What then does the mound of Troy tell us about the events up to and following the legendary Trojan War?

Troy

"She has climbed the great Tower of Ilium."
[*Iliad* 6.386 (Rieu 1950, 127)]

"Cry, Trojans, cry! practise your eyes with tears!
    Troy must not be, nor goodly Ilion stand;
Our firebrand brother, Paris, burns us all.
    Cry, Trojans, cry! a Helen and a woe!
Cry, cry! Troy burns, or else let Helen go."
[Prophetic words of Cassandra in Shakespeare's *Troilus and Cressida*, act 2, sc. 2, lines 108–12]

Troy! A generation ago only a few students of the Bible would have imagined that the legendary battle on the plains around Troy would have any connection with the battles of the biblical judges and Saul and David with the Philistines. Today, due to instant transcontinental communication and jet travel, we say that the world is getting smaller. Now too, because of the refinements in archaeological method and the explosion in the number of excavations, we are beginning to realize that what were once thought of as different and distant worlds, the world of the Israelites and the world of the Aegean, clashed in the Valley of Elah with the contest between David and Goliath (1 Sam. 17).

One very important tool for archaeologists is pottery typology. Consider this: modern soda and beer containers have changed in composition, size, shape, label design, and how they open over the past century; we would be able to set up a bottle/can chronology, dating each piece according to its characteristics. The archaeologist is able to set up such a chronology with the pottery of the ancient world. Chapter 4 will detail how this chronology works, but suffice it to say for now that enough artifacts have been recovered at Sea People/Philistine sites on Cyprus and in Israel that archaeologists have been able to set up a chronology of their particular ceramic forms.

Before the ancient Near Eastern empires of the Hittites and the Egyptians broke up in the second half of the thirteenth century B.C., countless sites along the eastern Mediterranean coast traded ceramic forms referred to today as Mycenaean IIIB imports. This designation refers to ceramic vessels that were made in Mycenae or its environs and filled with goods to be traded throughout the Near East. These well-crafted, beautiful vessels are immediately identified by any veteran excavator. The thirteenth-century B.C. breakup of the empires in the Near East and Greece brought a halt to this far-reaching trade. All seasoned archaeologists excavating near the seacoast in Israel or on Cyprus look for an end to Mycenaean IIIB imports, signaling the break between the Late Bronze Age and the Iron Age. At numerous sites on Cyprus and in Israel, the pottery that follows this break is a locally made imitation of the imports and is referred to as monochrome Mycenaean IIIC:1b pottery. At a few sites in Israel, this locally made imitation pottery is followed by a bichrome "Philistine" pottery (see pp. 40–41 for details).

Since the 1930s scholarly debate about the mound of Troy has focused on which stratigraphic level of the mound holds the city of Priam and Hector. Is it the level known as Troy VI or the level known as VIIA? To answer this question, I have focused my research on the pottery. Can we find the same pottery sequence at Troy as on Cyprus and in Israel: the Mycenaean IIIB imports (which would cease presumably after the destruction of Troy by the Mycenaeans), followed by locally made IIIC:1b pottery?

The *Iliad* and the *Odyssey* make it very clear that there was trade between Troy and the Mycenaean cities in Greece. Helen was taken during one such trip to the Achaean mainland. Would the thirteenth-century Mycenaean IIIB pottery imports have ceased while the Mycenaeans were besieging Troy? If the city was sacked as Homer states and resettled by poor survivors, did the new inhabitants make the local Mycenaean IIIC pottery? These are the questions that need to be considered.

Beginning in 1870, the first excavator of Troy was the famed Heinrich Schliemann, followed by Wilhelm Dörpfeld. They both believed that Troy VI was the city that Homer wrote about, since it was "well built" and "finely towered" (Vermeule 1972, 275; M. Wood 1986, 113). Due to the findings of Carl Blegen's seven seasons at Troy from 1932–1938, several scholars of ancient Greek history

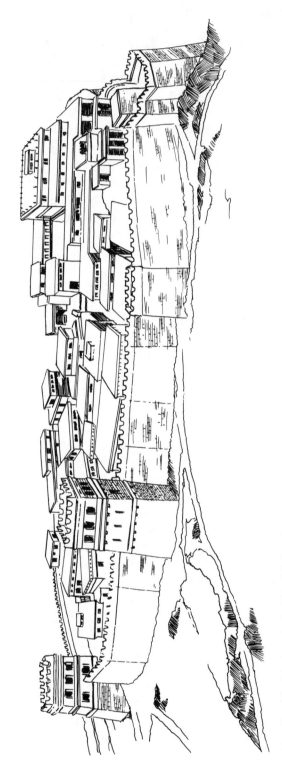

How Troy VI might have looked (ca. 1300 B.C.).

How Troy VI looks today.

came to believe that Troy VIIA was the Troy of Priam recounted in the *Iliad*. "Troy VIIa was then Priam's city, and VIIb 1 was built on its ruins by those who survived" (Desborough 1964, 164–65). "It [Troy VIIA] was smaller and more rubbly than before [Troy VI] . . . and in spite of its shoddy aspect is generally felt to be the city Homer sang about" (Vermeule 1972, 276; see also Chadwick 1976, 184–85). Blegen and those who came after him using his excavation reports recognized that Troy VI was a "great city." But they were troubled by the fact that Troy VI seemed to end around 1300 B.C. with an earthquake and by the fact that they saw no evidence of fire, counter to Homer's epic (Vermeule 1972, 273; see Cottrell 1963, 200ff. for Blegen's words). According to Vermeule, Troy VI could have witnessed the earlier raid by the Achaeans mentioned in the *Iliad*—the one led by Heracles, who raided not only Troy but went further inland as well, into Hittite territory (1972, 275–76; M. Wood 1986, 164).

When I first began my research about Troy in the 1960s, I too became convinced that Troy VIIA was Priam's city, in spite of the fact that it was Troy VI that had the "wide streets, beautiful walls and great gates just as the *Iliad* had told" (M. Wood 1986, 91). It was Troy VI that had the luxury goods. One holdout for Troy VI at that time, I remember, was O. R. Gurney, whose words about Troy VI as well as the evidence that the practice of cremation was widespread there, fit well with the demise of numerous heroes depicted in the *Iliad* (Gurney 1952, 168–69; M. Wood 1986, 168).

However, the pottery chronology that we utilize in our work in Israel made me reinvestigate my earlier conclusion. If Troy had Mycenaean imports, at which level did these imports end? Secondly, what type of pottery followed the imports? Blegen appears to agree to the *sequence* of pottery in our chronology, "but," he cautions, "to convert it into a specific year B.C. is another matter on which one finds no close agreement among the specialists" (1975, 163).

Imported Mycenaean pottery and other imported goods have been found throughout Troy VI (M. Wood 1986, 91). The luxury imports on this level other than ceramics are of such a quantity that Blegen, too, believed that trade of this extent implied a direct route between Mycenae and Troy. But such trade between Mycenae and other cities ceased around 1250 B.C. (M. Wood 1986, 164). Therefore, I agree with Blegen concerning the date for the demise of Priam's Troy—circa 1250 B.C.—but I believe that Priam's city was Troy VI, not VIIA (Blegen 1975, 163). Troy VIIA was, as Vermeule describes it, small, rubbly, and shoddy, with a shantytown, and as M. Wood states, it had "no imported luxuries, and few (if any) sherds from imported pots—*mainly poor imitations of Myceanaean wares* [emphasis mine]" (1986, 115). The shantytown, with its locally made Mycenaean imitations, fell around 1180 B.C. (M. Wood 1986, 224).

Wood goes on to answer the earthquake question posed by Blegen. Troy VIIA appears to have had no royalty. None of the great or royal houses appear to have been utilized in accordance with their original function, thus pointing to an earthquake destruction of Troy VI. In its weakened state Troy VI was attacked, its royal house was killed or enslaved, and the succeeding Troy VIIA became a squatter town. Wood also cites evidence that Troy VI was indeed burned, as the earlier excavator Dörpfeld documented (M. Wood 1986, 91). Weapons of war were recovered as well (M. Wood 1986, 227–28; see also Blegen's words on the fire in Troy VI in Cottrell 1963, 201). The dates of 1250 B.C. for the downfall of Troy VI and then 1180 B.C. for the destruction of Troy VIIA fit in well with the movement and destruction of the Sea Peoples as they migrated through western and southern Anatolia towards Cyprus and Egypt.

One further question about Troy VI is significant to this discussion. What did the Trojans trade? The *Iliad* mentions the horses of Troy, and the quantity of horse bones found in Troy VI bears witness to this. The extensive artifacts associated with textiles suggest another means of support. A third item of export seems to have been ceramics known as Grey Minyan ware, or Trojan ware (Blegen 1975, 161–63; M. Wood 1986, 165–66). This type of pottery was common throughout the region at the time; therefore, it is difficult to come to any definite conclusions about where it was produced. To my knowledge, neutron activation tests on it have not been completed. Grey Minyan ware/Trojan ware has been found at other sites in Palestine, Syria, and Cyprus, and we have recovered such sherds at Tel Miqne-Ekron dating to the second half of the thirteenth century B.C. This pottery will be discussed further in chapter 4 (M. Wood 1986, 71–72, 86–87, 165–66; Buchholz 1974, 175–87).

The Sackers of Cities

Already in book 1 of the *Iliad*, Achilles and Agamemnon argue over booty gathered while raiding and sacking cities. The sacking of cities for booty was not unusual during the Late Bronze Age; according to the *Iliad*, to be called a "Sacker of Cities" was evidently an honor (Tritsch 1974, 233–39; M. Wood 1986, 159–61). The *Odyssey* records the numerous adventures, wanderings, and sackings of cities throughout the Near East (including raids on Egypt) by Odysseus, as well as by other survivors of the Trojan War. If Troy VI was the city of Priam and Hector and the wanderings of Odysseus followed, then the destruction of Troy VI around 1250 B.C. would have happened just prior to the raids on Egypt against Pharaoh Merneptah. The Peoples of the Sea continued to sack cities.

However, there is a difference in the raiding and sacking at the end of the Bronze Age, circa 1200 B.C. About this time Israel was moving into the Promised Land in the hill country of Canaan, and large numbers of families from the Aegean were also on the move to their promised lands. Whereas earlier groups of men from the Sea Peoples had traveled as mercenaries for the Hittites or the Egyptians, at the end of the Bronze Age Sea People men were moving with their household goods and entire families. They were raiding not only for booty, but to establish new settlements. It was not just Troy VIIA, the squatter city that followed Troy VI, that was destroyed by the Sea Peoples; a number of major population centers throughout

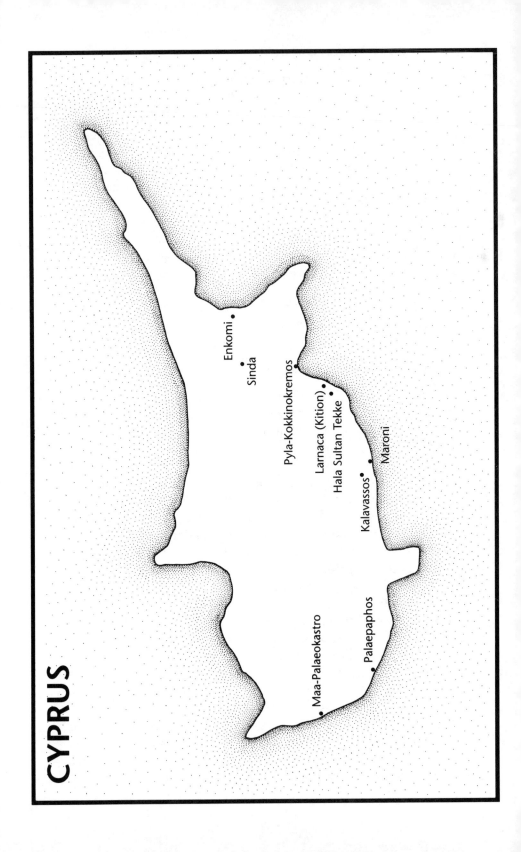

CYPRUS

Enkomi

Sinda

Pyla-Kokkinokremos

Larnaca (Kition)

Hala Sultan Tekke

Maroni

Kalavassos

Maa-Palaeokastro

Palaepaphos

Mycenaean Greece were devastated (Bright 1981, 115; Desborough 1964, 217–57; Stiebing 1980, 8; Vermeule 1972, 269–74; M. Wood 1986, 222–23). Knossos, on Crete, was sacked at some point during the thirteenth century B.C., but then the pace of destruction increased, and by the end of thirteenth or early twelfth century Mycenae, Thebes, Tiryns, and numerous other cities had been destroyed. The Hittite and Egyptian empires collapsed; that this was due solely to the Sea Peoples is doubtful, but both empires were definitely weakened by them. The Sea Peoples' path of destruction can be traced along the southern coast of Anatolia to Cyprus, to Syria, and then down the coast of Canaan to Egypt.

So by the beginning of the twelfth century, Troy and many Mycenaean city-states had been destroyed, and the survivors had moved on. From Troy, we will pick up the story of the Sea Peoples on Cyprus, for Cyprus apparently became a staging area for further moves of these people east and south and eventually into the Bible stories of Joshua, the judges, and others.

Cyprus, the Staging Area[12]

The descendants of Javan: . . . Kittim. . . . From these the coastland peoples spread.
[Gen. 10:4–5]

Cyprus has been mentioned repeatedly in our study thus far. Experts in ancient Near Eastern history do not dispute the theory that the Sea People invaders of the late thirteenth and early twelfth centuries mentioned in contemporary Egyptian texts were from western Anatolia and the Aegean. In order for them to have gotten to Egypt, they probably would have passed by or through the island of Cyprus in the eastern Mediterranean; therefore, that is a logical place to search for evidence of Sea People/Philistine activity.

In the Bible, Cyprus is first mentioned in Genesis 10:4–5 as Kittim (ISBE 3:45; Elwell 1988, 1:563). Here it is viewed as a staging area for the coastland peoples. The next scriptural reference to Kittim or Cyprus is found in Numbers 24:23–24. This passage is part of Balaam's final oracle, and in one translation of these verses (following Albright, in part), Balak finally receives satisfaction through Balaam's prediction that the Philistines (Kittim/Kition, explained below) would overpower the Hebrews (Eber) before they themselves would be subdued.

83

> Sea-peoples shall gather from the north;
>   and ships, from the district of Kittim.
> I look, and they shall afflict Eber;
>   but they too shall perish forever!
> [*ISBE* 3:45]

Eber is Abraham's ancestor, according to Genesis 10:21–25 and 11:14–26 (Achtemeier 1985, 233–34; Elwell 1988, 1:648). However, not all scholars are agreed that *Eber* equals *Hebrew* (Hebrew is consonantal, and both words have the same consonants). In Numbers 24 the word could mean simply "region beyond" (*ISBE* 2:8; Achtemeier 1985, 233–34). Nor are all scholars agreed that Numbers 24:24 refers to the Sea Peoples. If it does and if the dating of the Sea People/Philistine attacks in the Egyptian records of Pharaohs Merneptah and Ramesses III is applied here, an approximate date for the Numbers 24 passage could be established, since all translations of verse 24 read in the future tense: "But ships shall come from Kittim." In any case, Cyprus is described again here as a staging area, and it is believed widely that the Sea Peoples did depart from there for Canaan and Egypt beginning late in the thirteenth century B.C.

The island of Cyprus is only 43 miles from the shores of Anatolia to the north, 76 miles from the Syrian coast to the east, 264 miles from Egypt in the south, and 500 miles from Athens in the west. The Late Bronze Age, especially the fourteenth and thirteenth centuries, was a prosperous period for Cyprus. Crete had previously been using the island as a convenient trading stop when going to and from the Palestinian coast. Then, in the fourteenth century B.C., the Mycenaeans replaced the Cretans, probably due to the downfall of Knossos on Crete. Imported Mycenaean pottery has been found at numerous Late Bronze Age sites on Cyprus. But the island had another advantage besides its convenient geographic location—its abundant supply of copper. Copper plus tin are the major ingredients for bronze, and this was, after all, the Bronze Age. Cyprus became a focal point for trade going east and west between Greece and Mesopotamia and north and south between Anatolia and Egypt.

Shortly after the mid-thirteenth century B.C., Cyprus went through a drastic change because of the destruction of numerous centers in Mycenaean Greece and Anatolia, including Troy. Some of the survivors of those defeats moved on and evidently settled on Cyprus; others became plunderers throughout the region, according to records from Ugarit (Karageorghis 1984, 21), a major trading port on the Palestinian coast opposite Cyprus. In response, new settlements were constructed on Cyprus strictly for defensive purposes; among them were two sites named Pyla-Kokkinokremos (Pyla for short) and Maa-Palaeokastro (Maa for short) on the southeastern and western coasts. The artifacts that were uncovered at both sites, as well as the finely cut ashlar block masonry used for some of the construction, show that the builders and inhabitants were from Crete, Greece, and Anatolia. (Ashlar construction was known at Troy VI but not on mainland Greece. See also Raban and Stieglitz 1991, 37–38.) Both Pyla and Maa were destroyed in 1210 B.C. or shortly thereafter. Pyla had no good source of water, no agriculture. It existed strictly for military purposes, and after its 1210 destruction, the inhabitants did not return. They may have moved instead to Kition, seven miles away. Maa was resettled, and its pottery, Mycenaean IIIC:1b, gives us a clue about the new inhabitants. Following the familiar pattern, this pottery was locally made, imitating the Mycenaean pottery of the Greek mainland. Specimens of this local pottery were the first artifacts I picked up off the surface during my visit to Maa. After excavating Mycenaean IIIC:1b pottery for several seasons at Ekron in Israel, I was excited at finding identical pottery at this site on Cyprus.

According to Dr. Karageorghis, the excavator, both Pyla and Maa were military outposts originally built by invaders, possibly Sea Peoples, at previously uninhabited sites. Then after its 1210 B.C. destruction, Maa was inhabited by a new wave of Sea Peoples from the Peloponnese or the Greek islands off southwest Turkey, the Dodecanese. Dr. Karageorghis has concluded that these new invaders were Achaeans who were somehow related ethnically to the other Sea Peoples.

The Late Bronze Age on Cyprus had witnessed a great deal of trade and coexistence between peoples, including people from the Mycenaean orbit, until the mid-thirteenth century B.C. Other interesting finds which can be traced to the earlier mid-thirteenth-century wave of invaders at Pyla include a large amount of Late Minoan (Cretan) pottery as well as stone "horns of consecration" like those made famous at Knossos. Grey Minyan ware (Trojan ware) has also been recovered at various Cypriot sites, indicating contact with Anatolia.

The sequence of events at Maa and Pyla was apparently duplicated at Sinda and Enkomi, sites to the north of Pyla. The Sea People invaders often destroyed Late Bronze Age settlements on

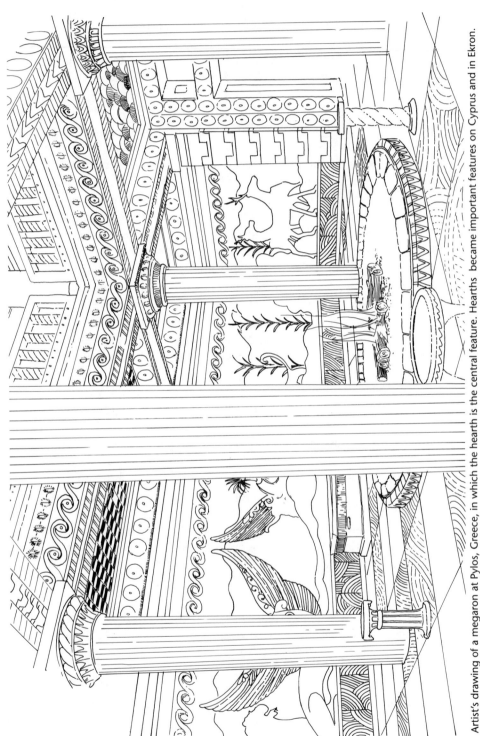

Artist's drawing of a megaron at Pylos, Greece, in which the hearth is the central feature. Hearths became important features on Cyprus and in Ekron.

Cyprus such as at Enkomi and Kition (called Larnaca today, but the old name may also be the source of the biblical Kittim; see Achtemeier 1985, 532–33), only to rebuild them utilizing ashlar block construction in part. The rebuilt defensive wall at Maa as well as other walls at Kition, Sinda, and Enkomi are sometimes called "Cyclopean," because they call to mind the great boulder walls in the Peloponnese at Mycenae and Tiryns.

There are two finds that provide a direct link between Cyprus and the Philistine Sea Peoples. The first is a stamp seal of the late thirteenth century, which was found sealed below a floor at the southern end of a megaron at Enkomi, a site that had been destroyed and rebuilt by the Sea Peoples. A megaron is an Aegean-style palace, a long building with a central hall, a hearth, side rooms, and an open-faced porch. The seal shows a warrior crouched behind a shield in a defensive position. The warrior's headgear includes the feathered headdress characteristic of the Philistine invaders of Egypt pictured on reliefs at Medinet Habu during the reign of Pharaoh Ramesses III. It is suggested that the seal represents an enemy invader, due to his unheroic pose behind the shield.

The other artifact, also from Enkomi and this time from a tomb, is a beautiful ivory game box. The rectangular box with legs holds the pieces needed to play the game. The side of the box has a hunting scene carved into it: The wheeled chariot depicted is pulled by horses and bears a charioteer and a hunter carrying a drawn bow. On foot are two men wearing the feathered headgear. One of these men is spearing an animal, and the other, standing behind the chariot, is bearing an ax. His headgear is very clear, as is his kilt with its pointed tassel. This second man especially resembles some of the Philistines who attacked Ramesses III early in the twelfth century B.C. The men on the seal and on the game box are all bearded. Whereas most of the Philistines pictured at Medinet Habu are clean-shaven, a few of them are bearded.

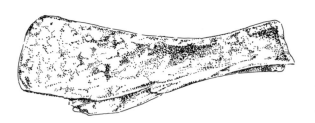

Bovine scapula which may have been used to foretell the future.

In addition, bovine scapulae, both incised and non-incised, have been found at Tel Miqne-Ekron in Israel. Such scapulae have also been found at Kition and elsewhere on Cyprus, in the stratigraphic context of Late Cypriot IIIA (1225 B.C. and later). Scapulomancy is a divination technique that may have been used on Cyprus (Webb 1986), whereby priests tried to determine future events by studying the natural features of bovine shoulder blades. The incisions or notches must have played a role, since the incisions present on some of the scapulae at Ekron and on Cyprus appear not to have occurred naturally, but to have been cut into the bone. However, their purpose is not known. Scapulomancy was practiced elsewhere in the Mediterranean basin, but at present it is impossible to explain how or if these incised scapulae were used in cultic practices on Cyprus and at Ekron. There are other possible explanations for the presence of numbers of bovine scapulae. Oxen were common sacrificial animals on Cyprus, and of course the Old Testament also specifies the ox as one of the sacrificial animals to be used by the Israelites (e.g., Exod. 20:24; 24:5).

To summarize, Sea People settlers came to Cyprus (Maa, Pyla, Sinda, Enkomi, Kition, and other sites) late in the thirteenth century B.C., after the Trojan War, from Crete, Greece, and Anatolia. At the end of the thirteenth and the beginning of the twelfth centuries more Sea People settlers arrived, this time Achaeans from the Peloponnese or from the islands off western Anatolia, according to Dr. Karageorghis, and one of their distinguishing features was their Mycenaean IIIC:1b pottery, made locally. Mycenaean IIIB imports ceased, and the new Sea Peoples evidently became the ruling class at Enkomi, Kition, and other sites. As will be demonstrated in later chapters, the sequence of events on Cyprus was reflected in findings about the Philistine sites in Canaan. Cyprus seems to have been the bridge between the Aegean and Canaan. The presence of the Sea Peoples is evident at various sites on Cyprus, and from these sites they launched their attacks on the Eastern Mediterranean coast and down into Egypt, to be repulsed first by Pharaoh Merneptah and finally by Ramesses III.

4

The Philistines
from Joshua to David

The Way of the Philistines

When Pharaoh let the people go, God did not lead them
by way of the land of the Philistines, although that was
nearer. . . .
[Exod. 13:17]

The stage has been set. We have looked briefly at the biblical references to the Philistines. We have also looked briefly at the archaeological record of Tel Miqne-Ekron, one of the five major Philistine cities
mentioned in the Bible. We have examined the possible origins of the
"Sea Peoples," a diverse and extensive collection of tribes which likely
included the group we know today as the Philistines, and we have
seen that they came from Greece, Crete, and western Anatolia. In this
chapter we will utilize the archaeological records of Tel Miqne-Ekron
as well as those of other Philistine sites along the eastern coast of the
Mediterranean, and, in conjunction with data from ancient Egypt and
the Aegean, we will develop a chronological record of events that
allows us a better understanding of the social and religious life of
God's people Israel in its encounters with the Philistines.

We begin this study at the end of the Late Bronze Age and the
beginning of the early Iron Age. The traditional date for this transition is 1200 B.C., but period shifts are of their very nature gradual.

The various dig sites in an extended basin frequently indicate a gradual shift, and the dig results throughout the Eastern Mediterranean support this fact. The history of this area during the Late Bronze Age was full of momentous events. The last half of the thirteenth century B.C. witnessed the collapse of the Hittite empire in Anatolia, the Trojan War, the collapse of Aegean civilization and culture at numerous Greek mainland and island sites, and the end of Egypt's domination over Syro-Palestine.

This collapse of the dominant powers allowed for the maritime migration of various ethnic groups out of the Aegean to travel, plunder, trade, and settle along the Anatolian coast and in Cyprus, Syria, Palestine, and Egypt. The material remains uncovered in excavations on Cyprus and along the coast of Syria and Palestine indicate not just a destruction level in many sites, but also evidence of a new people moving in to establish new cultures. For example, along the southern coast of Canaan, there is no mistaking the new "Philistine" pottery for the earlier Canaanite pottery of the Late Bronze Age. At the various dig sites a sequence of cultures is seen, as well as an overlap of Aegean, Canaanite, Egyptian, and Israelite cultures. Although this study focuses on the Philistines, who settled primarily south of modern Tel Aviv to the Negeb and from the Mediterranean to the mountains of Judea, it is important to realize that there are sites within this area that were not affected by the Philistines and their culture. While it is not possible to establish an "absolute" chronology of events—even when considering Egyptian historical records that list the various pharaohs and their actions against the Sea Peoples and the Canaanites—"low" and "high" Egyptian chronologies have been developed upon which archaeologists generally agree. The two chronologies differ by only about fifteen years.

The chart below includes the Egyptian rulers most relevant to our study of the Philistines and other Sea Peoples.[1]

	High Chronology	Low Chronology
Merneptah	1224–1214 B.C.	1212–1202 B.C.
(Queen) Tausert	1209–1200	1193–1185
Ramesses III	1198–1166	1182–1151

Figure 1 incorporates the chronologies with the dating of the stratigraphic levels of the digs at various sites. The identification of the bulk of the finds at each level is indicated by the shaded bars.

Figure 1. Comparative chronology of the emergence of Philistine culture in Palestine.

(Adapted from T. Dothan 1989, 8. Also Kelm and Mazar 1982, 4; 1989, 41; Oren 1982, 41; Oren 1982, 163–66; Seger 1984, 50–51; Stager 1991a, 35.)

Low Chronology	1185	1175			1070		
High Chronology	1200	1191			1085		
Egyptian Dynasties	XIX	yr. 8 Ramesses III	XX		XXI		
Ekron	VIIIB VIIIA	VII	VIC	VIB	VIA	V	IV
Ashdod	XIV	XIIIB	XIIIA	XII		XI	X
Qasile				XII		XI	X
Sera'	X		IX	∘Ramesses III?			VIII
Halif	VIII	VII					
Gezer	XV		XIV	XIII	XII		XI
Timnah	VI		∘Ramesses III		V		
Ashkelon							

Legend:

- LB (Canaanite/Mycenaean)
- Mycenaean IIIC:1b
- Egyptian
- Philistine
- Local Tradition
- Not Occupied
- * Scarab
- • Other artifact

There are clearly two locally made pottery types associated with the Philistines, the monochrome Mycenaean IIIC:1b and the later Philistine bichrome ware. Some scholars, such as T. Dothan, refer to two waves of migrating Sea Peoples beginning in the second half of the thirteenth century B.C., with the Philistines coming in the second wave early in the twelfth century (during the reign of Pharaoh Ramesses III). According to this theory, the first wave of invaders made the monochrome Mycenaean IIIC:1b pottery, and the second wave made the bichrome pottery, which replaced the monochrome. Other scholars, such as Stager, speculate that there was one basic group of Philistines that moved into the area in the twelfth century (during the reign of Pharaoh Ramesses III); this group soon adapted its Mycenaean IIIC:1b pottery style to that encountered locally and developed the Philistine bichrome. All scholars, however, agree that the Philistines were on Canaan's seacoast by the middle of the twelfth century B.C.

The events surrounding the scriptural references to the Philistines and their first encounters with Israel in the Promised Land probably occurred shortly after the beginning of the twelfth century B.C. It was then that the Lord said to Joshua, "You are old and advanced in years. . . . This is the land that still remains: all the regions of the Philistines . . . " (Josh. 13:1–2).

In Exodus 13:17 we read that when Pharaoh let the Israelites go, they were not immediately led to the land of the Philistines, even though that land was nearest Egypt, for God is said to have thought, "If the people face war, they may change their minds and return to Egypt." Later, while at Mount Sinai, Israel was told that the borders of the Promised Land would be "from the Red Sea to the sea of the Philistines, and from the wilderness to the Euphrates" (Exod. 23:31).

The exodus is generally placed in the first half of the thirteenth century, during the reign of Ramesses II or earlier. To date, archaeologists have not found any evidence of Philistines living in Canaan prior to the turn of the twelfth century. Evidence for Sea Peoples, yes, but there is no record of a group of people called by the name Philistines until Ramesses III names and describes them at Medinet Habu. For this reason, some biblical scholars have concluded that this early reference in Exodus 13:17 to the Philistines is an anachronism. They believe the word *Philistine* is used in Exodus to speak to a later audience who by then knew this way into the Promised Land as the "Way of the Philistines."

Historical records inform us that the Egyptians knew this coastal artery leading to Canaan and Syria as the "Way of Horus." Fortunately, recent archaeological digging has uncovered material relevant to understanding the Exodus 13:17 passage. Digging has uncovered evidence of six fortresses on this route described in Exodus as the road through the Philistine country. The most dramatic of these finds is the fortress found at Deir el-Balah (T. Dothan 1982a and c). This site is located approximately seven miles south of Gaza and a scant mile east of the Mediterranean. For centuries the prevailing westerly winds have blown the beach sands there, creating dunes which long ago covered the settlement.

Extensively excavated in the 1970s and the early 1980s, this Gaza Strip town, Deir el-Balah, covers a large residence or palace that dates back to the mid-fourteenth century B.C., the Amarna period of Pharaoh Akhenaton. Superimposed on the large residence was a fortress with massive walls seven feet thick. This second structure and the artifacts it contained can be dated to the period of Pharaoh Seti I, the father of the great Ramesses II. Seti I recorded his achievements on the Temple of Amon at Karnak in Upper Egypt. The reliefs there also describe the Way of Horus and the fortresses built along this highway.

A reconstructed Philistine tomb with coffin at Kibbutz Revadim.

The pottery analysis at Deir el-Balah has led T. Dothan to conclude that the existence of this fortress continued through the reign of Ramesses II (ca. 1304–1237 B.C.), who is thought by many to have been the pharaoh of the exodus. In the sediment immediately above the fortress a settlement was found containing artisan quarters and an industrial area with kilns that probably were used to prepare clay burial coffins. The next higher layer proved to be a Philistine settlement containing numerous pits holding Philistine pottery. This was the layer immediately under the covering sand dune, which was over forty-five feet deep. The Philistine pottery in the top layer has been dated to the end of the twelfth or the beginning of the eleventh century B.C.

The most striking finds in this Deir el-Balah dig site were uncovered while excavating the cemetery, namely, anthropoid clay coffins with removable lids in the shape of heads. None of the heads pictured on these coffins, however, wore the feathered headdress of the Sea Peoples (see p. 59); their headgear was of an Egyptian style. Nonetheless, these Egyptian clay coffins, dated to the fourteenth-thirteenth centuries B.C., may have influenced later Philistine burial customs, as the Philistine settlement succeeded that of the Egyptian fortress built on the Way of Horus.

To date there are no Philistine burial sites positively identified as belonging to any one of the five chief Philistine cities mentioned in the Old Testament. Tel el-Far'ah, in southern Israel (see pp. 70–71), has numerous tombs in its cemetery 500 containing Philistine grave goods, and Beth-shean (see p. 163) has Philistine clay coffins. Because the clay coffins found at Deir el-Balah contained numerous Mycenaean and Cypriot pottery imports, T. Dothan would like to reexamine all the artifacts from its cemetery in order to study more precisely the cultural influences on the Philistines.

The Deir el-Balah site serves as an important link to understanding Exodus 13:17. The site confirms that the Egyptians of the fourteenth-thirteenth centuries B.C. had a string of fortresses on this route that they called the Way of Horus and that Exodus calls the "way of the land of the Philistines." First mentioned by Pharaoh Seti I (ca. 1316–1304), Deir el-Balah was possibly used later by Pharaoh Ramesses III as a location to settle the Philistines he conquered during the twelfth century B.C. The finding of forty anthropoid clay coffins holding artifacts from the Aegean world, Cyprus, and Canaan, as well as from Egypt, not only reflects the international flavor of the area, but also explains where the Philistines may have picked up the idea of using clay coffins like those found at Tell el-Far'ah in the Negeb and at Beth-shean.

The archaeology done at Deir el-Balah shows that Philistines were on the southern coast of Canaan in the twelfth century B.C. Their presence is even more evident archaeologically at the five sites mentioned in Joshua 13:2–3: "This is the land that still remains: all the regions of the Philistines . . . ; there are five rulers of the Philistines, those of Gaza, Ashdod, Ashkelon, Gath, and Ekron. . . ." Also, in the allotments of the Philistines given to Judah, Simeon, and Dan, we read of two additional cities that must be considered in this study: Timnah (Josh. 15:10; 19:43), which we will encounter later in the Samson stories, and Ziklag (Josh. 19:5), which was given to David by Achish, the king of Philistine Gath.

What the archaeological record says about these various sites is more than simply interesting, since the biblical record is at best ambiguous and at times confusing. In Joshua 13:6 we read, "I will myself drive them [the Philistines and other enemies] out from before the Israelites; only allot the land to Israel for an inheritance, as I have commanded you." And in Judges 1:18 we read, "Judah took Gaza with its territory, Ashkelon with its territory, and Ekron with its territory." Yet, the following verse states, ". . . but [Judah] could not drive out the inhabitants of the plain, because they had chariots of iron." Then, two chapters later, in Judges 3:1, 3, we read, "Now these are the nations that the LORD left to test all those in Israel who had no experience of any war in Canaan . . . : the five lords of the

Tell Ashkelon and its fortifications.

Philistines. . . ." What exactly happened on the coastal plain of Canaan and in the hills of Judea?

Due to the political situation, the Gaza Strip has not been excavated extensively since 1967. In fact, Tell Harube, which may be the biblical Gaza, has not been examined by archaeologists since 1922. Even in that year only a few soundings were done on the mound itself. Philistine pottery was found, but since both the excavation and the publication of the material have been incomplete, all that can be said currently is that the Philistines were present at the site.

The Ashkelon site on the coast north of Gaza is being worked today (Stager 1985b, 1986, 1987, 1991a). It is a huge site topped by impressive ruins left by the medieval crusaders. The debris layers there are up to forty-two feet deep. The Philistine layers have been exposed to any great extent only since 1985. In spite of the massive amount of debris present at Ashkelon, Philistine fortifications were finally uncovered there during the 1990 season. An impressive mud-brick tower, thirty-four feet by twenty feet, was revealed. This tower was part of the fortification system protecting a Philistine city of over one hundred fifty acres. (Jericho and Jerusalem in the same time period covered approximately thirteen acres each.) What had been found at the extensively excavated Ashdod site has now been found true for Ashkelon as well: the imported pottery from Greece (Mycenaean IIIB) was present exclusively during the Late Bronze Age and was followed by monochrome Mycenaean IIIC:1b, the locally made pottery.

The later monochrome pottery has been tested by neutron activation analysis. This analysis has confirmed that—as was true for Ashdod and Ekron in Israel and Enkomi, Kition, and other sites on Cyprus—local clays were used to make the IIIC:1b pots. For Stager, the excavator at Ashkelon, the presence of an abundance of locally made Mycenaean pottery marks the arrival of the Philistines on the East Mediterranean coast. This pottery is in turn followed by the classic Philistine bichrome variety.

This is the same pottery sequence found at most Philistine sites. However, Mycenaean IIIC:1b does not show up at Timnah nor at Tell Qasile (in modern Tel Aviv). A. Mazar, the excavator of both Timnah and Qasile, believes that the Philistines arrived at those sites later than they did at Ashdod, Ekron, and Ashkelon.

Quite naturally, the pottery sequence plays an important role in determining precisely when the Sea Peoples first arrived on the southern seacoast of Canaan. While nearly all scholars agree that this

occurred around the end of the thirteenth century B.C. or the beginning of the twelfth century, they do not agree about the exact date.
The Egyptian reliefs discussed in chapter 3 and the many excavated
Philistine artifacts are all major factors in attempting to date the stories of the judges and to understand Israel's encounters with the
Philistines. What happened at Ashkelon figures very importantly in
the argument.

Three Egyptian inscriptions need to be considered. First is the
stele inscription of Pharaoh Merneptah relating how he repulsed the
invasion of the Sea Peoples allied with the Libyans (*ANET,* 376–78)
in the fifth year of his reign (during the final quarter of the thirteenth
century). This was found alongside his list of invaders, which was
cited in chapter 3 (p. 64). Second, on the bottom of the same stele,
sometimes referred to as the "Israel Stele," is an inscription from
Merneptah that may allude to an earlier campaign into Canaan. This
inscription contains the only mention of the name Israel in Egyptian
writings of the period. That part of the Israel Stele reads:

> The princes, prostrated, say "Shalom";
>   None raises his head among the Nine Bows.
> Now that Tehenu has come to ruin, Hatti is pacified.
>   Canaan has been plundered into every sort of woe.
>   Ashkelon has been overcome.
>   Gezer has been captured.
>   Yano'am was made non-existent.
>   Israel is laid waste (and) his seed is not.
>   Hurru has become a widow because of Egypt.
> All lands have united themselves in peace.
> [Yurco 1990, 27; a similar translation can be found in *ANET*, 378]

The third inscription is a series of reliefs on a wall at Karnak in
Upper Egypt, which in the past had been credited to Merneptah's
father, Ramesses II, and to Merneptah's brother, Khaemwase.
Stager, in a detailed article, presents the case that Merneptah's cartouche (name), and not that of his father, was the original one mentioned in parts of the battle scene reliefs (1985b; Yurco 1990, with
pictures).

Stager believes that four of the battle scenes on the reliefs at
Karnak are likely to have originated with Merneptah rather than with
his predecessor, Ramesses II. He also argues that credit for the four
Merneptah battle scenes was later usurped by Merneptah's succes-
sors. In stating his conclusions, Stager focuses his attention on the
Ashkelon battle scene. He points out that in it the inhabitants of

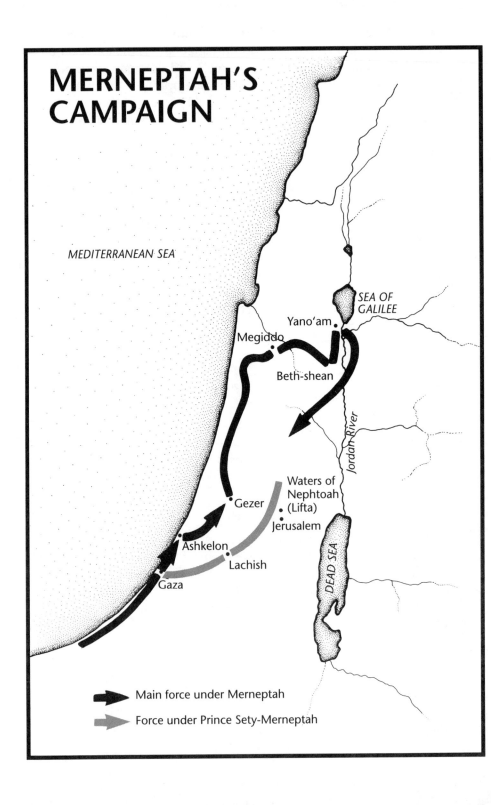

MERNEPTAH'S CAMPAIGN

MEDITERRANEAN SEA

SEA OF GALILEE

Yano'am

Megiddo

Beth-shean

Jordan River

Waters of
Nephtoah
(Lifta)

Gezer

Jerusalem

Ashkelon

DEAD SEA

Lachish

Gaza

→ Main force under Merneptah

→ Force under Prince Sety-Merneptah

Ashkelon, which is a named city on the relief, are dressed and armed as Canaanites, not as Sea Peoples. (We know the dress of the Sea Peoples from the later reliefs of Ramesses III at Medinet Habu.) In addition, these people at Ashkelon on the Karnak reliefs are seen to be besieged within their citadel high on a mound. The picture presented above the Ashkelon scene is the same, except for one major change—the besieged people being vanquished are missing both a mound and a fortress with walls. They are fighting, instead, in open, rolling countryside. Though the top part of this relief, where the mound or fortress could have been, is missing, Stager believes, after closely studying the battle scenes, that this particular enemy had no citadel (see also Yurco 1990, 27–32). The other two battle scenes at Karnak are similar to the Ashkelon scene, in which the besieged inhabitants are within their citadel on a mound. Stager concludes his article by arguing that the three citadels with mounds are those of Ashkelon, Gezer, and Yano'am, even though only Ashkelon is specifically named. He points out that the determinative that Egyptians regularly used on stelae for cities, countries, and provinces is syntactically feminine, and this is how the three cities are presented on the Israel Stele. The type of determinative usually used by Egyptian scribes for people without a fixed city is used for Israel. The linguistic gender of this determinative is masculine: "his seed is not" (Stager 1985b, 60–61; Yurco 1990, 28). Stager does not believe this to be a haphazard designation.

Using the reliefs at Karnak and the Israel Stele, Stager drives home his point that during the reign of Pharaoh Merneptah, Ashkelon (as well as Gezer and Yano'am) was a Canaanite city and not yet a city belonging to the Sea Peoples. If all four battle reliefs at Karnak are credited to Merneptah and correspond to the stele, then this conclusion by Stager (and Yurco) is obvious. In addition, if the enemy without the mound or fortress on the relief is indeed the Israel mentioned on the stele, that would constitute pictorial evidence for Israel's presence in Canaan by the end of the thirteenth century. The depiction on the relief also fits well with our conception of a non-urbanized Israel during the beginning years of the conquest (see Stager 1985b and Yurco 1990 for additional discussion on Israel). The main focus of the Israel Stele, however, is the attack on Egypt by the Libyans and their Sea People allies; therefore, the stele and the four battle reliefs at Karnak have important implications for dating the arrival of the Sea Peoples into Canaan. If Stager's evaluation is correct, Ashkelon clearly was still a Canaanite city during the reign of Merneptah.

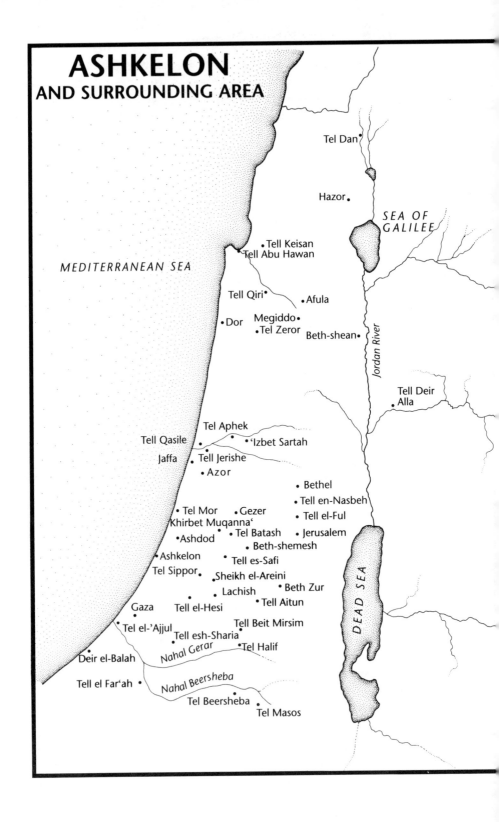

ASHKELON
AND SURROUNDING AREA

MEDITERRANEAN SEA

Tel Dan•

Hazor•

SEA OF GALILEE

• Tell Keisan
Tell Abu Hawan•

Tell Qiri•   • Afula

• Dor   Megiddo•
        • Tel Zeror   Beth-shean•

Jordan River

Tell Deir
Alla•

Tel Aphek
Tell Qasile•   •• 'Izbet Sartah
Jaffa • • Tell Jerishe
      • Azor

                    • Bethel
                    • Tell en-Nasbeh
• Tel Mor   • Gezer   • Tell el-Ful
•Khirbet Muqanna'
•Ashdod   • Tel Batash   • Jerusalem
            • Beth-shemesh
•Ashkelon
Tel Sippor•   • Tell es-Safi
        •Sheikh el-Areini
            • Beth Zur
          • Lachish   • Tell Aitun
Gaza•   Tell el-Hesi
    •   Tell Beit Mirsim
Tel el-'Ajjul•
        •Tell esh-Sharia
Deir el-Balah•   *Nahal Gerar*   •Tel Halif

Tell el Far'ah •   *Nahal Beersheba*
        Tel Beersheba•
            Tel Masos•

DEAD SEA

Keeping the pottery sequence and the reliefs in mind, we can propose a well-informed dating of the Sea Peoples' arrival at Ashkelon. If the imported Mycenaean IIIB ware was still used and in place there through the reign of Merneptah, and if Canaanites controlled Ashkelon during the fifth year of Merneptah, then the Sea Peoples could not have controlled the city before Ramesses III defeated them (ca. 1175 B.C.) and settled them in southern Canaan.

We do not have evidence of an early wave of Sea Peoples coming down and settling in Ashkelon before the attack on Egypt during Merneptah's reign, circa 1207 B.C. Stager is convinced that the Philistines arrived at Ashkelon a generation later, circa 1175 B.C., during the reign of Ramesses III. These people began to make Mycenaean-style pottery (IIIC:1b) from the local clays. It was still another generation later, circa 1150, according to Stager, before the inhabitants of Ashkelon made the classic Philistine bichrome pottery assimilating Egyptian, Canaanite, and other motifs. As will be demonstrated when we look at the archaeological evidence of Ashdod and Ekron, this arrival date of 1175 B.C. is twenty-five years or so later than archaeologists date the settlement of the Sea Peoples at those sites.

Israel's Test[2]

> Now these are the nations that the LORD left to test . . .
> Israel. . . .
> [Judg. 3:1]

Ashdod, according to Joshua 15:45–47, was allotted to Judah, but Ashdod is missing from the list in Judges 1:18 (except in the Septuagint) of the Philistine cities that Judah captured. Instead, Ashdod was probably one of the cities referred to in verse 19: "but [Judah] could not drive out the inhabitants of the plain, because they had chariots of iron." In any event, Israel could not effectively control any of the Philistine territories for very long, according to Judges 3:1, 3: "Now these are the nations that the LORD left to test all those in Israel . . . ; the five lords of the Philistines. . . ."

Ashdod was on the trade and military route to and from Egypt that also went through Ashkelon and Gaza. The city was not mentioned in Pharaoh Merneptah's inscription on the Israel Stele about his attack on Ashkelon, Gezer, and Yano'am. This may indicate that it, like Gaza (which was Egypt's headquarters for the area), remained loyal to Egypt; indeed, Ashdod's last Late Bronze stratum indicates that it was a Canaanite-Egyptian fortress at the time. Its Late Bronze

Ashdoda (twelfth century B.C.). Her decor is in the Philistine style, but the head may echo the Mycenaean "Great Mother" goddess.

city held local Canaanite pottery forms, imported Mycenaean IIIB and Cypriot pottery, a Ramesses II scarab and cartouches, and a stone doorpost with a hieroglyphic inscription possibly dating to the Ramesses II period or earlier. This Late Bronze stratum of the mound suffered destruction circa 1200 B.C., most likely due to the Sea Peoples; the destruction debris was up to 40 inches deep in places. Only parts of the mound were immediately resettled; other parts remained abandoned. At Ashdod the classic scenario for sites connected with the Sea Peoples—in this case, perhaps, the ones we will be naming the Philistines—is evident. Its Late Bronze inhabitants used imported Mycenaean IIIB pottery, which was replaced by locally made Mycenaean IIIC:1b pottery, which, in turn, was followed by the classic Philistine pottery.

The sequence is the same as cited earlier for Ashkelon, but the Ashdod excavator has a basic disagreement with the excavator of Ashkelon in interpreting the presence of Mycenaean IIIC:1b pottery. The excavator of Ashdod, Moshe Dothan, believes that, on the basis of the cultic artifacts, the pottery and its decorative styles, and the architecture, there were clearly two waves of migrating Sea Peoples: the first arriving circa 1200 B.C., after Pharaoh Ramesses II but before Ramesses III, and using locally made Mycenaean IIIC:1b pottery; and the second wave during the days of Ramesses III and using the classic Philistine pottery. Remember that Stager confirms the same pottery sequence at Ashkelon, but believes that no Sea Peoples/Philistines arrived at the site before the time of Ramesses III (ca. 1175 B.C.). I am convinced that Stager's conclusions about the four battle reliefs and Merneptah's stele are correct concerning the chronology of events—for Ashkelon, that is.

Before proceeding with the Ashdod site material, note the importance of what has been presented thus far in the verses from Joshua and Judges about the Philistines. According to Joshua 15 and Judges 1, the coastal plain was to belong to Israel, but if Israel ever conquered the Philistines there, it governed the area only for a short period of time. Remember, too, that, using the available archaeological data, we have seen that the Sea Peoples did not appear on the southern seacoast of Canaan until the twelfth century B.C. or, at the earliest, the very end of the thirteenth century.

At Ashdod, the transition from the people of the Late Bronze Age (imported Myc. IIIB pottery) to the Sea Peoples (locally made Myc. IIIC:1b pottery) was not a smooth one, as the deep destruction layer displays. However, the transition from the Sea Peoples with the Mycenaean IIIC:1b pottery to the people making the classic Philistine bichrome does appear to have been a smooth one, although the materials in the two strata reflect distinct cultural differences between the peoples whose possessions are contained therein. Whereas Stager attributes the transition at Ashkelon to assimilation to local Canaanite and Egyptian influences, Moshe Dothan believes that there are enough distinct cultural differences in the two Ashdod strata to indicate two waves of Sea People migration. The first Sea Peoples to arrive were the vanguard for those who would come later (M. Dothan 1979, 131; 1989, 67). The second wave, arriving in Canaan during the reign of Ramesses III, included the Philistines who had been defeated by him and, as he describes it, had been settled "in strongholds, bound in my name. Their military classes were as numerous as hundred-thousands. I assigned portions for them all with clothing and provisions from the treasuries and granaries every year" (*ANET*, 262).

103

For Moshe Dothan the most distinctive element illustrating cultural differences between the two waves is the figurine known today as the "Ashdoda," which is representative of a ceramic motif introduced into Canaan during the Philistine period. Moshe Dothan believes that this seated clay figurine links the Philistine world with the Mycenaean world through their shared mother goddess, and he also points to other examples of Mycenaean influence. The Ashdoda figurine is unique among all those of its type in that it was found in such fine condition, but the Ashdod excavations have also come up with numerous fragments of similar figurines. These finds, along with other artifacts such as jewelry, metal, gold objects, faience, scarabs, a stamp seal bearing an inscription, and ivory, reflect Aegean *and* Egyptian origins for this second wave of Sea Peoples. One specific indicator of the connection between Egypt and this second wave is that Philistine bichrome pottery makers had by then adopted an Egyptian jug form as one of their own, adapting it by using their white slip with bichrome paint but using Egyptian motifs such as the lotus flower. For Moshe Dothan, it was this second wave of immigration bringing the Philistines that "established the foundation of a long-lasting political and cultural entity at Ashdod" (M. Dothan 1989, 67).

Stager believes that during Pharaoh Merneptah's military campaign into Canaan Ashkelon was Canaanite, and I believe Stager is correct. But Pharaoh Merneptah did record his battles with the Sea Peoples, and it is logical to assume, on the basis of the artifacts at Ashdod as well as the extensive corpus of ceramics and other artifacts at Ekron, that some of the Sea Peoples on the pharaoh's list had settled in other parts of the southern coast of Canaan during his time or shortly thereafter—perhaps at Ashdod and Ekron, for example. It is also logical to assume that, since Ashkelon was a large seaport city (more than 150 acres) serving the entire Eastern Mediterranean, it would have had among its polyglot population some Aegeans (with Myc. IIIC:1b pottery). Ashkelon, however, remained under Canaanite control at least until the time of Ramesses III.

Checking various excavations along the coast of Canaan, Syria, and Cyprus to determine when Mycenaean IIIB pottery ended and IIIC:1b began, one learns that this break occurred some time during the reigns of Merneptah and Tausert and before the reign of Ramesses III. Ugarit, Tell Abu Hawam (near Haifa), Tell Deir Alla, and other Syro-Palestinian sites show clear signs of attack and destruction in the levels corresponding to the days of Merneptah or

A. Mazar gives a tour of his site to the staff of Tel Miqne-Ekron.

some time before Ramesses III. Artifacts dated to the pharaohs just prior to Ramesses III have also been recovered from these levels (M. Dothan 1979, 125–34; 1989, 67–68; T. Dothan 1982a, 289–96; 1985, 166). I believe that the evidence from Cyprus and the Mediterranean coast along Syria, as well as from a few other sites in Canaan (some still to be discussed in this chapter), clearly demonstrates an initial settlement, or wave, of Sea Peoples in Canaan before the attack on Egypt by a second wave during the time of Ramesses III. It was this second movement of Sea Peoples—of which the Philistines were a part—that became a dominant force in the history of Canaan.

As was already mentioned, when the Late Bronze fortress of Ashdod was destroyed by the first wave of Sea People, only parts of the mound were resettled and rebuilt. But during the Philistine bichrome days the city became a thriving, fortified metropolis, which flourished until the mid-eleventh century B.C. The archaeological evidence does, then, reflect the situation recorded in Joshua 15 and especially in Judges 1 and 3. The Sea Peoples' presence at Ashdod at the end of the thirteenth century was not very strong, not until the time of Ramesses III early in the twelfth century when the Philistines moved in.

Samson[3]

Samson went down to Timnah and saw there a young Philistine woman.
[Judg. 14:1 NIV]

One of my first memories of the Timnah excavation, or Tel Batash, was of the volunteers wearing T-shirts saying, "Samson dug Timnah and so do we." It is easy to see why the volunteers would enjoy working there. The mound is small but impressive and is square, an unusual shape for a tell. It measures about six hundred feet on a side, and the ruins rise about forty feet above the floor of the plain. Whereas Ekron lies on the eastern edge of the coastal plain, Tel Batash is in the area called the Shephelah, the foothills beginning just five miles east of Ekron which surround part of the Sorek Valley. The valley runs east-west, and Ekron and Timnah are both in the western part of it. Driving to Timnah from Ekron, one passes by fertile cotton fields, as well as groves of almond trees, fed in part by the perennial stream that also flowed by Timnah in the ancient past. Even today a glimmer of the city's past glory is visible whenever the train speeds past the mound on its run to Jerusalem, for the tell sits astride an ancient east-west highway that followed the Sorek Valley and linked the coastal plain on the west to the Judean hills and Jerusalem on the east.

The unique shape of Timnah dates back to the Middle Bronze Age (ca. the eighteenth century B.C.), when its inhabitants constructed a huge earth rampart in the shape of a square of approximately six acres. (These may be the years of the Judah and Tamar story of Genesis 38.) I wish to focus here, however, on the transition years between the Late Bronze Age and Iron Age I, the thirteenth/twelfth century B.C. At Tel Batash-Timnah the Late Bronze Age witnessed a flourishing Canaanite town with an international flavor, but also a town that suffered continual attacks as at Ashkelon and Ashdod. The excavators believe that a large Canaanite building, razed in the fourteenth century B.C. and uncovered in stratum VII, may have quartered the governor (see A. Mazar 1985c, 67 for drawing). Among the debris of this Late Bronze building were seals and scarabs from Egypt, as well as numerous imported Cypriot and Mycenaean objects. A storage room beneath the steps leading to the second floor contained five storage jars, three of which still contained carbonized kernels of wheat. Nearby, the base of a jug containing almonds still in their outer shells was recovered; the almonds were also carbonized. A poignant reminder of what may have happened here became visible with the recovery nearby of two human skeletons surrounded by bronze spearheads and arrowheads. Canaanite occupation of the city continued through stratum VI to the thirteenth century, until the

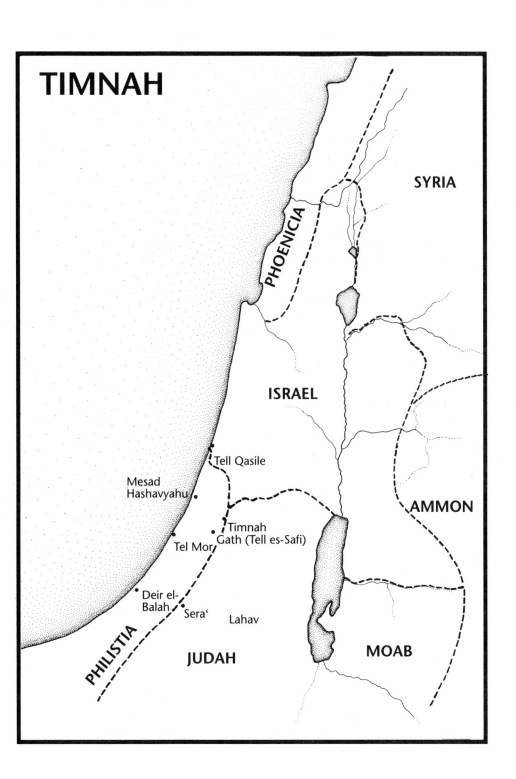

TIMNAH

SYRIA

PHOENICIA

ISRAEL

AMMON

Tell Qasile

Mesad
Hashavyahu

Timnah
Gath (Tell es-Safi)

Tel Mor

MOAB

Deir el-
Balah
Sera'

Lahav

PHILISTIA

JUDAH

Philistines appear on the scene. In the Old Testament, it is the Book of Joshua that first mentions Timnah in this Philistine context.

Joshua 15:10–11 puts Timnah on a roughly east-west line along with Beth-shemesh and Ekron as part of the territory that will belong to the tribe of Judah. On the other hand, Joshua 19:43 squeezes the tribe of Dan between Judah and Ephraim and states that Timnah and Ekron are to be Dan's. Verse 47 adds, however, that Dan could not hold its inheritance and later migrated north.

The excavators associate Timnah's next stratum, stratum V, with the Philistines and the Samson stories. Stratum V is the earliest Iron Age level city (ca. 1150–1000 B.C.) and will be the focus of this section. A basic question that needs to be asked is whether or not the pottery sequence here is the same as that of neighboring Ekron, namely, the Mycenaean IIIB imports of the Late Bronze Age, followed by the locally made Mycenaean IIIC:1b pottery, which in turn is followed by the classic Philistine bichrome ware. As with Ashkelon and Ashdod, pottery sequences are crucial in trying to pinpoint when the Philistines arrived at the site.

As already noted, imported Mycenaean IIIB ware was found in the Late Bronze Age stratum in the building that may have housed the area's governor. However, the locally made Mycenaean IIIC:1b ware so prevalent at the neighboring Ekron is not present at Timnah. The excavators interpret this to mean that the Philistines arrived at Timnah later than they did at Ekron. Since Timnah's Philistine ceramics began with the classic bichrome ware, the Philistines probably arrived there sometime around 1150–1100 B.C. This phase of Philistine occupation apparently ended around 1000 B.C.; it appears that the city was then abandoned for a period of time.

Amihai Mazar, one of the principal excavators of Tel Batash, agrees with Stager of Ashkelon that both pottery forms, Mycenaean IIIC:1b and the classic Philistine bichrome ware, represent just one group of people—the Philistines. Furthermore, just as the excavators on Cyprus refer to the makers and users of Mycenaean IIIC:1b ware as Achaeans, Mazar calls the pottery makers of Mycenaean IIIC:1b ware in Canaan Mycenaean Greeks or Philistines. For Mazar, the logical conclusion is that the Achaean immigrants on Cyprus were the same peoples as the Mycenaean Greek refugees on Canaan's coastal plain. Mazar, like Stager of the Ashkelon excavations, believes that the Philistines initially came to Canaan during the reign of Ramesses III, circa 1175 B.C., made their monochrome IIIC:1b pottery locally, and then after a couple of decades started producing their bichrome pottery in the decoration of which the Philistines used adaptations of Egyptian and Canaanite motifs (1990, 307–8). Thus, for Mazar, there was only one wave of Sea Peoples to this area, and since at Timnah there is no Mycenaean IIIC:1b pottery, the Philistines must have arrived at Timnah later than at Ashkelon, Ashdod, and Ekron.

Before we look at the Samson stories in this context, I would like to mention a couple of interesting finds from stratum V at Tel Batash. To date, no archaeologist has found a Philistine "archive," and we still do not have clear evidence of Philistine writing. However, a stone seal used to make identifying impressions on clay seals, or bullae, for papyrus documents was found at Timnah. It showed a stick figure playing a lyre. A bulla from the same Philistine period was also recovered. The climate at Timnah is not conducive to preserving papyrus, but these two artifacts give an indication that evidence of writing may yet be found there.

Both the seal and the bulla are examples of Philistine glyptic (stone carving) art. At Ashdod, a better specimen of a Philistine seal from the same time period has been recovered. Ashdod's stamp seal is more than just an example of glyptic art; it also has a linear script on it similar to a script on some clay tablets found at Deir Alla in the

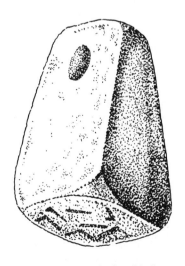

Seal and bulla found at Timnah.

109

Transjordan by the Jordan Valley. The Deir Alla tablets were uncovered in association with Philistine pottery. The script on Ashdod's seal and on the Deir Alla tablets is still undeciphered, but it may be related to a Cypro-Minoan script, providing another link between the Philistines and the Greeks from the Aegean. The tablets, seals, and bullae provide hope that a Philistine archive will be uncovered eventually, and when Philistine writing is found, the script may well be Mycenaean Greek.[4]

Now let us continue with Judges 13 and the Samson stories. Samson, of the tribe of Dan, was from Zorah, which today is believed to be under the ruins of the Arab village of Sar'ah some five miles east of Tel Batash-Timnah, on the northern ridge of the Sorek Valley just north of Beth-shemesh. Zorah was also mentioned in Joshua 15:33 as a town assigned to Judah, but later, in 19:41, it was assigned to Dan. It was also from Zorah that the tribe of Dan, after the Samson stories, left to stake out a new land for the tribe far to the north (Judg. 18).

> Now be careful not to drink wine or strong drink, or to eat anything unclean, for you shall conceive and bear a son. No razor is to come upon his head, for the boy shall be a nazirite to God from birth. It is he who shall begin to deliver Israel from the hand of the Philistines. [Judg. 13:4–5]

Before his birth, Samson's mother was commanded to abstain from "wine or strong drink" (vv. 4, 7, 14). The injunctions that a Nazirite must follow are found in Numbers 6:1–8. In the New International Version, Judges 13:4, 7, and 14 read "wine or other fermented drink," and in all likelihood this strong or fermented drink was beer, which may have been higher in alcoholic content than wine, since wine was generally mixed with water. It is interesting to note this possibility since beer jugs were very common vessels in the days of Samson, judging from the quantity of ceramic sherds recovered at various Philistine sites.

". . . for the boy shall be a nazirite to God from birth" (Judg. 13:5). While Samson was growing, "the LORD blessed him. The spirit of the LORD began to stir him . . ." (Judg. 13:24–25). Imagine how chagrined his parents must have been when suddenly Samson told them to get a Philistine girl for his wife. A young Israelite man, a Nazirite, one who had vowed "to separate [himself] to the LORD" (Num. 6:2), wanted a wife from the uncircumcised Philistines! The Bible is quick to point out that God would use this deed to help deliver Israel from Philistine domination (Judg. 14:4). The wife Samson chose was from Timnah, the Timnah referred to earlier —stratum V. This is the Philistine layer with the distinctive pottery and the Philistine seal and bulla. This was the Timnah with the surrounding wheat fields and almond groves. According to the excavators, the Samson stories had to have taken place some time after 1150 B.C. Timnah at this time was an urban center with numerous mudbrick houses.

Samson continued to be reckless with his Nazirite vows, for while on the way to get his wife, he killed a lion, and sometime later he noticed a beehive in the carcass and scraped some honey from it into his hands. This is in violation of the Nazirite code of Numbers 6:6: "they shall not go near a corpse." Samson knew this and did not tell his parents where he had gotten the honey that he shared with them.

While at the wedding feast, no doubt a drinking feast, Samson told a difficult riddle involving the lion that he had killed earlier. He fooled the Philistines with his riddle, but he in turn was fooled by them. He wreaked vengeance on thirty victims in Ashkelon, also a Philistine city at this time. In a rage Samson returned home to his parents; his in-laws believed that he was divorcing their daughter, and they then gave her in marriage to his best man, evidently a resident of Timnah. Later, about the time of the wheat harvest (which would have been preceded by some hot, dry weather), Samson returned to Timnah. He was carrying our equivalent of a dozen roses—a young goat. Samson expected to be given his "wife" again, but the father-in-law, who followed practices normal for the age, graciously offered his younger daughter to Samson instead, trying not to compound the problem. Samson's retaliation of setting the fields on fire led to the death of his former wife and her family in Timnah by Philistine hands.

Samson countered by smiting the Philistines "hip and thigh with great slaughter" (Judg. 15:8) before escaping to the south or southeast. Here another interesting event developed. Samson was evidently in the territory of Judah, and the men of Judah mounted up a force—not to fight the Philistines but instead to stop Samson and turn him over to his pursuers. They pointed out to him, "Do you not know that the Philistines are rulers over us?" (Judg. 15:11). It is rare to find references to Judah in the Book of Judges (except in the opening chapters), but they are included in the promise of Judges 13:5: "It is he who shall begin to deliver Israel from the hand of the Philistines."

So Samson exacted a promise from the Judahites that they would not harm him; then he allowed them to tie him up and take him to a

111

place called Lehi, which means jawbone." When he came to Lehi, the Philistines came shouting to meet him . . ." (15:14). In other words, the Philistine jaws were clamoring for revenge, but Samson used the "fresh jawbone of an ass" to stop them! The Spirit of the Lord helped him out of this situation, and the Lord also provided him with water after the battle.

However, the man who could kill a lion with his bare hands and kill an armed Philistine force with a donkey's jawbone could not control his sexual lusts. Samson went next to Gaza, another one of the five Philistine cities, where he found a prostitute. Some of the Gazaites, hearing he was spending the night with her, lay in wait all night at the city gates to kill Samson. He instead got up at midnight and carried off the city gates. Unfortunately, Gaza is a site, as mentioned above, that will not be excavated in the near future. However, from what we know about the city gates of other Philistine sites, the Gazaites evidently were hiding in one of the guardrooms in the gate complex. Why would Samson have taken the gates and carried "them to the top of the hill that is in front of Hebron" (Judg. 16:3) in Judah's territory rather than towards his own home or elsewhere? Perhaps he was embarrassing weak-kneed Judah for turning him over to the Philistines.

Next we come to one of the last episodes in the life of Samson—his intriguing relationship with Delilah. She is a puzzle. Scripture does not state specifically where she was from, only that she came from the valley of Sorek, meaning the "valley (wadi) of the choice vine." This name would, no doubt, have been affirmed by Samson, since both his wife and now Delilah were from the valley. Samson's home was just to the north of the Sorek, with Ekron and Timnah to the west down in the Sorek Valley.

Where Delilah lived in relation to these towns we do not know. But the lords of the Philistines, which would have included the lord of Ekron, came to her with a lavish offer—pounds of silver if she could figure out the secret to Samson's strength so that they might subdue him. There is no sure way of determining if Delilah was even a Philistine. Would the Philistine lords have to have made such an extravagant offer if she was one of them? Her name may mean "flirtatious" (Boling 1975, 248), which seems appropriate. But it may also be a pun on the Hebrew word for night (*laylah*), whereas Samson's name is related to the Hebrew word for sun (*semes*). The night would win, and the sun would forever be taken away from Samson.

Samson had always been able to move about Philistine territory freely, as attested by his marriage to a daughter of Timnah and his trips to Ashkelon (Judg. 14:19) and Gaza (Judg. 16:1). Apparently the Philistines were confident in their domination over Israel. The location for this story with Delilah is in the Sorek Valley but probably is not Timnah, considering what havoc Samson had created there earlier. Ekron cannot be excluded as a possibility, since the text states that "the lords of the Philistines came to her" (Judg. 16:5). And again, later "she sent and called the lords of the Philistines. . . . Then the lords of the Philistines came up to her, and brought the money in their hands" (Judg. 16:18). Ekron would have been a logical location for the gathering of the Philistine lords; however, we cannot be certain. The lords, though, did travel to her with the money unobserved, implying that this was *not* Israelite territory.[5]

Samson was a Nazirite who never seemed to take his vows seriously. While he was in the arms of Delilah, his hair was cut in violation of those vows (Judg. 13:5). Sadly, he was so captivated by his lover that "he did not know that the LORD had left him" (Judg. 16:20). Samson had forgotten that God was the source of his strength; he was captured and blinded and taken deep into Philistine territory, to Gaza, scene of an earlier escapade of his. The words *down to Gaza* (Judg. 16:21) provide another clue that the scene with Delilah took place up in the valley, in or near the foothills, since Gaza is on the coastal plain down by the Mediterranean Sea.

Samson's Death[6]

"Let me die with the Philistines."
[Judg. 16:30]

We are not yet finished with Samson. What was perhaps the most significant victory of his life occurred at the moment of his death in a Philistine temple at Gaza. Questions have been raised about what this temple looked like. To give a possible answer, I would like to move to another Philistine site, that of Tell Qasile, which has a temple and, unlike Gaza, has been excavated.

Tell Qasile, on the north side of the Yarkon River and encompassed by modern Tel Aviv, was not one of the five chief Philistine cities. We do not know its name during the Philistine period, and we do not know which biblical site would correspond to it. The material remains excavated here identify it as a Philistine site. This tell is a small one,

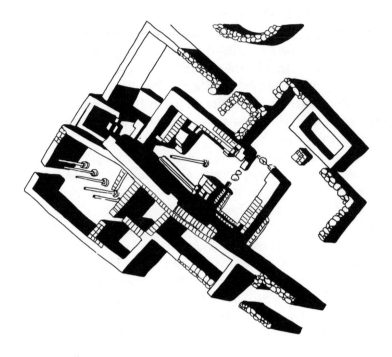

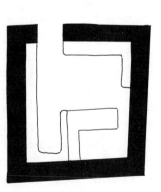

Sketch of a Philistine temple at Tell Qasile, near Tel Aviv.

encompassing only four acres, and was first settled in the twelfth century B.C.—the Philistine/judges period. The town was constructed at the mouth of the Yarkon River and was used as an inland port. Archaeologist Benjamin Mazar, excavating here in the late 1940s and 1950s, identified it with the "Sea of Joppa" where the cedarwood from Lebanon for the temples of Solomon and Zerubbabel arrived.

Excavation beginning in 1971 under Amihai Mazar, nephew of Benjamin Mazar, has uncovered three Philistine temples built in succession on top of one another over a time span of approximately 180 years. The first temple was built when the site was first settled in the mid-twelfth century B.C. and was in use into the eleventh century. The second temple, which seems, more precisely, to have been a second phase of the first temple, was built in the eleventh century. The final temple, the most elaborate one, was used from the eleventh century into the tenth and was destroyed by fire in approximately 980 B.C. The destruction of the settlement and this final temple may be attributed to the conquest of Philistia by David, according to both Benjamin Mazar and Amihai Mazar.

Several miles to the south of Qasile lies Gaza, and Gaza is where the captive Samson milled the grain in darkness. We are led to suspect that something is going to happen when the biblical writer states: "But the hair of his head began to grow . . ." (Judg. 16:22).

> Now the lords of the Philistines gathered to offer a great sacrifice to their god Dagon, and to rejoice; for they said, "Our god has given Samson our enemy into our hand." When the people saw him, they praised their god; for they said, "Our god has given our enemy into our hand, the ravager of our country, who has killed many of us." And when their hearts were merry, they said, "Call Samson, and let him entertain us." So they called Samson out of the prison, and he performed for them. They made him stand between the *pillars* [emphasis mine]; and Samson said to the attendant who held him by the hand, "Let me feel the pillars on which the house rests, so that I may lean against them." Now the house was full of men and women; all the lords of the Philistines were there, and on the roof there were about three thousand men and women, who looked on while Samson performed. [Judg. 16:23–27]

The third and final temple of Tell Qasile appears to have had a construction similar to the biblical description of the Philistine temple at Gaza, but smaller. Its roof was supported by two cedarwood pillars resting on cylindrical limestone bases. The temple measured approximately forty-seven by twenty-six feet—not the size of the temple in the Samson story, but remember that this is Tell Qasile and not Gaza. The orientation of the temple was east-west, and the sacred rites were performed at the west end. The entrance from the courtyard on the north side of the temple led into an antechamber that had inside dimensions of nineteen by twelve feet. Next, a ninety-degree turn to the west led into the main hall with its two supporting pillars. This main hall measured twenty-four by nineteen feet. The north and south walls of this room had stepped benches that had been plastered over. The walls of the antechamber also had similar benches. A raised platform approximately three feet high was constructed near the west wall of the main hall. In Hebrew this type of platform is referred to as a *bamah*. The *bamah* ran up to the benches on the north wall, and at the south end of the *bamah* were two steps leading up onto it. The lower of the two steps covered the stone base on which one of the two wooden pillars had rested. The imprint of the pillar had been visible on the stone base so that the excavators could measure its dimensions. The two pillars had been placed on an east-west line in the main hall, with the *bamah* just to the north and in front of the western pillar (A. Mazar 1990, 322 for drawing). Anyone entering the main hall would have had an unobstructed view of the *bamah* and the objects that were placed on or by it.

Near the third temple was a courtyard containing a square stone structure four feet by four feet. Due to the numerous animal bones

Reconstruction of a *bamah* at Kibbutz Revadim.

found in the courtyard around the structure, the excavators believe that the temple sacrifices were conducted here. Just west of the temple and abutting its west wall was a small shrine (called temple 300) containing benches, a *bamah*, and numerous Philistine vessels, including cultic ones. The excavator believes that it was dedicated to a minor god or to the consort of Qasile's god (Shanks 1984, 57–59 with pictures). Also, on the south side of the third temple and abutting its south wall stood a house with two square rooms and a courtyard whose partial roof was supported by wooden pillars with stone bases. Among the numerous artifacts found there were Philistine storage jars, as well as two imported Egyptian ones. The wealth of

Replica of a clay figurine of a mourning woman (purchased in the Aegean); figurines from Tell Qasile reflect the Mycenaean traditions of the Philistines.

the finds in these rooms and the proximity of these buildings to the third temple suggest that their use may have been linked to that of the temple and its priests.

It is easy to picture Samson between the two main pillars of a temple like this third one, with the jeering crowd seated both in front of and behind him along the north and south walls. The sacred objects, including Dagon, would have been nearby on the *bamah*. And since Samson "brought the house down" with his performance, Dagon, all the cultic objects, Samson himself, and the merry crowd both within the temple and on the roof would have been crushed.

In the third and final temple at Tell Qasile, which may have been brought down by David and his men, some beautiful cult objects have been recovered among the heaps of ashes and burnt wooden beams. These cult objects, quite eclectic in nature, have Canaanite, Egyptian, and Aegean origins. Vessels have also been found that are unique to Qasile. For A. Mazar, two pottery motifs indicate the continuation of the Mycenaean traditions of the Philistines (1990, 323–26). The first is the Ashdoda (see p. 102), fragments of which were found during excavation at Qasile. The second depicts a woman mourning, with her hands on or above her head; the representative find at Qasile is a clay figurine. Variations on this mourning-woman motif are seen throughout the museums of Cyprus and Greece that have Mycenaean material on display.

According to its excavators, the architecture of the third temple at Qasile has no close parallels among other temples in Palestine, but it does resemble temples in Mycenae, as well as others on the Aegean island of Melos and at Kition on Cyprus. The similar temples at these three places date to the thirteenth and twelfth centuries B.C., and themselves do not have earlier architectural roots elsewhere in the Aegean. These places are linked, however, to the Sea Peoples, and other references will be made to them.

Chronologically, the third temple at Qasile dates to slightly later than the Samson era. Qasile, like Timnah, does not have the Mycenaean IIIC:1b pottery indicative, in my view, of the first wave of the Sea Peoples. Qasile seems to have been settled around the time of the Philistine phase of Timnah (stratum V), approximately 1150 B.C. The two earlier temples at Qasile, underneath the one described in detail above, were considerably smaller and not as elaborate. The earliest one, circa 1150 B.C., was approximately twenty-one by twenty-two feet. The second one was twenty-five by twenty-eight feet. Both of these earlier temples had benches and a raised platform (*bamah*) for the cult objects, but neither had pillars. These first two temples would have been the ones that belonged to the Samson era.

The final minutes of Samson's life brought to light the only recorded prayer of Samson the Nazirite.

> Then Samson called to the LORD and said, "Lord GOD, remember me and strengthen me only this once, O God, so that with this one act of revenge I may pay back the Philistines for my two eyes." And Samson grasped the two middle pillars on which the house rested. . . . Then Samson said, "Let me die with the Philistines." He strained with all his might; and the house fell on the lords and all the people who were in it. So those he killed at his death were more than those he had killed during his life. Then his brothers and all his family came down and took him and brought him up and buried him . . . in the tomb of his father Manoah. He had judged Israel twenty years. [Judg. 16:28–31]

Reckless Samson turned to the Lord and the Lord heard his cry. Note that his family was able to come en masse into Philistia to retrieve the body. There is no hint that Samson's body was violated, a treatment totally different from what King Saul would receive. Samson died honorably doing the task that was prophesied of him in Judges 13:5: "It is he who shall begin to deliver Israel from the hand of the Philistines." The Philistines, I have no doubt, recognized the valor of Samson in spite of their tremendous losses.

"Drive Them Out"[7]

> . . . but [Judah] could not drive out the inhabitants of the plain. . . .
> [Judg. 1:19]

Chapter 1 pointed out that in the books of Joshua and Judges, Ekron is assigned to both the tribes of Judah and Dan, but evidently neither tribe could drive the Philistines from the city. The Book of Judges also tells the stories of Samson, which are set in the Sorek Valley but do not even mention Ekron. The "lords of the Philistines" visited Delilah, but the specific cities they came from are not named. The biblical record tells us very little about Ekron during this Late Bronze/Iron I period of the judges before Samuel. What does the archaeological record tell us?

This is an appropriate time for such a question, since Ekron is currently part of an ongoing interregional study of the settlement pattern in the Shephelah and on the coastal plain of Canaan during the Iron Age. The archaeologists of the sites that have been discussed thus far are constantly consulting with one another about the finds of their respective sites. A wealth of new information has come to light that demands a reassessment of the Philistines, who became residents of the coastal plain during the transition years of the Late Bronze Age to the Iron Age I. This reassessment also demands that the archaeological evidence on Cyprus be reexamined, since this island seems to have been the staging area for Philistine migrations to Canaan.

We have already noted that there are diverse opinions among archaeologists on four key issues: 1) Were there one or two waves of Sea Peoples who settled on the coast of Canaan? 2) Do the two major pottery forms, Mycenaean IIIC:1b and Philistine bichrome, indicate one group of invading people who assimilated neighboring forms or two groups of invaders, the second of which included the Philistines who introduced the bichrome pottery? 3) Did the Philistines settle in Canaan just after the reign of Pharaoh Merneptah or later, during the reign of Ramesses III? 4) Is the high chronology or the low chronology of the Egyptian rulers more accurate?

Most archaeologists agree that by the first half of the twelfth century B.C. the generic term *Philistines* was the appropriate name for the invaders of Canaan and Egypt who evidently came by land and sea. Furthermore, they are in agreement that these Philistines were either Mycenaean Greeks (which may include Cretans) or western Anatolians who, from various points in the Aegean, fled the collapse of their society that is exemplified in the *Iliad* and the *Odyssey*.

At Ekron striking discoveries from the end of the thirteenth century B.C. have been made at a couple of places in the Late Bronze layer of the tell. This is the period of the Canaanite Ekron from which ceramic imports from Cyprus and elsewhere in the Aegean world (Mycenaean IIIB) have been uncovered. A few dark brown krater sherds bearing wavy incised decorations with heavy burnishing have also been recovered. This type of pottery is commonly called Trojan ware or Anatolian grey polished ware. These few sherds do not necessarily indicate that Trojans or Anatolians had migrated to Ekron. They may simply indicate the movements of pots as objects of trade.

However, the abundance of Mycenaean IIIC:1b pottery found at Ekron and Ashdod does indicate, I believe, the arrival of a new ethnic element. The pottery, as mentioned numerous times above, is locally made but is definitely linked stylistically and decoratively to

120

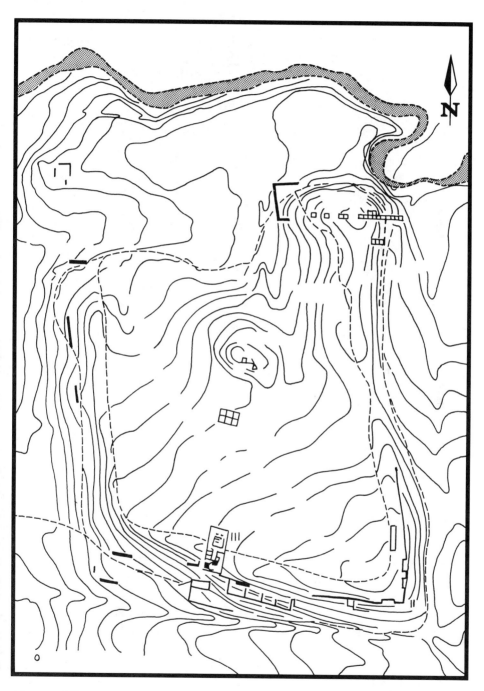

Site map of Ekron.

Reconstruction of a kiln at Kibbutz Revadim.

Cypriot sites as well as to other sites in the Aegean. On Cyprus, archaeologists link similar locally made pottery to the arrival of Achaean immigrants. One such distinctive pottery find at Ekron which has created considerable interest is the recovery of numerous *lekane* bowls. In Cypriot and Greek literature, these bowls are also referred to as *kalathos* bowls. They were well known from the end of the Late Minoan period (corresponding to the Late Bronze Age; see Cottrell 1957, 234–37).

At Ekron, along with the lekane bowls and numerous other Mycenaean IIIC:1b pottery sherds from the Iron I period, some kilns were uncovered, including a large square kiln. No evidence has been found in connection with this kiln to reveal whether it was used for pottery or for metal items. The whole field I area was enclosed by a massive eleven-foot-thick mudbrick wall, which evidently encompassed the entire fifty-acre tell. Twelfth-century B.C. Ekron was a site worthy of a Philistine lord.

Enough Mycenaean IIIC:1b pottery has been recovered from Ekron for Trude Dothan to posit the following chronology. The Canaanite city of Ekron in the Late Bronze Age (more specifically,

122

Reconstruction of a pottery workshop at Kibbutz Revadim.

the thirteenth century B.C.) was destroyed during the first third of the twelfth century, and its northeast sector (field I of the tell; see map, p. 121) was replaced with an industrial area (stratum VII) in which appears locally made Mycenaean IIIC:1b pottery with plain horizontal bands or spirals similar to those found on sites on Cyprus and in the Aegean. The final two-thirds of the twelfth century saw still another change; architecturally this northeast sector (field I) changed to domestic dwellings (stratum VI) in which were found a slightly altered style of pottery called Elaborate Mycenaean IIIC:1b. These vessels were pictorial, with highly stylized fish and bird decor. The same trend is seen at sites on Cyprus. It is in stratum VI that we also find the earliest Philistine bichrome pottery at Ekron. T. Dothan sees through this data the influx of two waves of peoples—those of stratum VII followed by those of stratum VI—both tied to Cyprus and the Aegean. According to T. Dothan, the first wave came at the beginning of the twelfth century (after the reign of Merneptah) and the second came still during the first third of that century (the reign of Ramesses III). The Philistine bichrome pottery, according to her, is an outgrowth of the Elaborate Mycenaean IIIC:1b pottery of stra-

123

The author with a Philistine bowl from Ekron.

tum VI. This schema seems entirely possible when one considers that the Egyptian records of Merneptah do tell of attacks by the Sea Peoples at the end of the thirteenth century, and some of these peoples could have settled in Ekron and Ashdod (Breasted 1906, 4:41). It is also possible that Ashkelon continued to be Canaanite throughout the reign of Merneptah, as did Timnah.

It is the second wave during the reign of Ramesses III that T. Dothan sees as the Philistine invasion. Ramesses III specifically identified one of the attacking groups as the Philistines, and I believe they became the dominant group in Palestine and, therefore, are named as such in the Bible. The Ekron of stratum VI with the Elaborate Mycenaean IIIC:1b pottery and the Philistine bichrome ware is the city associated with the defeat of the Sea Peoples by Ramesses III (according to his own records), around 1175 B.C. Two pieces of evidence that Trude Dothan cites are the cartouche of Ramesses III found in the same stratum with Philistine pottery at

124

Gezer and the scarab of Ramesses III likewise found in the Philistine stratum at Ashdod.

Another intriguing find of stratum VI was uncovered in a pit in the northeast sector of the tell (field I). There, a bovine scapula was found alongside large fragments of lekane bowls. (More cattle scapulae have been found in stratum V.) The well-defined, cylindrical pit in which the scapula was discovered was not cut haphazardly, leading me to surmise that perhaps this was a *favissa*, where objects used in cultic observances were discarded. This whole area was strewn with objects that may have been of cultic significance: clay figurines reminiscent of the Ashdoda, miniature vessels, clay fragments of various sexual body parts, and a lion-headed rhyton, that is, an Aegean drinking cup. The lekane bowls have ties to Cyprus, and the scapulae found in the pit may be related to scapulomancy, the divination technique using sacrificed oxen mentioned earlier (pp. 87–88). Oxen were the chief sacrificial animals on Cyprus. These scapulae will be discussed in detail when I relate the finds of stratum V at Ekron, the period that coincides with Samuel.

I have one final comment concerning the diversity of opinion among scholars about the four questions raised above. I accept Stager's conclusion that Ashkelon was a Canaanite city at the time Pharaoh Merneptah repulsed the Libyans and their Sea People allies. I can also accept that Ashkelon did not become Philistine until the time of Pharaoh Ramesses III, the time when, according to Stager, Mycenaean IIIC:1b pottery was followed generally by Philistine bichrome ware. However, Ashkelon is a very large site with meters of debris above the Philistine strata, and I also believe that Sea Peoples could have been living in Canaanite-controlled Ashkelon, a polyglot seaport, while making and using their Mycenaean IIIC:1b pottery. A. Mazar believes that the Philistines came to both Tell Qasile and Timnah in the mid-twelfth century; at these sites there was no Mycenaean IIIC:1b pottery, only the Philistine bichrome. This too, I believe, is a correct conclusion. The excavators of Ekron and Ashdod have concluded that the Sea Peoples came earlier to these cities, perhaps at the end of Pharaoh Merneptah's reign. From my involvement in the Ekron project since 1984, I have been convinced that we have unearthed sufficient artifacts along with ceramics to warrant this conclusion, as well.

Is it possible for regional cultural changes and movements of peoples to be uniform and simultaneous? I think not. The Egyptian records of Merneptah and the succeeding pharaohs speak of migrations occurring over a period of years. The *Iliad* and the *Odyssey* speak of wars and movements of peoples stretching also over a long period of time. Even the biblical exodus and the subsequent conquest occurred over many years. Perhaps it was at Ekron and Ashdod where the core of the Sea Peoples first settled before the second wave moved down into Canaan—the complete Sea People migration thereby spanning some fifty years.

Israel's Battle[8]

In those days the Philistines mustered for war against Israel,
and Israel went out to battle against them. . . .
[1 Sam. 4:1]

Samson was unable to provide any permanent solution to the Philistine problem; he afforded only temporary local relief. Where Samson belongs in the picture chronologically is not known definitely, but he probably fits best into the second half of the twelfth century B.C. or slightly later. The Philistines were on the coastal plain, and the tribe of Dan felt the pressure some time after Samson to move north (Judg. 18). At least one of the tribal representatives sent north to spy out a new land was from Zorah, Samson's hometown (Judg. 18:2). The territory that appealed to them was in the area of Laish north of the Sea of Galilee, formerly under the sphere of influence of Sidon. Sidon too had suffered attacks from the Sea Peoples, the occurrence of which may have aided the Danites in their conquest of Laish, soon to be renamed Dan. Laish was far removed from Sidon and isolated from the coast by mountains. The presence of the Sea Peoples on the coast would have hindered the Sidonians from exercising their control over any territory to the east.

During Samuel's time, the tribal league of Israel was at war with the confederation of the five Philistine city-states. The Philistines appear to have had parts of Israel almost completely surrounded. They lived on the coastal plain that extended north to the Mount Carmel Range. They controlled the Jezreel Valley, which would figure in the battle with Saul, and they also controlled parts of the Jordan Valley south towards Jericho (that is, to Deir Alla). Samson obviously was a big thorn in the side of the Philistines, and maybe because of the damage Samson had inflicted, the Philistines decided war with Israel was a necessity. Further war between the Philistines

126

and the Israelites began some time around 1050 B.C. The Philistines decided on a bold thrust to cut a gap through the center of Israel. "In those days the Philistines mustered for war against Israel; . . . [Israel] encamped at Ebenezer, and the Philistines encamped at Aphek" (1 Sam. 4:1).

The biblical Aphek is believed to have been east of modern Tel Aviv near the source of the Yarkon River, which flows through Tel Aviv into the Mediterranean Sea. Aphek would then have been east of Qasile, which is at the mouth of the Yarkon River. At Aphek also, the Canaanite culture ended in the second half of the thirteenth century B.C., and here, too, the excavator believes that the destruction of the Canaanite city was due to the "enigmatic 'Sea Peoples' that marauded the coasts of the Levant and brought an end to the Late Bronze civilization" (Kochavi 1981, 81). The culture that followed the Canaanite one was the Philistine culture, with its ubiquitous pottery among other features. The Yarkon River may have been the northern border of Philistine territory, and it is from Aphek that the Philistines made their attack on the Israelites, who were in the hills to the east of Aphek. The neighboring eastern hills of Ephraim show what are believed to be signs of Israelite settlement, and it is one of these settlements, 'Izbet Sartah, that is believed to have been the Ebenezer of 1 Samuel 4. The material culture of both Aphek and 'Izbet Sartah display the fluidity of the times. When the Philistine culture at Tell Aphek later was buried into the ground, perhaps during King David's time, the Israelite occupation at 'Izbet Sartah also ended, perhaps because Israel was now able to leave this outpost in the hill country.

Here, then, in the area of Aphek, is where the fateful battle of 1 Samuel 4 took place. This battle was the nadir, the lowest point in Israelite history up to that time, and it may be the source of the negative reputation that Philistines have been accorded to this day. The Israelites lost the initial battle with heavy loss of life. Therefore, they resolved to do a deed not unknown among their neighboring cultures; they brought the presence of their God into the battlefield area. Earlier, when the Israelites had left Mount Sinai and wandered through the desert, had not the ark of the covenant always been in front with the priests? "Whenever the ark set out, Moses would say, 'Arise, O LORD, let your enemies be scattered, and your foes flee before you'" (Num. 10:35). And when Israel crossed the Jordan River to enter the land, did not the ark again lead the way? "When the people set out from their tents to cross over the Jordan, the priests bearing the ark of the covenant were in front of the people" (Josh. 3:14).

No doubt the Israelites thought of this history as they sent word to Shiloh, twenty miles to the east of Ebenezer, to bring the ark to the battlefield. And so, "The two sons of Eli, Hophni and Phinehas, were there with the ark of the covenant of God" (1 Sam. 4:4). The ploy worked—temporarily—for the spirits of the Israelites were buoyed: "all Israel gave a mighty shout, so that the earth resounded" (v. 5). And the Philistines in response cried out, "Woe to us! Who can deliver us from the power of these mighty gods? These are the gods who struck the Egyptians with every sort of plague in the wilderness" (v. 8). But someone there was able to remind the Philistines, "Take courage, and be men, O Philistines, in order not to become slaves to the Hebrews as they have been to you; be men and fight" (v. 9).

Note the reference in verse 8 to "gods" (*elohim* in Hebrew, a word commonly used to refer to deity) in the plural form. This is not unusual, coming from the Philistines. Even though we do not yet have much specific information on their religion, we do know that, as was typical of Aegean peoples, they were polytheistic and that evidently they had adopted the Canaanite pantheon. Verse 9 states that the Israelites had been slaves to the Philistines, which no doubt accurately describes the plight of the Judahites, Danites, and Simeonites who bore the brunt of Philistine forays into the Judean hills.

Israel lost the battle near Aphek, and even more importantly, it lost the ark of the covenant. The phrase "and they fled, everyone to his home [tent]" (v. 10) illustrates just how bad the situation was; the soldiers were deserting the army in fear (McCarter 1980, 107). The Israelites had given up on God; the Philistine gods were apparently more powerful than the Holy One of Israel. (Even when the ark was returned later, it was still rejected by Israel for at least twenty years, during which they accepted other gods, "Baals and the Astartes" [1 Sam. 7:4]). The ark of the covenant, containing the tablets of the law, a pot of manna, and the rod of Aaron (Exod. 16:31ff. with NIV Study Bible notes; 25:16, 21; Num. 17; and Heb. 9:4), was now gone. The Philistines evidently continued their attack deep into Israelite territory and destroyed Israel's religious center at Shiloh. Eli died at Shiloh, and the place where Samuel grew up played no further role as a religious center in the life the nation.

Shiloh is a fairly easy site to find, thanks in part to a clear geographical description in Judges 21:19: "So they said, 'Look, the yearly festival of the LORD is taking place at Shiloh, which is north of Bethel, on the east of the highway that goes up from Bethel to Shechem, and south of Lebonah.'" The tell of Shiloh, though a small

128

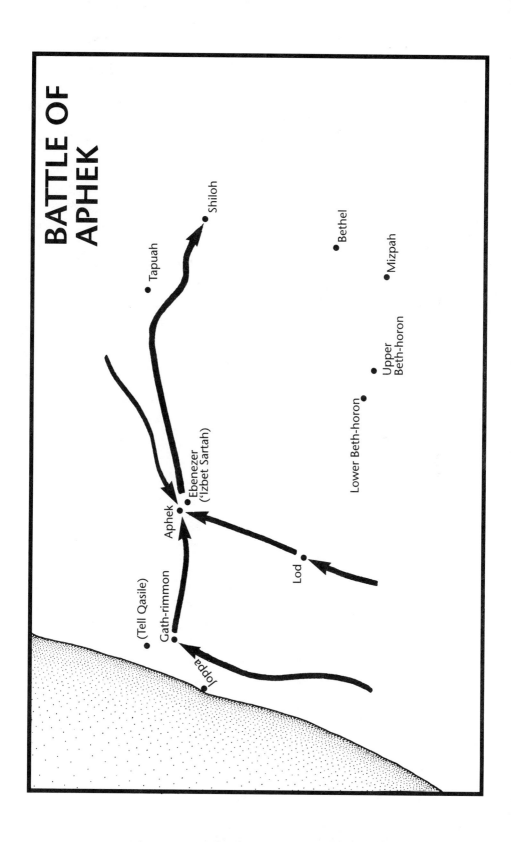

BATTLE OF APHEK

one of eight acres, is a rich one going back to the Middle Bronze IIB period of approximately 1750 B.C. Its excavators believe that already during this period Shiloh had a Canaanite shrine. Destroyed during the sixteenth century B.C. and occupied in part during the Late Bronze period, Shiloh was abandoned before the end of the Late Bronze Age. It was reoccupied in the twelfth century B.C. by Israelites. The material remains in that layer are typical of those associated with the Israelites, namely, collar-rimmed storage jars (according to some but not all archaeologists) and stone-lined silos (five feet in diameter). These are the same type of remains as found from this period at Ebenezer ('Izbet Sartah), twenty miles to the west (see also A. Mazar 1990, 330–48). A total of twenty large storage jars have been found, together with numerous stone-lined silos and other vessels. Carbonized raisins have been recovered, as well as large quantities of carbonized wheat from two of the silos, offerings such as those Hannah brought on a yearly basis (Judg. 21:19; 1 Sam. 1:21, 24; 2:19). With all these discoveries, 1 Samuel 1:24, which describes Hannah's offering to the Lord at Shiloh, comes alive.

Shiloh suffered a fiery destruction in the mid-eleventh century B.C., a destruction its excavators associate with the Philistine defeat of Israel near Aphek and Ebenezer. The excavations at Shiloh attest to the fact that this religious center never regained its prominence. This brings to mind the words spoken by Jeremiah some 450 years later:

> Go now to my place that was in Shiloh, where I made my name dwell at first, and see what I did to it for the wickedness of my people Israel. . . . therefore I will do to the house that is called by my name, in which you trust, and to the place that I gave to you and to your ancestors, just what I did to Shiloh. And I will cast you out of my sight, just as I cast out all your kinsfolk, all the offspring of Ephraim. [Jer. 7:12, 14–15]

It was mentioned earlier that after the battle near Aphek and Ebenezer the Israelites fled to their tents, demonstrating that they were no longer willing to fight in the army of the Lord. In losing the ark of the covenant, they believed that they had lost their God. What Israel did not realize in the eleventh century B.C. and again 450 years later in Jeremiah's time was that the Lord God of Israel was in control. The sequence of events in 1 Samuel 5 teaches this lesson, but the lesson was not learned at the time. There is also an irony in Jeremiah 7:15b, "as I cast out all your kinsfolk, all the offspring of Ephraim." The Judeans of Jeremiah's day would realize that Jeremiah was referring to the conquest of the northern tribes by Assyria in 722 B.C., but Jeremiah's words also applied to Israel of the eleventh century B.C., for Shiloh was located in Ephraim. The Lord God could not tolerate what the sons of Eli were doing, nor the fact that the Israelite army was trying to manipulate God by bringing the ark of the covenant into the battlefield without seeking his will.

Ichabod[9]

She named the child Ichabod, meaning "The glory has departed
from Israel."
[1 Sam. 4:21]

In addition to the capture of the ark, 1 Samuel 4 records the deaths of numerous Israelites, including Eli and his daughter-in-law, the wife of Phinehas. Eli, we are told, had judged Israel for forty years but was unable to control his sons, who served as priests at Shiloh. Earlier, a "man of God" had come to Eli and had predicted doom on Eli's house (1 Sam. 2:27–36), a prediction that was fulfilled in part in the battle during which the ark was captured by the Philistines. The crushing blow for Eli, which brought on his death, was not the death of his two sons in battle but the realization that they had been instrumental in the loss of the ark. The wife of Phinehas grieved for the loss of the ark as well as for the loss of her father-in-law and husband. Her dying wish, after a traumatic childbirth, was that her infant son be named Ichabod, for "the glory has departed from Israel, for the ark of God has been captured" (1 Sam. 4:22).

The focus of the passage is on the ark, the object that the Israelite army thought they could use to manipulate God and the outcome of the battle. God, though, had not been defeated, nor had he abandoned them. He was definitely in control, as the events of chapters 5 and 6 would show.

The Philistines then took the ark to Ashdod: "When the Philistines captured the ark of God, they brought it from Ebenezer to Ashdod; then the Philistines took the ark of God and brought it into the house of Dagon and placed it beside Dagon" (1 Sam. 5:1–2).

The stratum or layer of earth at Ashdod that is believed to belong to the period of Samuel and Saul is stratum X (mid-eleventh century B.C.). However, archaeologists have not yet uncovered the remains of a temple from that period in the areas excavated. At this time Ashdod was a well-built Philistine city with a distinctive pottery now referred to as Ashdod ware. (It was the earlier strata XIII–XI that had the Mycenaean IIIC:1b and the Philistine bichrome ware). The Ashdod of this period expanded outside its walls and was not destroyed until the tenth century B.C., perhaps by King David or by the Egyptian pharaoh Siamun, who conducted a military campaign in this region around 960 B.C. It was Ashdod stratum XII of the late twelfth century that produced the Ashdoda, and the building associated with the Ashdoda may have had cultic significance. But it was the still earlier stratum XIII of the early twelfth century where the Philistine "High Place" was found. The High Place contained a square altar of plastered bricks and a round stone pillar base, which may have been used as a stand for the god of the city; it may have been this type of altar and pillar base that appeared in our story of the ark.

First Samuel 5 tells us that the god of Ashdod was Dagon.[10] The god Dagon was also mentioned in the earlier Samson story when the Philistines of Gaza thanked him for having delivered "Samson our enemy into our hand" (Judg. 16:23). The Philistine god of Ekron of the eighth century B.C., whom we will be studying later (2 Kings 1:2), was Baal-zebub (or Baal-zebul). As has been explained previously, very little epigraphic material of any type has been recovered at the Philistine sites thus far; therefore, no one is sure if the Philistines simply adopted the local gods of Palestine or if they identified the gods of their places of origin with the local gods. Dagon is known to have been an ancient Semitic god of the northern Mesopotamian area, who was worshiped as far back as the third millennium B.C. A northwest Semitic word for grain is *dagan*, so it is thought that Dagon was the god of grain, a fertility god. This Semitic god is well known from the excavated eighteenth-century B.C. archives at Mari in the mid-Euphrates Valley. The name Dagon is used not only in reference to the god, but also as part of a Semitic personal name and even in the name of a month.

Additionally, Dagon is known from some Ugaritic materials as the father of Baal Haddu. Ugarit was on the East Mediterranean coast just opposite the island of Cyprus. It was a major seaport, accepting trade on the east-west routes between Mesopotamia and Greece as well as on the trade routes moving north-south between Egypt and Anatolia. Ugarit was destroyed at the beginning of the twelfth century B.C., and for a time its excavator, Claude Schaeffer, suspected that the Sea Peoples, of whom the Philistines were a part, had razed it on their march south towards Egypt. Schaeffer later determined that a major earthquake had destroyed Ugarit, implying that the Sea

Peoples may have bypassed its ruins (Schaeffer 1983, 74–75). Because of Ugarit's prominent role in the Eastern Mediterranean as a trading center and the importance of Dagon there as a major fertility god, it is unlikely that Dagon would have remained unknown to anyone conducting trade in the region.

A great temple was dedicated to Baal at Ugarit, as well as a house for Baal's high priest, but just to the east of this was a still greater temple, one dedicated to Dagon (Curtis 1985, 36, 88, 91). Two dedicatory stelae in Dagon's name have been found there. Another site, Beth-shean in lower Galilee, also had a temple dedicated to Dagon (Douglas 1962, 287 with picture). The Philistines evidently had a garrison in Beth-shean, which is located in the Valley of Jezreel north of Philistia. This was the place where Saul's body would be hung after his death in battle with the Philistines. The temple there is in the correct time frame for our 1 Samuel 5 story, but we will leave Beth-shean for now and will return later.

Ashdod evidently had a temple dedicated to Dagon that was used until around 150 B.C., for 1 Maccabees 10:83–84 and 11:4 describe Jonathan Maccabeus going there and "burning down the temple of Dagon with all the fugitives who had crowded into it." Presently, however, in order to find a temple in Philistia, a "house of Dagon" comparable to the temple the Bible refers to in 1 Samuel 5, we must turn to the three successive temples at Tell Qasile (see pp. 113–18). It is the third of these temples that is the largest and that fits into the time frame of the Philistine capture of the ark. Again, this is the stratum X (ca. 1050–980 B.C.) temple, referred to in the archaeological literature as temple 131. Tell Qasile is not Ashdod, but viewing the temples at Qasile provides an excellent glimpse into the Philistine cult. T. Dothan believes that the architecture of the temples at Tell Qasile demonstrates links between the Aegean and the Philistine worlds. She mentions that at Qasile there is evidently a fusion of Canaanite temple styles and of temple styles from Mycenae in Greece, from shrines on the isle of Melos in the Cyclades, and from shrines at Kition on Cyprus (T. Dothan 1985, 170). Amihai Mazar, the excavator at Qasile, has elaborated on the nature of this fusion (1980, 61–73). He compares various architectural components of some of the temples of the Late Bronze Age in Palestine (among them the temples at Lachish and Beth-shean), with thirteenth-century temples of Mycenae and Cyprus. He also includes in his comparisons the twelfth-eleventh-century temples at Tell Qasile and on Cyprus. The architectural components that he surveys are 1) the entrances, 2) raised platforms within the temples, 3) benches, 4) pillars, 5) chambers in the backs of the temples, 6) the location and orientation of the temples, and 7) courtyards containing sacrificial altars.

Amihai Mazar suggests that the architectural tradition of the temples at Qasile differs from the West Semitic temple traditions of the Late Bronze and Iron Ages in Palestine. He believes, however, that a connection between the temples of Qasile and those of Cyprus and other Aegean sites is undeniable (1980, 68). He recognizes that this may be due in part to trade between the Near East and the Aegean during the fourteenth and thirteenth centuries B.C., but adds that this resemblance could also be due to the coming of the Sea Peoples during the thirteenth/twelfth century B.C. Through the work of T. Dothan and Mazar, we are better able to understand the journey of the ark of the covenant from one Philistine shrine to the next. As the ark of the Lord was brought into Ashdod and carried into the temple, the people would probably have gathered in the temple courtyard as they would have gathered during cultic ceremonies.[11] First Samuel 5 describes a contest between two gods, Dagon and the Lord God of Israel. It is true that the ark of the covenant had been captured, but does this mean that God had also been captured?

> When the people of Ashdod rose early the next day, there was Dagon, fallen on his face to the ground before the ark of the LORD. So they took Dagon and put him back in his place. But when they rose early on the next morning, Dagon had fallen on his face to the ground before the ark of the LORD, and the head of Dagon and both his hands were lying cut off upon the threshold; only the trunk of Dagon was left to him. [1 Sam. 5:3–4]

At Qasile, each of the three successive temples had a "holy of holies" where the god would have been venerated. Two of the three definitely had a stepped, raised platform, a *bamah* in the holy of holies (see diagram on p. 114). It is easy to picture Dagon falling off such a platform to a prostrate position before the ark of the Lord.

The Hand of the Lord[12]

> The hand of the LORD was heavy upon the people of Ashdod,
> and he terrified and struck them with tumors. . . .
> [1 Sam. 5:6]

For the Israelites in the Lord's army at Ebenezer, the loss of the ark meant that their God had been vanquished. The final outrage for a captured god was to be paraded through a city and then placed in the victor's temple, as at Ashdod. The Israelites were to understand only later that the Lord had allowed this to happen, perhaps to show his displeasure with Eli's sons at Shiloh.

The battle between the deities in Ashdod's temple was not witnessed by any Philistine priest, but was fought at night. After the third night the Philistines realized which deity had been victorious. This realization was reinforced by the fact that the people of Ashdod were afflicted with "tumors," which, when linked to the Philistine remedy "five gold tumors and five gold mice" (1 Sam. 6:4), has been thought to have been the bubonic plague (McCarter 1980, 123; Lind 1980, 97).

This is the passage that I cited earlier and linked with the plague account in the *Iliad* (pp. 71–76). Note that the biblical writer describes this plague as coming from the "hand of the LORD" (1 Sam. 5:6). The Lord had used this means before to wreak havoc on an enemy (Mendenhall 1973, 106–8). When the Philistines learned that the Israelites had brought the ark of the covenant into their camp before battle, they said, "Woe to us! Who can deliver us from the power of these mighty gods? These are the gods who struck the Egyptians with every sort of plague in the wilderness" (1 Sam. 4:8). And after the plague of tumors had struck them, the Philistines wondered, "Why should you harden your hearts as the Egyptians and Pharaoh hardened their hearts?" (1 Sam. 6:6). The events in Egypt, where the Philistines had also been and had fought, were similar enough to the present plague to influence their response. God would deliver the ark as he had delivered Israel from Egypt (Lind 1980, 97–98).

"So they sent and gathered together all the lords of the Philistines. . . " (1 Sam. 5:8). The word used in reference to the Philistine rulers in this passage, in the Samson saga, and later in 1 Samuel 29:2 is *seren* (plural *seranim*), a word whose precise meaning remains unclear to philologists. Most scholars believe it to be a Philistine word with either a Greek origin or a hieroglyphic Hittite origin (McCarter 1980, 123; *ISBE* 3:158). Here again is another possible signpost on the quest to determine the origin of the Philistines.

The Philistine lords operated together when necessary, as we have seen in the Samson stories (Judg. 16). In 1 Samuel 5 the lords decided to send the ark from Ashdod to another Philistine site. We are not told their reasoning here, but it seems a strange decision, knowing, as they did, that the ark was the source of their problems. One commentator suggests that perhaps the ark traveled to Ashkelon and Gaza before arriving in Gath as reported in 1 Samuel 5:8 (McCarter 1980, 101). This is hinted at later perhaps in 1 Samuel 6:4. However, we are told plainly that "the hand of the LORD was against the city [Gath], causing a very great panic; he struck the inhabitants of the city, both young and old, so that tumors broke out on them" (1 Sam. 5:9). So the ark was sent on to Ekron.

Here the story builds to a climax, for the ark's notoriety had preceded its arrival. "As the ark of God was entering Ekron, the people of Ekron cried out, 'They have brought the ark of the god of Israel around to kill us and our people'" (v. 10 NIV). The Ekronites did not want the ark to enter their city due to what had happened at its previous stopping points. Ironically, as seems evident today, it was not the ark that was spreading the plague but the bearers of the ark and those who accompanied it ("Beware of Greeks bearing gifts"). The Ekronites even accused the bearers of trying to kill them. Note the phrase *us and our people*. These words may reflect a city-state mentality as found in their former homes in the Aegean.

Recent excavating seasons at Ekron have brought to light several intriguing finds that may help locate the events of this story. Remember that the city of Ekron was surrounded at the time by a massive mudbrick wall nearly eleven feet thick. A gateway has been uncovered that may have been the location for the scene where the Ekronites tried to prevent the ark from entering the town. This Iron II gateway, probably covering an Iron I gateway, is on the southern side of the city, and directly north of it, in the center of the city, are the remains of some monumental buildings. Two of them, one on top of the other, are labeled building 351 and building 350. It is the upper one (350) that probably dates to the time of the ark story in 1 Samuel 5. Building 350 was constructed in the eleventh century B.C. with a four-foot-thick foundation of boulder-sized stones, suggesting to the excavators that the structure may have been multi-storied. The mudbrick walls above the foundation were plastered white. Excavators T. Dothan and Gitin believe that building 350 was either a temple or a palace/temple complex, due to its architecture and the finds within.

Like the temple in Qasile, this building had a plastered mudbrick *bamah* or platform, which in this case was in one of the three rooms to the west of the main hall. If the ark made it into the city and within this building, it would most likely have been placed in front of the *bamah*. Trude Dothan likens this *bamah* to others at Qasile and Mycenae and on Cyprus.

Among the more interesting finds from building 350 in Ekron are three bronze wheels, each with eight spokes. These, together with a couple of other bronze pieces, have been enough for Dothan and Gitin to suggest that they were part of a bronze cultic stand like those known from a twelfth-century site on Cyprus. The top of this stand would have supported a basin, and the stand itself would have been a smaller version of those made by King Hiram of Tyre for Solomon's temple in Jerusalem about one century later (1 Kings 7:27–37).

In another one of the rooms of this building a cache of unusual ceramic bottles was found. Some of the bottles were crushed; others were whole or were missing only the neck. The various decorative styles were similar to the Philistine bichrome style of the twelfth/eleventh century. A large, ivory, Egyptian earring was recovered in the same room.

In the third room of building 350 a beautiful, whole specimen of an iron knife, with an ivory handle and bronze rivets holding the handle in place, was found. The Philistines of the Bible were noted for their iron chariots and weapons. Near the knife lay a bronze linchpin, a pin that would have kept the wheel of a chariot in place. This third room also contained a small *bamah*, and on top if that was a lump of iron, the significance of which is not known. (Perhaps a gift of iron as in the *Iliad*?)

The entryway into the twenty-six-by-thirty-three-foot main hall of this building was on the north side, and on the north-south axis of the building are two pillar bases seven and a half feet apart. Earlier, in discussing the story of Samson at Gaza, I described a temple at Qasile for comparative purposes. Here now is a possible second example of a temple with pillars.

The main hall also contained a series of three hearths, each about three feet in diameter. A hearth was a common central feature of a megaron at Aegean sites such as Mycenae and Cyprus (see p. 86). The only other Philistine hearths uncovered in Palestine thus far are at Qasile. Each of these hearths built on top of one another was lined with a layer of stream-washed (wadi) pebbles that was covered with a thick layer of ash and charcoal containing a mixture of animal bones.

This hall may have been the location for the gathering of the Philistine lords mentioned in 1 Samuel 5:11: "They sent therefore and gathered together all the lords of the Philistines, and said, 'Send away the ark of the God of Israel, and let it return to its own place, that it may not kill us and our people.'" Note the translation *its own place*. The Hebrew word there is *maqom*, a common word sometimes used to refer to a shrine or a *bamah*. This is a reference to the platform upon which the ark would rest in its own sanctuary. The Philistines realized who had been afflicting them and wished to make amends by returning the ark of the Lord to Israel (McCarter 1980, 124).

The Philistine lords decided on an immediate but appropriate response to the God of the ark, "For there was a deathly panic throughout the whole city. The hand of God was very heavy there; those who did not die were stricken with tumors, and the cry of the city went up to heaven" (vv. 11b–12). Exodus 2:23–24 records another cry to heaven, which God heard and answered. Here in 1 Samuel, we should not anticipate such a favorable response (McCarter 1980, 124). According to Mendenhall, the Philistines used diviners and priests to accomplish the following: "[1] a consultation of the gods through various kinds of specialized divination to ascertain the cause of the outbreak, usually identified as a moral or ethical delict, [2] a confession of sin, and [3] appropriate action as a propitiatory ritual in order to remove the cause of the wrath" (1973, 107).

First Samuel 6 reports all three activities:

> . . . the priests and the diviners . . . said, "If you send away the ark of the God of Israel, do not send it empty, but by all means return him a guilt offering. Then you will be healed and will be ransomed; will not his hand then turn from you?" And they [the Philistine people] said, "What is the guilt offering that we shall return to him?" They [the priests and diviners] answered, "Five gold tumors and five gold mice, according to the number of the lords of the Philistines; for the same plague was upon all of you and upon your lords. So you must make images of your tumors and images of your mice that ravage the land, and give glory to the God of Israel; perhaps he will lighten his hand on you and your gods and your land." [1 Sam. 6:2–5]

Is it possible that the models of the mice and the tumors were crafted at Ekron? Kilns and other industrial installations have been uncovered at two different locations in the tell thus far. Near the gateway in the industrial area of the city a large installation with a crucible containing traces of silver was found. This installation was lined with *hamra*, a hard, red, rough, sandy plaster. This is solid evidence that some metal crafting was being done there during the early

Iron Age I. A gold, double-coiled hair ring was also found in the area. Several kilns were uncovered in field I (the upper tell), including a well-preserved one. It is certainly possible that the models of the tumors and mice were crafted in one of these kilns.

From Ekron the ark of the covenant was drawn on a cart by cows up the Sorek Valley to Beth-shemesh. Ownership of this city was disputed, according to archaeological research and biblical references (Josh. 15:10 assigns it to Judah; Josh. 19:41 to Dan [Ir-shemesh]). According to 1 Samuel 6:8–15, it was then an Israelite town. Its tell has only one Iron Age I level, which contains much Philistine pottery. As has been noted, its material culture is indistinguishable from that of its neighbor Timnah. The contention over this city alerts one to the care required in trying to determine ethnicity of material cultural remains. At the time that the story of the ark took place, Beth-shemesh, whose name means literally "House of the Sun (god)," evidently was controlled by Israelites but had a Philistine presence (A. Mazar 1990, 312; Wright 1966, 74–76; T. Dothan 1982a, 50–51). Disaster struck there, just as in the Philistine cities where the ark had been, for quite a few inhabitants died, according to the 1 Samuel account. The plague probably killed those men as well, but in this case they were said to have died because they had "looked into the ark of the LORD" (1 Sam. 6:19 NIV, RSV). Perhaps because Beth-shemesh did not appear to have priests present or perhaps because the people feared further judgment from the Lord, the ark was sent on to Kiriath-jearim, to remain there for some twenty years.

The Lord Delivers

". . . and he [God] will deliver you out of the hand of the Philistines."
[1 Sam. 7:3]

Before beginning our study of the life and times of Saul and his encounters with the Philistines, let us look briefly at 1 Samuel 7, which deals with Samuel in his role as judge. There is little in this chapter about Philistia, but the battle between Samuel and the Philistines and its results are well known: " . . . the Philistines drew near to attack Israel; but the LORD thundered with a mighty voice that day against the Philistines and threw them into confusion; and they were routed before Israel" (v. 10). It was after this battle that Samuel set up his stone of help or "Ebenezer." We have encountered the name before, in 1 Samuel 4, since it was at Ebenezer that Israel had lost an earlier battle and the ark of the covenant. Now, twenty years after the recovery of the ark, Israel was able to push back and defeat the Philistines at Ebenezer through the help of the Lord God. Whether or not the Ebenezer of chapter 7 is at the same location as the Ebenezer of chapter 4 is difficult to determine, but the significance of the name would not have been lost on the Israelites (McCarter 1980, 146–47, 149).

The most intriguing verse of this passage, however, is 14: "The towns that the Philistines had taken from Israel were restored to Israel, from Ekron to Gath; and Israel recovered their territory from the hand of the Philistines." Perhaps what is meant here is that due to Samuel the cities *up to* the borders of Ekron and Gath were restored to Israel but not Ekron or Gath itself. The excavations at Ekron have not detected any type of destruction or transition of material culture during this time, but it is possible that the environs around the city were taken by Israel. The verse goes on to say, "There was peace also between Israel and the Amorites." However, there soon would be no peace between Israel and Philistia.

Metal Crafting

"He [Saul] shall save my people from the hand of the Philistines. . . . "
[1 Sam. 9:16]

The battle of Mizpah where Samuel raised his Ebenezer demonstrated to Israel what God could do for his people. Alas, though, Samuel grew old, his sons did not follow in the ways of the Lord, and the people came to Samuel with a request for a king, a man to lead them as kings in the surrounding nations did. The Israelites had forgotten what the Lord could do, and they wished instead to follow a man who would lead them against the Philistines.

They were rebelling against God as back in the days of Moses: "they have rejected me from being king over them" (1 Sam. 8:7). After the people were warned about what a king would do (1 Sam. 8:10–22), they were sent home, and God set in motion the choosing of the king. Saul was anointed and crowned, but not everyone supported him until after the battle for Jabesh-gilead against Nahash the Ammonite. God was willing to operate through Saul (chap. 11), and Saul's kingship was reaffirmed by "all the Israelites" (v. 15) at Gilgal. However, his kingship was soon repudiated.

It is in chapter 13 that we again encounter the Philistines. The text is broken in verse 1, which tells Saul's age when he began to reign and the length of his reign. However, the following story took place shortly after 1050 B.C. Saul was in command of the main Israelite striking force at Michmash, and Saul's son Jonathan seemed to be the head of the reserve force back in Gibeah. It was Jonathan who began this episode of what would turn out to be a long conflict with the Philistines by making a preemptive strike against them; Jonathan left Gibeah and successfully hit the Philistine garrison at Geba (or was it Gibeah? McCarter 1980, 181–82, 227, as well as 1 Sam. 10:5 and 13:3). This led both the Philistines and Israelites to muster their men.

Saul took his men down to Gilgal where Samuel was to meet them, but Saul, in a wrongheaded attempt to keep his force together, took on the role of the priest and offered the burnt offering just before Samuel made his appearance. Therefore, Samuel denounced Saul and his kingship, declaring that Saul would not leave a dynasty after him. Samuel then left for Gibeah.

What follows are verses that can be better understood now that pertinent artifacts are being excavated and studied.

> Now there was no smith to be found throughout all the land of Israel; for the Philistines said, "The Hebrews must not make swords or spears for themselves"; so all the Israelites went down to the Philistines to sharpen their plowshare, mattocks, axes, or sickles; the charge was two-thirds of a shekel [a pim] for the plowshares and for the mattocks, and one-third of a shekel for sharpening the axes and for setting the goads. So on the day of the battle neither sword nor spear was to be found in the possession of any of the people with Saul and Jonathan; but Saul and his son Jonathan had them. [1 Sam. 13:19–22]

That the Philistines had iron has been shown by the excavations throughout Philistia. Recall a previous section where I stated that an iron knife with an ivory handle and bronze rivets, as well as an ingot of iron, had been recovered during a recent season at Ekron. These and other metal implements belong to stratum V, around 1050 B.C. They date to the time of our story in 1 Samuel 13. An iron knife with a similar ivory handle and bronze rivets was recovered at Tell Qasile from an earlier period (stratum XII), cirea 1150–1100 B.C. (A. Mazar 1985b, 1, 6–8). At both Qasile and Ekron the knives were found in context with the Philistine pottery, and at Ekron they were found beside a *bamah*, a high place. "Such iron knives with bronze rivets have been found in twelfth to early eleventh century contexts

141

throughout the Aegean and the eastern Mediterranean, from Perati in Attica to Hama in Syria, almost always uncovered in association with typical Mycenaean IIIC1 pottery of the twelfth century B.C. (or its local imitations)" (Muhly 1982, 49).

The ingots and iron knives call to mind several passages in the *Iliad*. At the funeral and games for Patroclus after the death of Hector by Achilles' hand, the animals were sacrificed with an iron knife: "Many a white ox fell with his last gasp to the iron knife . . ." (23.30–31, Rieu 1950, 413). The *Iliad* also contains several passages where iron is offered either as part of a ransom or as a prize. For example, when one Trojan is captured, he begs his captor, "Take me alive, son of Atreus, and take appropriate ransom. In my father's house the treasures lie piled in abundance; bronze is there, and gold, and difficultly wrought iron . . ." (6.46–48, Lattimore 1951, 154). And at the funeral games for Patroclus, prizes for a chariot race included a woman skilled in the fine crafts and a large tripod as the top prize; two talents of gold as fourth-place prize, and a third-place prize of a bright grey iron kettle (23.257–70, Rieu 1950, 419). In another contest the prize was a lump of pig iron, large enough, according to Achilles, "'to keep the winner in iron for five years or more, even if his *farm is out in the wilds*. It will not be lack of iron that sends his *shepherd or his ploughman in to town*. He will have plenty on the spot'" (emphasis mine; 23.833–35, Rieu 1950, 434).

The Philistines possessed the technology of working with metal for both weapons and farming implements, according to 1 Samuel 13:19–22. Likewise, the *Iliad* presents the Aegean Greeks as having the technology for producing both iron weapons and iron farming implements. Moses, in Deuteronomy 8:9, mentions that among the blessings of the Promised Land are its mountains of iron. Yet, in the days of Saul, the Israelites were not yet as skilled in working with metal as the Philistines were. Even three hundred years earlier and probably at least a full century before Moses, Pharaoh Tut-ankh-Amon was buried in a tomb containing, among other things, a beautiful iron knife. Iron was known in the Late Bronze Age, but the technology for working the ore was not available throughout the Near East until well into the Iron Age.

First Samuel 13:19–22 includes a word that has been troublesome for a long time. The word is *pim* in verse 21. That word is used only once in the Hebrew Bible—here in this verse. Neither the translators of the King James Version nor those of the Authorized Version knew what it meant, so they translated it as "file," an implement for sharp-

pim

Pim weight; its equivalent weight in silver was the price a Philistine smith charged to sharpen a plow or a mattock.

ening farm tools. The translators of the Revised Standard Version knew it to be a weight used for payment but did not know its value. By now, however, at least a dozen weights bearing the inscription *pim* have been uncovered at various sites such as Tells Gezer, Timnah, Ashdod, and Ekron. The weight of a pim is about one-fourth of an ounce of silver, or two-thirds of a shekel. This is the way that the New International Version and the New Revised Standard Version have translated the word. Interestingly enough, one Bible encyclopedia mentions that *pim* is probably a non-Hebrew word belonging to the Philistines (*ISBE* 4:1054). This reasoning may be due to the fact that the word occurs only here, in a Philistine context. In any case, the Philistines charged around one-fourth of an ounce (of silver) to sharpen a plow or a mattock and half that for sharpening an axe or setting the point on an oxgoad.

The mention of "no smith" in 1 Samuel 13:19 has also puzzled readers for a long time. We assume that the reference here is to iron and the working of iron (see, for example, the NIV Study Bible note, p. 393). This assumption leads to other questions. What was the secret in making iron weapons? Was it so difficult that the few accomplished people could keep the technique to themselves for such a long time? And, if the protagonists in the *Iliad* had iron ingots and gave iron as gifts, why did they fight with bronze weapons? Thanks to the definitive works of James Muhly and Jane Waldbaum pertaining to metalworking in the ancient Near East, these questions and others can now be answered (Muhly 1982; Waldbaum 1978, 1990; A. Mazar 1990, 356–66).

143

Bronze weapons were made of an alloy of 90 percent copper and 10 percent tin. Iron ore was more plentiful in the Near East than copper ore and easier to dig out. Tin had to be imported from, it is thought, as far away as England and Afghanistan. Why, then, did the ancient Near Eastern peoples continue to make bronze weapons instead of iron ones? There are two reasons, according to Muhly, and Waldbaum adds a third.

First, fashioning iron into feasible weapons required melting it in a kiln that could heat to 1530 degrees Celsius, whereas melting copper required a temperature of 1100 degrees Celsius. Weapons made from iron not heated to this high temperature were inferior to those made of bronze.

Second, archaeology in recent years has demonstrated that there was extensive trade throughout the ancient Near East and to regions beyond it during the Late Bronze Age. While this extensive trade, which included tin, lasted, there was no need to devise kilns that could melt the iron at 1530 degrees Celsius. Around 1200 B.C., the Near East and the Aegean witnessed the collapse of empires, the Trojan War, and the movements of the Sea Peoples. Needless to say, trade was disrupted. It appears that tin was then in short supply. Necessity became the mother of invention, and a better kiln was developed.

It also appears that many of the early iron implements that were around in the Late Bronze Age, like those mentioned in the *Iliad*, were made of wrought iron rather than of the carburized iron produced in the hotter kiln. Wrought iron is shaped by hammering, and this was done after the iron was smelted and was still in a pliable state. Since iron weapons produced in this manner are inferior to bronze weapons, the plentiful supplies of iron ore in the ground were worthless until the turmoil at the end of the Bronze Age forced the smithy to develop a hotter furnace in order to work an ore other than copper and tin.

Even when the hotter furnace is used, a superior weapon does not automatically result. The process is still quite complicated, and a smithy would probably have to have done considerable experimentation before discovering that iron, after it has reached its melting point, must be quenched (by plunging it into a vat of cold water) and tempered (by further heat treatments at different temperatures). Only then does a carburized iron implement superior to any bronze one result. The people who possessed this technology could garner power, as 1 Samuel 13:19–22 explains. The Philistines restricted the spread of their superior metalworking technology to maintain their power over the Israelites.

Interestingly, the word for iron is not even used in the 1 Samuel 13:19 passage, nor is there any reference there to a Philistine monopoly of iron. Perhaps the passage intends to show that the Philistines were technologically superior to the Israelites in all metalworking and were able to control access to the metals and the technology. However, tests that have been done on iron artifacts from Philistine sites do not show a consistent pattern of carburizing the iron.

Jane Waldbaum suggests a third reason for a switch from bronze weapons to iron, an ecological one. Bronzeworking required two to four times more wood charcoal than ironworking. Perhaps the ancient Near East was becoming deforested and the smithy was forced to develop a better way. Waldbaum recognizes, however, that at present there is not enough evidence to support this hypothesis.

The technological advance in ironworking could only be used for implements having a simple shape to mold; therefore, iron was used for weapons of war and for farming tools. Bronze, evidently, had been the metal of choice for making weapons in the eleventh century B.C. before iron began to dominate, and through the centuries bronze has continued to be chosen for casting objects with a more intricate design, such as statues.

Tests have been conducted on some Iron Age objects excavated in Israel and Cyprus to determine if they were carburized or wrought, and one hopes this testing will become a standard practice in order to better determine when and where advanced iron technology developed. No tests have been conducted yet on the iron knife with the ivory handle found at Ekron during the 1988 season. The iron knife from King Tut's tomb that I mentioned also has not had any technical tests done on it, but it is suspected that it was made from meteoritic iron rather than from iron ores found naturally in the earth. Other iron objects from the Late Bronze period that have been tested have been shown to be from meteorite iron.

Based on tests of iron artifacts from the 1200–900 B.C. time frame, Muhly believes that iron technology was developed in the East Mediterranean—the dominant role belonging to the Greeks and the Greek colonists who arrived on Cyprus early in the twelfth century. These are the same people who made the Mycenaean IIIC:1b pottery. He further believes that from Cyprus the iron metallurgy was introduced to Canaan via the Sea Peoples, which included the Philistines.

First Samuel 13:19–22 states that the Israelites had to go to Philistia to maintain their metal farm implements. Of the iron artifacts found in Israel from this Iron I period, iron weapons (such as the iron knife at Ekron) are found only at Philistine sites, whereas iron farm implements (such as an iron plowshare found at Gibeah, Saul's hometown) have been found throughout Palestine. Muhly believes, however, that Philistine control over the Israelites was political rather than simply technological. King David was the Israelite who would break the Philistine confederation.

"Hebrews Are Coming"

"Look, Hebrews are coming out of the holes. . . ."
[1 Sam. 14:11]

There is an interesting anecdotal story from World War I in connection with the events related in 1 Samuel 14 (Gidal 1985, 9–10). In the biblical account, the Israelites under Saul were facing the Philistines at a site five miles northeast of Gibeah and fifteen miles west of Gilgal. This was an unusual locale for the Philistines since it is in the central hill country, at Michmash, and not on the coastal plain. Michmash was strategically important, since it guarded the entrance of a pass to the Israelite highlands. The Israelite army was gathered on the opposite side of the pass at Geba with additional forces at Gibeah. Jonathan with his armor-bearer decided to try to break the stalemate by conducting a frontal assault on the Philistine outpost at Michmash. Jonathan waited for the Lord to give the proper sign, climbed the crag, and successfully routed the Philistine troops in the outpost, leading to a general rout of the enemy. Saul joined in chasing the Philistines back towards the coastal plain.

The World War I anecdote involves the English forces who were battling the Turks in the area of Michmash. Orders were given to take the Turkish outpost there. It is said that an English staff officer remembered dimly a biblical story happening in the area. He went to his Bible and found the incident of 1 Samuel 14. The officer then went to his general and read him the account of how Jonathan defeated the Philistine garrison by climbing the crag and killing about twenty Philistines in an area no larger than a half an acre. Some versions of the story say it was General Allenby himself who then devised the plan for the British.

In any event, scouts were sent out to find the trail that Jonathan might have taken up to this half-acre site. They found a pass with a "rocky crag on one side and a rocky crag on the other. . . . One crag rose on the north in front of Michmash, and the other on the south in front of Geba" (1 Sam. 14:4–5). Allenby's staff officer, a brigadier, sent a detachment of men up this trail to the half-acre plot before the Turkish squad awoke, and the Turkish army, a short distance away, was routed by the English as the Philistines had been routed by the Israelites.

There is another interesting part to the story in the Bible. The passage in 1 Samuel 14:21 states, "Those Hebrews who had previously been with the Philistines and had gone up with them to their camp went over to the Israelites who were with Saul and Jonathan" (NIV). Evidently because of Philistine domination, some Israelites had gone over to the Philistine side, but now that the Philistines were on the run, these Hebrews switched sides again. Later, we will encounter other examples of Hebrews in the Philistine camp (or hiding, as in v. 22) and the consequences of their actions.

A Giant Philistine

"Am I not a Philistine? . . . Choose a man for yourselves, and let him come down to me."
[1 Sam. 17:8]

The seventeenth chapter of Samuel contains one of the best-known stories of the Bible. The battle it describes between David and Goliath took place in the foothills, the Shephelah, some fourteen miles west of Bethlehem. This would have been a day's journey away from home for young David, who was sent by his father to deliver food to his brothers at the battle front. The valley the Philistines and Israelites were fighting over led out onto the coastal plain. Later, in 2 Chronicles 11:7, Rehoboam would build a fortress at Soco in the same valley, but by the time of 2 Chronicles 28:18, the Philistines would capture it (Myers 1986b, 290).

First Samuel 17 contains several episodes reminiscent of the *Iliad* with its encounters between the Achaean Greeks and the Trojans. Since the Philistines came from the Aegean orb, it is logical to assume that they shared some customs with the heroes of the *Iliad*. Consider, for example, the armor that Goliath wore:

He had a helmet of bronze on his head, and he was armed with a coat of mail [plated cuirass/scale armor]; the weight of the coat was five thousand shekels of bronze. He had greaves of bronze on his legs and a javelin [scimitar] of bronze slung between his shoulders. The shaft of his spear was like a weaver's beam, and his spear's head weighed six hundred shekels of iron; and his shield-bearer went before him. [1 Sam. 17:5–7; additions in brackets are from McCarter 1980, 284 and NIV]

The *Iliad* describes the armor for the one-on-one combat between Paris and Menelaus in book 3, lines 330–40 (Rieu 1950, 72–73):

[Paris] began by tying round his legs a pair of splendid greaves, which were fitted with silver clips for the ankles. Next he put a cuirass [plated armor] on his breast. . . . Over his shoulder he slung a bronze sword with a silver-studded hilt, and then a great thick shield. On his sturdy head he set a well-made helmet. It had a horsehair crest, and the plume nodded grimly from the top. Last, he took up a powerful spear, which was fitted to his grip.

Battle-loving Menelaus also equipped himself in the same way. . . . [brackets mine]

Note that I made two additions in brackets in the quote from 1 Samuel. Where the New Revised Standard Version reads "coat of mail," the New International Version has "coat of scale armor," similar to the Anchor Bible's "plated cuirass" or plated armor. My second addition, from the Anchor Bible, illustrates the dissimilarity between its translation and those of the New Revised Standard and New International Versions. I prefer the translation *scimitar* because descriptions and reliefs of battle scenes of warfare in the ancient Near East never show a javelin "slung between [the] shoulders" (see Yadin 1963, 1 and 2). In addition, the translations of 17:5–7 do not mention that Goliath carried a sword. Yet, later, in verse 45, David points out, "You come to me with sword and spear and with a javelin [read *scimitar*]. . . ." And lastly, note verses 50–51: "So David prevailed over the Philistine with a sling and with a stone, striking down the Philistine and killing him; there was no sword in David's hand. Then David ran and stood over the Philistine; he grasped his sword, drew it out of its sheath, and killed him; then he cut off his head with it."

The translation problem lies with the Hebrew word used in verse 6—*kidon*. Both the New International Version and the New Revised Standard Version translate the word "javelin," but the 1 Samuel Anchor Bible Commentary (McCarter 1980, 284, 291–93) and its supporting references suggest that a *kidon* was a scimitar (see also Molin 1956). This was a sword with a single-edged, curved cutting blade on its outer, convex side. The Joshua volume of the Anchor Bible series uses a similar word, *sicklesword,* to translate *kidon* in Joshua 8:18, 26. These and two references in Job 39:23 and 41:29 are the only biblical references to a *kidon.* Yadin, in his discussion of the Egyptian sicklesword (a *khopesh,* meaning the "foreleg of an animal," which it does resemble), states that it was a very common weapon used from Anatolia to Egypt and that it continued to be used into the twelfth century B.C., the period of the judges (Yadin 1963, 2:349–50; pictures in 1:172, especially 204–7, where Pharaoh Ramesses III is shown carrying one). The sicklesword was out of use by the end of the eleventh century B.C. (Boling and Wright 1982, 240).

All this suggests that 1 Samuel 17:45 should read, "You [Goliath] come to me with sword and spear and scimitar. . . ." The first weapon mentioned, the double-edged, pointed sword, was used for thrusting, and the scimitar, in contrast, was used for slashing. The Hebrew word for sword used here and in verses 39, 47, 50, and 51 but omitted in the description of Goliath in verses 5–7 is *hereb,* a very common word for a sword. David used the *hereb,* the double-edged sword, to decapitate Goliath, even though the scimitar would have worked better. It is Goliath's double-edged sword that David later picked up from Ahimelech the priest when he was fleeing from Saul in chapter 21.

The Anchor Bible suggests that the references in 17:7 and in 2 Samuel 21:19 ("the shaft of his spear was like a weaver's beam") are actually describing a device attached to the spear for slinging purposes, making the spear into a type of javelin. These are depicted in battle scenes from both Egypt and Greece and in the *Iliad,* where the spear is tossed first by one contestant and then the other in one-on-one combat.

Goliath's armor, for the most part, was similar to that of the protagonists in the *Iliad.* His cuirass, though, was probably a coat of mail or scale armor, whereas those described in the *Iliad* may have had two solid halves clasped together. Although it may have been Aegean in type, Goliath's armor was not similar to Philistine dress as pictured on the Egyptian reliefs at Medinet Habu. This is not necessarily an obstacle to assigning Goliath an Aegean heritage, since the biblical Philistines were a confederation of several group of Sea Peoples, one of which would have included Goliath's forebears.

The challenge shouted by the champion Goliath was typically Aegean; similar calls are found repeatedly in the *Iliad.* In book 3 Paris, the new husband of the lady Helen, challenged Menelaus, her former husband, to a duel that would decide once and for all who would receive her. Afterward, the others were to have made a treaty of peace. Alas, the duel did not settle the matter (neither did the duel between David and Goliath), and there would be more challenges before the Achaeans sailed for home. This type of battle, choosing representatives from each army to fight to decide an outcome without heavy loss of life, was foreign to the Israelites, but it was not foreign to the Aegean Philistines.

In the biblical story, the Philistines fled and were chased by the Israelites to Gath and the gates of Ekron to continue their battles another day: "The troops of Israel and Judah rose up with a shout and pursued the Philistines as far as Gath and the gates of Ekron, so that the wounded Philistines fell on the way from Shaaraim as far as Gath and Ekron" (1 Sam. 17:52).

Gath, Tell es-Safi, has not been excavated extensively, but the excavations at Ekron do show that Ekron was a large urban center with strong fortifications during the time depicted in 1 Samuel 17 (stratum V). In fact, the city was then at a peak according to the excavations thus far; the rich, eleventh-century finds (described earlier) include the particularly fine iron knife with an ivory handle and bronze rivets. The city had a large industrial area, including kilns and cultic areas. The bronze wheels of an incense stand and the bronze pin for a chariot wheel reflect its Aegean background. The time frame of Ekron's stratum V is the end of the Iron I period there and elsewhere in Palestine and coincides with the arrival of David, who would later become king over Israel.

✺5✺

The Philistines
from David to Solomon

David's Flight

David rose and fled that day from Saul; he went to King
Achish of Gath.
[1 Sam. 21:10]

We have now reached the apex of the struggle between Philistia
and Israel. Near the end of the Iron I period, in the succeeding stories of David's relationship with Achish, king of Gath, there seems to
be a definite shift in the strategy of the Philistines. They seem to have
become very expansionist minded. No longer content with the
coastal plain, they made inroads into the foothills, the Shephelah,
beginning in Saul's day. Initially, they had the upper hand with their
superior skills in metalworking and in the strength that their confederation provided, as illustrated by 1 Samuel 13, especially by verses
19–22. But this superiority would be affected by David's shrewd
relationship with Achish. Who was this king of Gath?

The Anchor Bible (McCarter 1980, 356–57) states that the name
Achish may be Philistine in origin.[1] Since we do not yet possess sufficient epigraphic material of a Philistine language (with the excep-

tions perhaps of the Deir Alla tablets and the seal at Ashdod, both still undeciphered), this etymology for Achish may be premature. The commentary also cites Mitchell (1967, 415), who points out that the name Achish was found on an Eighteenth Dynasty (Late Bronze Age) Egyptian writing board with Cretan (*kftyw*) names. Mitchell further links the name Achish to that of Anchises, a Trojan, the father of Aeneas, making the same connection I proposed in chapter 3 (p. 69; McCarter 1980, 356; Mitchell 1967, 415). So too does Wainwright (1959, 76–78), who concludes his discussion on the plague and Apollo Smintheus by stating, "There is, thus, much to connect the Philistines with Dardanians and originally at some point with the Troad."

The name Goliath, like Achish, is not Semitic, but rather Anatolian (McCarter 1980, 291, Mitchell 1967, 415; Wainwright 1959, 79). Not all agree though; the *International Standard Bible Encyclopedia* (2:524) proposes that Goliath may have been a remnant of one of the aboriginal groups of giants of Palestine who now were in the employ of the Philistines.

This discussion of names provides some background to the major story of David's encounter with King Achish of Gath.

Gift of Achish

> So that day Achish gave him Ziklag. . . .
> [1 Sam. 27:6]

The relationship between Saul and David deteriorated so badly that David decided to go to the Philistine territory, knowing that Saul would be reluctant to attack him there. So David and the six hundred men with him offered their services to Achish, king of Gath (ca. 1020 B.C.). David entered into an arrangement, receiving a military fief in exchange for his services to Achish, maybe an arrangement similar to what the Philistines had with their Egyptian overlords.

Verse 5 of chapter 27, in which David asks to live in a country town, may already foreshadow his plan, which is found beginning in verse 8. David needed to get out from under King Achish's eye. Achish honored his request and gave him the city of Ziklag, a town which we are still not able to locate definitively today.

Initially during the days of the conquest of Canaan by Joshua, the tribe of Simeon seems to have received Ziklag through the casting of

Boundary stone from Gezer. The Hebrew reads *thm gzr;* the Greek, *Alkion.*

lots (Josh. 19:5; 1 Chron. 4:30); however, Ziklag is also listed as part of Judah's inheritance in Joshua 15:31. By the time of David, Ziklag must have fallen into the Philistine sphere of influence, since Achish was able to grant it to David. In 1 Samuel 30:14, the words of the Egyptian servant imply that Ziklag was in the vicinity of "the Negeb of the Cherethites" (or "Cretans"). And still much later, when the Jews returned to Palestine from captivity in Babylon, some of them settled in Ziklag (Neh. 11:28).

All of the above passages locate Ziklag by placing it in context with other cities or within a region. Ziklag must have been north of Beer-sheba on the Nahal Gerar, but was it to the northwest or northeast? Much of the recent dispute has centered on two sites, Tel Sera' (Tell esh-Shariah in Arabic), which is about ten miles northwest of Beer-sheba, and Tel Halif (Tell Khuweilifeh in Arabic), which is about ten miles northeast of Beer-sheba.

Using the biblical passages mentioned above, we can make the following assumptions: The mound of Ziklag would have been of modest size in the period of the Israelite conquest of Canaan; it would have had a Philistine occupation before the kings of Judah took over and would have had a Persian occupation period after the Jews returned from captivity. Both Tel Sera' and Tel Halif meet these

153

qualifications. If only the ancient peoples had put up city limit signs (as at Gezer, which was rare), site identification would be so much easier! The uncertainty over the location of Ziklag shows that archaeologists need to be cautious (as do those who use the published results of their excavations) when drawing conclusions from their findings.

Ziklag is particularly important, since it was in this town that David was able to establish a base of operations and develop his shrewd (or brutal?) administrative capabilities (1 Sam. 27:8–12; 30:26–31). David's stay in Ziklag preceded his move to Hebron to be anointed king of Judah (2 Sam. 2) and his later move to Jerusalem to become king over all Israel. So let us study the two sites of Tels Seraʻ and Halif, particularly the Philistine layers, to determine what they reveal of the Sea Peoples' presence around the end of the eleventh century B.C. and into the tenth century.

Both sites are located on the Nahal Gerar (or Wadi esh-Shariah), with Tel Halif lying about eight miles to the east of Tel Seraʻ. The excavations at Tel Seraʻ were conducted from 1972 to 1978 by Eliezer Oren of Ben Gurion University of the Negev (Oren 1982). This tell covers approximately four acres; the stratum that provides ample evidence of a Philistine presence is called stratum VIII. The earlier Canaanite stratum X, of the thirteenth century, contained numerous imported Egyptian, Mycenaean, and Cypriot vessels—the same type of pottery we have observed in various other sites during the same period. The final Canaanite stratum, stratum IX (1200–1150 B.C.), was destroyed in the mid-twelfth century B.C. This stratum contained no Mycenaean or Cypriot imports, the same finding that we observed at other nearby sites, but neither did stratum IX contain Philistine sherds. Philistine pottery did not appear until the following stratum, stratum VIII. Oren believes that the Philistine pottery did not appear before the end of the reign of Pharaoh Ramesses III in the mid-twelfth century B.C. (Oren 1982, 166). He also believes that the destruction of stratum IX may have been due to a group of the Sea Peoples or possibly the Amalekites (mentioned in 1 Sam. 30). The eleventh-century B.C. buildings of stratum VIII contained late Philistine pottery of various types, such as common bell-shaped bowls, beer jugs, and Ashdod ware, a type of pottery that is decorated by applying black and white over a red background. Oren emphasizes that there is continuity *without* a destruction layer between the Philistine stratum VIII and the following Israelite stratum VII, which would be logical if Tel Seraʻ were

Fertility
figurine with
feathered
headdress
from Tel Halif.

David's Ziklag. There would have been no reason for David to destory this town before moving to Hebron to become the king of Judah; ". . . therefore Ziklag has belonged to the kings of Judah to this day" (1 Sam. 27:6).

For Oren, the continued presence of the Philistines into stratum VII without a destruction layer is crucial. What caps the argument for him that Tel Sera' is Ziklag is an architectural feature of stratum VII that in Palestinian archaeology has been commonly associated with the royal house of Judah: buildings constructed of stone ashlars. The stone blocks were finely cut, squared, and quite often placed in what is called a header-stretcher fashion (alternating the stones, first the wide side and then the narrow side facing out). Use of this ashlar building technique would have been logical in David's Ziklag, if David and his successors maintained the town as they did Hazor, Megiddo, Samaria, Gezer, and other sites with "royal architecture."

Stratum VI comes next, and its artifacts and other features show that Tel Sera' was occupied for a time by the Assyrians. This layer

Tel Halif, perhaps the site of Ziklag.

suffered a destruction, and Oren conjectures that perhaps this destruction was by the hands of Nebuchadnezzar, Josiah, or an Egyptian pharaoh. The Persian period comes next (stratum V), and this layer shows that the city may have become a storage center for grain. This evidence would be compatible with our understanding of the Jews' return from captivity. They would have needed to plant and then plan for storage for their crops, especially because of the problems the returnees had with their neighbors.

All of the evidence from Tel Sera' meshes neatly with the biblical texts on Ziklag. Next, let us go to Tel Halif, examine it, and compare the results with those from Tel Sera'.

Joe Seger of Mississippi State University spent four summers excavating Tel Halif between 1976 and 1980, with follow-up sessions throughout the 1980s (Seger 1983, 1984). I mentioned above that Tels Sera' and Halif lie on an east-west plane within eight miles of each other. Both are approximately twenty-three miles south of Tell es-Safi, which may have been the Gath of Achish the Philistine. Either of the tells qualify according to David's words to Achish (1 Sam. 27:5), ". . . let a place be given me in one of the country towns . . . for why should your servant live in the royal city with you?" Twenty-three miles would have been far enough away to have been out of the direct eye of Achish. Tell Halif, according to Seger, would have been even more out of the view of the king than Tel Seraʿ. It is eight miles *east* of Seraʿ (and therefore eight miles further away from the Philistine coastal plain), at the head of the Wadi esh-Shariah (Nahal Gerar) and at the westernmost ridge of hills that compose the hills of Judea. In other words, from this location David would have been better able to skirt around Philistine territory, avoid detection by them, and get to the south to conduct his raids against the Amalekites and others (1 Sam. 27:8–11). If David had been at Tel Seraʿ, he would have to have avoided Tel Halif in going to Judea to divide the spoils (1 Sam. 30:26–31). So, the location of Tel Halif looks very favorable for the site of Ziklag. What about the archaeological record?

Tel Seraʿ had a clear-cut Philistine presence during the days that we ascribe to David, but Seger interprets this as evidence that it was *not* Ziklag. Would Achish have given a thriving Philistine country town over to a recent enemy, an enemy of whom the Philistines had asked,

> "Is this not David the king of the land?
> Did they not sing to one another of him in dances,
> > 'Saul has killed his thousands,
> > > and David his ten thousands'?"
> [1 Sam. 21:11]

Wouldn't it have been more logical for Achish to have turned over to David an outpost on the periphery—like Tel Halif? During the eleventh century B.C., Halif had a very modest Philistine presence, which, according to Seger, would have made it easy for David and his men to take it over with Achish's blessing.

According to Seger, due to the raid on the town by the Amalekites (1 Sam. 30), there should be some sort of destruction debris at Ziklag; the Egyptian captive stated, ". . . and we burned Ziklag down" (v. 14). However, Oren spoke of the continuity between the Philistine and the Judean strata at Tel Seraʿ. Tel Halif also shows no sign of widespread burning, but it does show "willful destruction" of eleventh-century artifacts, including the Philistine type (Seger 1984, 50). Seger believes that enough evidence has been uncovered to indicate some sort of disturbance at the site at the end of the eleventh century B.C.

The tenth century at Tel Halif saw some modest reconstruction, and extensive rebuilding occurred at the end of the tenth century and into the ninth. This construction pattern makes sense for Seger, since it was soon after the Amalekite raid that David received word of Saul's death and moved to Hebron (2 Sam. 1–2). The move to Hebron would have forestalled any extensive rebuilding of the site until Solomon's time or later. The fact that no ashlar buildings or "royal architecture" have yet been found at Halif, according to Seger, should not rule out Halif as Ziklag. It is also important to remember that not all parts of the tell have been excavated.

The occupation of Halif was disrupted by the Assyrian conquest around 701 B.C. Halif was resettled shortly thereafter for a very short period and was not occupied during the Babylonian conquest. It was later resettled during the Persian period, Nehemiah's time, as was Tel Sera'.

In summary, Seger feels that Tel Halif presents as good a stratigraphic case for being David's Ziklag as does Tel Sera', and he believes that Tel Halif is in a better strategic position than Tel Sera'. According to Seger, if Tel Halif is not Ziklag, then another reasonable possibility would be that it is the biblical city of Rimmon. We will consider this briefly.

Oded Borowski, a former member of Kibbutz Lahav next to Tel Halif who is now teaching at Emory University in Georgia, has recently become co-director at Tel Halif (Borowski 1988). He adds some interesting insights to the site identification question of whether Tel Halif or Tel Sera' is David's Ziklag. Borowski begins his comments on Oren's identification of Tel Sera' as Ziklag by citing 1 Samuel 30. This chapter concerns David's return to Ziklag after a three-day march to discover that it had been attacked by the Amalekites. All the wives, sons, and daughters of David and his men had been taken captive. David hurried in pursuit, leaving in Ziklag two hundred men who were too exhausted to cross the Besor Brook (vv. 9–10)—now identified as the Wadi esh-Shariah/Nahal Gerar. Even though both Sera' and Halif are near the Besor Brook, it is wider and more difficult to cross by Tel Sera'; therefore, Borowski believes that Tel Sera' is the better candidate for Ziklag.

Borowski believes that his site, Tel Halif, is the biblical Rimmon (or En-rimmon), and he demonstrates that this name is preserved in the area. 'En means "spring of," and rimmon means "pomegranate." There are sufficient water sources in the area to justify the reference to springs. Pomegranates are a common fruit in the Near East, and the excavations at Halif have even uncovered a ceramic bowl with a pomegranate figure in its center. (However, ceramic containers in the shape of pomegranates were also recovered at Tel Sera' and at Ekron.) In addition, Rimmon is mentioned in biblical verses cited in connection with Ziklag, notably in Joshua 15:31–32; 19:7; and in Nehemiah 11:29 concerning the return of the Israelites from the Babylonian exile. Rimmon definitely was in the neighborhood of Ziklag, and due to the retention of the name En-rimmon in the area, as well as geographic and topographic data, Borowski feels that Tel Halif is Rimmon rather than Ziklag. He recognizes that the debate will continue, but so will the excavations at Tel Halif.

Although scholarly debate will continue on the question whether Tel Sera' or Tel Halif is David's Ziklag, considerable information about the Philistine world of King Achish of Gath and his "country town" of Ziklag has already been recovered. Both of the tells (Sera' more so than Halif) had a Philistine presence in the Iron I period (see fig. 1, p. 91). Even the town's name, Ziklag, displays its foreign character, for that is a non-Semitic name. Oren believes that the name may derive from one of the Sea People invaders, the Tjekker, who accompanied the Philistines and others in the attempt to invade Egypt during Ramesses III's time (see p. 64; Oren 1982, 156; also Wainwright 1959, 78). Even though we are not sure yet of the exact location of Ziklag, we know that the Philistines were present at Gath and the surrounding area during the Iron I period. Achish, king of Gath, appears in the biblical record around 1020 B.C. Later, he may have become a vassal of David when, according to 1 Chronicles 18:1, David took Gath from the Philistines. This relationship may have continued well into the days of Solomon (see 1 Kings 2:39–40). We will examine Gath again in a later chapter.

A Nailed Body[2]

. . . and they fastened his body to the wall of Beth-shan.
[1 Sam. 31:10]

The events of 1 Samuel 31 surrounding the death of King Saul began already back in chapter 28. David had been asked by King Achish of Gath to join the Philistine forces against Saul. Then David and Achish had joined up with the Philistine forces at Aphek (1 Sam. 29:1–3), the location of the Philistine victory and their capture of Israel's ark of the covenant a generation earlier. The other Philistine forces dismissed David since they did not trust him. While David headed back for Ziklag (as related in our previous section), the

Philistines joined their comrades at Shunem (28:4), north of Mount
Gilboa, just opposite Saul's forces.

There is no consensus today about why Saul allowed himself to be
in such a precarious position; he seems to have been playing into the
hands of the Philistines (Bright 1981, 194). His forces were on one
hill, and the Philistines were opposite him on another hill. The plains
between the hills provided excellent terrain for the Philistines and
their chariots (2 Sam. 1:6). Here Israel lost its king (and even lost his
corpse) when the Philistines killed Saul and recovered his body from
the field of battle.

> They cut off his head, stripped off his armor, and sent messengers throughout
> the land of the Philistines to carry the good news to the houses of their idols
> and to the people. They put his armor in the temple of Astarte; and they fas-
> tened his body to the wall of Beth-shan. [1 Sam. 31:9–10]

First Chronicles 10:10 adds some additional information: "They put
his armor in the temple of their gods, and fastened his head in the
temple of Dagon."

The excavation at Beth-shean has revealed multiple temples, clar-
ifying the information from Samuel and Chronicles about putting
the armor in one temple and the corpse in another. In earlier chapters I have already provided some information about findings at the
site. In our discussion about the ceramic anthropoid coffin lids at
Deir el-Balah, the lids were compared with similar coffin lids at
Beth-shean (p. 94). We also briefly compared the temples at Tell
Qasile with those at Beth-shean. This section will focus on the
archaeology of Beth-shean, primarily as it relates to the period of
Saul, including the temple in which his body might have been hung.

Beth-shean is at the eastern end of the Jezreel Valley, along a
rivulet that flows into the Jordan River a short distance to the east.
When you are at Beth-shean, it is hard to realize that you are 350
feet below sea level. The mound rises impressively above the surrounding terrain. Its location was important, since it lay at a cross-
roads for traffic going north-south or east-west. In New Testament
times, when its name was Scythopolis, it was a spot where caravans
would gather before traveling on together for safety reasons.

Already back in the Late Bronze Age and especially by the thirteenth century B.C., Beth-shean was controlled by the Egyptian
empire as an important fortified site helping to control the trade
routes. This control continued well into the twelfth century B.C. dur-

ing the reign of Ramesses III, the pharaoh who defeated the Sea Peoples and who evidently settled them, including the Philistines, in garrison towns such as Deir el-Balah and Beth-shean.

During the conquest of Canaan by Israel, Beth-shean became part of Manasseh's allotment (Josh. 17:11–13). The Joshua text points out a problem that is supported in Judges 1:27, "Manasseh did not drive out the inhabitants of Beth-shean and its villages." Beth-shean and its Canaanite population were then under the control of the Egyptians. The evidence suggests a strong Egyptian presence throughout the Late Bronze Age and especially during the reigns of the pharaohs of the Nineteenth and Twentieth Dynasties, which brings us into the Iron Age and Joshua's time. Some of the pharaohs of the Nineteenth and Twentieth Dynasties who had forces at Beth-shean were Seti I, Ramesses II (the pharaoh of the exodus?), Merneptah, who battled some of the Sea Peoples (see chap. 3, pp. 51–53), and Ramesses III.

Several stelae of the pharaohs have been found during the excavations at Beth-shean. A stele is an upright standing stone, and quite often it includes a text, images, and symbols. Stelae of Seti I, Ramesses II, and Ramesses III at Beth-shean describe military campaigns and also have the names of Egyptian gods inscribed on them.

The smaller finds at Beth-shean, such as Egyptian scarabs, amulets (some with an *ankh* symbol, an Egyptian sign of life), plaques, pottery and other ceramic objects, and jewelry decorated with various goddesses, all display a heavy Egyptian influence. Other objects demonstrate influence from the Aegean and from Mesopotamia; however, there is a scarcity of Philistine pottery at Beth-shean. But remember the Bible does not refer to Beth-shean as being either a Philistine or an Egyptian town; it only states that Manasseh did not drive out the inhabitants. All the evidence indicates that this was a Canaanite town dominated by Egypt during most of the Late Bronze Age and into the Iron Age, through the reign of Ramesses III in the mid-twelfth century B.C. There was definitely a Philistine presence there in the mid-twelfth century, but perhaps no more than a garrison force.

The stratum VI period of Ramesses III has been pinpointed by the finds of a pottery form well known to you by now—Mycenaean IIIC:1b, the form that may span most of the reign of Ramesses III (Dever et al. 1986, 87 n. 176). This is the pottery that appears at Philistine sites with the arrival of the Sea Peoples.

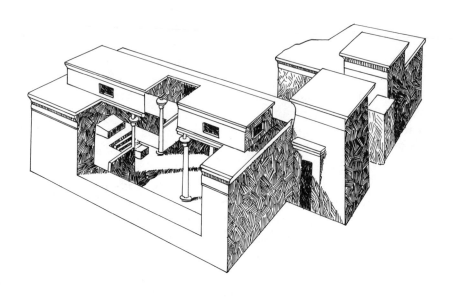

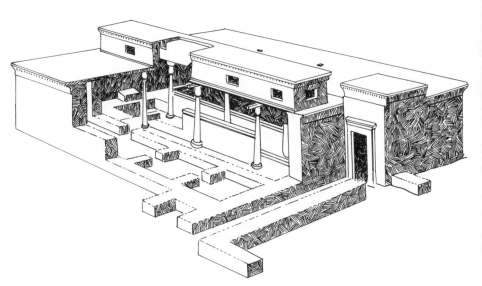

Temples at Beth-shean.

The strong Egyptian influence at Beth-shean during both the Nineteenth and Twentieth Dynasties, strata VII and VI, is illustrated by the fifty anthropoid coffin burials with grave goods, similar to those at Deir el-Balah. The later coffins of level VI from the Twentieth dynastic period, dated by the grave goods such as the pottery, can be assigned to the Sea Peoples, who were influenced by the way the Egyptians buried their dead. The Philistine pottery that was found at Beth-shean is not the classic, pretty bichrome pottery but is cruder. The unique headgear displayed on five coffin lids of tombs 66 and 90 in the Beth-shean burials is not duplicated in any other burials in Egypt or Canaan, but resembles the headgear of the Philistines at Medinet Habu, pictured by Ramesses III (T. Dothan 1982a, 271–72 with pictures). The feathered headgear can also be seen on the ivory game box and on the conical seal from Enkomi mentioned earlier on pages 60 and 87 (see also A. Mazar 1990, 305). Enkomi, on Cyprus, was one of the staging areas for the thrust of the Sea Peoples towards the south and eventually into Egypt. According to T. Dothan, the use of anthropoid coffin burials at Beth-shean began in the thirteenth century B.C., level VII, when the Nineteenth-Dynasty pharaohs controlled the site, and before the Philistine presence. This mode of burial continued there into the Twentieth Dynasty of Pharaoh Ramesses III, as evidenced by findings in level VI from the twelfth and eleventh centuries B.C. Tombs 66 and 90 support the conclusion that the Philistines had adopted the Egyptian mode of burial. These two tombs are dated to the time of Israel's King Saul.

Now let us look at the temples that have been excavated at Beth-shean. Both levels VII and VI of the thirteenth and twelfth centuries B.C. at Beth-shean contain temples sharing a similar design. The level VI temple is associated with Pharaoh Ramesses III of the early twelfth century B.C. It was constructed of sun-dried brick and was approximately fifty feet long, running north and south. It was almost as wide as it was long on the northern end. The temple was entered by passing through two courtyards. A ninety-degree turn led from the first to the second, and then from the second, a similar turn led into the sanctuary. In the sanctuary stood an altar, and behind it was a series of seven steps leading into the Holy of Holies, with another altar and storerooms on the left and right wings. The floor of the Holy of Holies was blue, and on it was the figure of the god Horus (a hawk figure) bearing the crown of Upper and Lower Egypt. From inscriptions, it is known that this temple dates to the reign of

163

Ramesses III. He may have been successful in defeating the Sea Peoples, but some time after these battles, Egypt appears to have lost control over Canaan, including Beth-shean, for the level VI buildings, including its temple, were found in ruins.

There are two temples above this one that are of particular interest. These are from level V (the beginning of the eleventh century), and the southernmost of the two was built directly over the ruins of the temple attributed to Ramesses III. This southern temple had a different orientation from the Ramesses III temple, west to east, and was about fifty feet long, with a twenty-six-foot-wide pillared hall leading to the eastern end, where the altar would have stood with steps leading up to it. On either side of the six-pillared hall were storerooms, making this temple almost square. The two center pillars had foundation deposits, one containing a jug of gold ingots and the other containing a pot of silver ingots.

This southern temple was separated from the northern level V temple by a corridor. The northern temple was rectangular, approximately forty feet by twenty-seven feet. It had four stone bases for roof supports. Like the southern temple, it had an entrance that prevented a passerby from glancing into the sanctuary.

We are now ready to return to 1 Samuel 31:9–10 and 1 Chronicles 10:10, where mention is made of the disposal of Saul's body and armor. Fitzgerald provides detail about clay figurines of

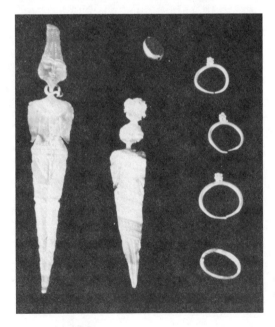

Gold pendants or inlays from dagger sheaths found at Middle Bronze Age (ca. 1550 B.C.) Gezer.

164

Astarte and other cult objects found in the level V temples (1967, 193–96; Rowe 1940, 22–24). Figurines of her and of other goddesses, either in gold pendant form or as clay figurines with the molds to make them, were found throughout the Late Bronze Age levels at Beth-shean. Fitzgerald mentions that a typical cult object of level V was the ceramic cult stand. These stands were cylindrical in shape, open at the top and bottom; on their sides were windows in which sculpted doves were perched. The stands had two handles, and also had snakes slithering up the sides (see Shanks 1984, 58–59 for pictures of similar stands). These cult stands, along with other cult objects, led Fitzgerald to conclude that it was the goddess Anat that dominated the cult at Beth-shean. She was the sister and consort of the god Baal, and she, like Astarte, was also a goddess of war and love. Her temple, the northern one described above, would have been the logical repository for the armor of Saul. The temples from level V were contemporaneous to the second and third of the three temples at Tell Qasile discussed on pages 113–18 in connection with Samson. Like the northern Beth-shean temple, the small shrine near the third temple at Qasile may have been used for the major deity's consort or for a minor god (A. Mazar 1977, 85).

The southern temple at Beth-shean was that of Dagon, where Saul's body was hung, as told to us in 1 Chronicles 10:10 (see also Rowe 1940, 22–24, 31, 33). The story of King Saul ends with the events related in 1 Samuel 31:11–13:

> But when the inhabitants of Jabesh-gilead heard what the Philistines had done to Saul, all the valiant men set out, traveled all night long, and took the body of Saul and the bodies of his sons from the wall of Beth-shan. They came to Jabesh and burned them there. Then they took their bones and buried them under the tamarisk tree in Jabesh, and fasted seven days.

Divide and Conquer[3]

> When the Philistines heard that David had been anointed king over Israel, all the Philistines went up in search of David.
> [2 Sam. 5:17]

Saul and Jonathan were now dead. David mourned their loss and was then anointed king of Judah in Hebron. His becoming king in Hebron did not antagonize the Philistines, specifically Achish, who still had no reason to believe that David was not a loyal vassal. Second Samuel 2–4 describes a civil war in Israel between David's forces and those loyal to Saul's family. The Philistines are not directly involved in the action of these chapters, though they no doubt encouraged David's endeavors—until the events described in chapter 5, that is. "So all the elders of Israel came to the king at Hebron; and King David made a covenant with them at Hebron before the LORD, and they anointed David king over Israel" (2 Sam. 5:3).

The Philistines finally recognized David as a threat. They knew that David, in uniting both Judah and Israel, could be more dangerous to them than Saul had been, under whom Israel and Judah had not always presented a united front. This David was the one who had killed his "ten thousands." Now, not only could the Philistines lose control of Judah, but of Israel as well, which they had defeated in the destruction of Saul and his forces at Mount Gilboa. The events described in 2 Samuel 5:17–25 spell the beginning of the end of Philistine domination over Israel.

The Philistine strategy was clear; they were going to try to split the two factions (Bright 1981, 198) of Israel and Judah. Perhaps they gathered their forces at Ekron, since the best way to "the valley of Rephaim" (v. 18) from the Philistine plain is to head east up the Sorek Valley. The valley, or lowlands, of Rephaim is located southwest of Jerusalem; it is cut at its northern end by the Valley of Hinnom, which is also southwest of Jerusalem (McCarter 1984, 153–54).

David consulted God, who gave him approval. He defeated the Philistines so suddenly and so decisively that he declared in verse 20, "The LORD has burst forth against my enemies before me, like a bursting flood." (He was picturing God rushing through the enemy like water rushing through a wadi, such as the Nahal Sorek, after a torrential rain.) There was now a breach in the Philistine record of victories. This battle was a reversal of the battle in 1 Samuel 4, in which the Israelites lost the ark of the covenant. Now it was the Philistines who left their religious treasures, their idols, behind. David not only carried them off (v. 21), he also had them burned (1 Chron. 14:12).

The Philistines tried again and attacked David in the Valley of Rephaim once more. Again David consulted the Lord; again he was victorious. This time he drove the Philistines out of the hill area, from Gibeon, which was just north of Jerusalem, to Gezer (1 Chron. 14:16). Driving the Philistines out of the central hill country from Gibeon westward served another purpose besides the military one.

The following chapter, 2 Samuel 6, describes the restoration of the ark of the covenant into Israelite society. This restoration could not have occurred earlier, because the Philistines had moved into the area of Kiriath-jearim under the sphere of Gibeon, where the ark had been held for some twenty years (due to the events of 1 Sam. 4). The Philistines had apparently left the ark alone after the plagues of rats and tumors ended. The victories of David and the fact that Israel was once again united set the stage for the return of the ark into the religious life of the nation. Philistia had begun to shrink in power and territory.

David's Obedience[4]

David did just as the LORD had commanded him; and he struck down the Philistines from Geba [Gibeon] all the way to Gezer.
[2 Sam. 5:25]

The Bible says that David pushed the Philistines out of the hill country surrounding Gibeon all the way west to Gezer (McCarter 1984, 152, 157). David was able to reintegrate the ark of the covenant into the religious life of Israel and to unify Israel under God and his reign. Did David, though, chase the Philistines to the gates of Gezer, or did he perhaps take Gezer? Can the archaeological record give us more information about the Philistine presence there?

The fortified city of Gezer was built on a hill that overlooks the coastal plain and is within eyesight of the Philistine city of Ekron. It is in the Shephelah, the foothills, overlooking the highways going to and from Egypt and Syria. At Gezer, one is high enough to see the sun set into the Mediterranean.

Gezer was one of the cities allotted the tribe of Ephraim (Josh. 16:10), but even though Joshua may have killed Horam, the king of Gezer (Josh. 10:33; 12:12), Gezer itself was not captured (Josh. 16:10; Judg. 1:29). Both Joshua 16 and Judges 1 refer to the Canaanites that dwelled there during the period of Joshua and the subsequent judges. The material excavated from Gezer indicates that there were Canaanite inhabitants there during the time of the judges, but the abundance and type of Philistine material in strata XIII–XI (ca. 1175 to 1050 B.C.) suggests to some that the Philistines were the overlords (Dever et al. 1986, 87f.; A. Mazar 1990, 312).

Gezer may have been unoccupied for a time at the end of the thirteenth and the beginning of the twelfth centuries B.C. Egyptian

Site plan of Gezer.

Pharaoh Merneptah in his famous stele (final quarter of the thirteenth century B.C.) claims to have conquered the people of Israel, as well as Ashkelon, Gezer, and other cities. An ivory pendant bearing the cartouche of Merneptah was found by an early excavator at Gezer. After what may have been a hiatus in occupation, the Philistines arrived circa 1175 B.C. No Mycenaean IIIC:1b pottery had been found at Gezer, similar to the situation at Timnah and Qasile. However, in the Gezer of the twelfth century B.C., we find an abundance of the classic Philistine pottery. On what is called the acropolis area of the tell a public building has been uncovered, which the excavators refer to as the "Cyclopean Complex." It was perhaps a public granary with threshing floors. Sometime around 1125 B.C., this structure was destroyed and then rebuilt. Perhaps this destruction was due to local disturbances, or perhaps some new Sea Peoples came to Gezer. After one more disturbance at the end of the twelfth century, the complex was converted into elaborate private housing. The transition from an industrial area into an elegant, patrician area may imply that the Philistines were mercenaries for the Egyptians at Gezer or simply were overlords of the local Canaanite population (Dever et al. 1986, 87f.). During the eleventh century these houses were destroyed, and by the middle of the eleventh century B.C., the Philistine culture was no longer distinctive. The bichrome pottery was no longer present at Gezer and had disappeared from other Philistine sites as well. This brings us to the time of Saul and David.

Let us return to the question asked earlier. Did David capture Gezer, or did he only smite the Philistines *to* Gezer? No destruction from this time can be found, and according to the Bible, Gezer presented a problem for David later on in his reign (see 1 Chron. 20:4). Furthermore, in 1 Kings 9:16–17, Gezer was given to Solomon by the pharaoh of Egypt *after* the pharaoh had attacked it, killed the Canaanites, and burned the city. This gracious pharaoh gave Solomon an Egyptian princess to be his wife, and he presented Gezer to Solomon as his daughter's dowry. The biblical record tells us that David had captured parts of the Philistine territory—such as Gath (1 Chron. 18:1)—all the way to the Mediterranean. This would have included Tell Qasile, according to B. Mazar (A. Mazar 1973, 46), but evidently David left Gezer alone. The Philistine town of Ashdod was also destroyed at the beginning of the tenth century B.C. (M. Dothan 1968, 254; 1969, 244), perhaps by King David or by Pharaoh Siamun, according to T. Dothan (1982a, 42). David was definitely powerful enough to have taken Gezer, in view of his other conquests, but perhaps he left it as a buffer between Israel and Philistia; or perhaps Philistia still had some sort of vassal relationship with Egypt, and David was being diplomatic in not wanting to anger the pharaoh (Lance 1967, 40–41; Dever, Lance, and Wright 1970, 4–5; Bright 1981, 199). After all, Egypt had controlled this area for centuries. At this time it simply is not known why David left part of Philistia alone.

As mentioned above, Chronicles records that a later pharaoh (perhaps Pharaoh Siamun of the Twenty-first Dynasty) attacked and burned Gezer and then turned it over to Solomon. According to the archaeological record, Gezer was burned sometime around the middle of the tenth century B.C. The Egyptian pharaoh was perhaps following an age-old custom of checking out a strong neighbor after the death of its king. (We will see this happening again after the death of Solomon, when Israel was split.) The pharaoh came north after Solomon became king, perhaps demonstrating by his display of power over Gezer: "This is my territory. I can still control it." Tel Mor, the port for Ashdod, was also destroyed, as was Beth-shemesh. It might be, however, attacking Gezer as well as other cities and then marrying off a daughter to Solomon indicates the weakness of the pharaoh and shows that Solomon was viewed by his neighbors as a power to be reckoned with (Dever, Lance, and Wright 1970, 5; Lance 1967, 41–42; Bright 1981, 212).

We will come back to Gezer when we discuss Solomon's reign and his links to Philistia. Let us move on now, however, to Ekron to illustrate that Philistia was definitely shrinking in power and size during the years of David's reign, regardless of whether it was a vassal to Egypt or to Israel. Philistia had been subdued (2 Sam. 8:11–12), and the archaeology of Ekron clearly demonstrates this.

Ekron was on the eastern end of Philistia, and it had been one of the Philistine staging areas to invade Israel and Judah, as we have discussed in previous sections. Full-scale excavation on the fifty-acre tell of Ekron began during the summer of 1984, and for the first few seasons the talk of the excavation centered on the problem of the "missing" tenth-eighth centuries B.C. (see pp. 41–43). Successive seasons revealed the story. Early in the tenth century B.C., circa 975, only the upper section of the tell was occupied. This was the acropolis area, approximately ten acres in size. The lower forty acres were basically abandoned for 270 years! Small wonder that the Bible rarely mentions Ekron during these three centuries. It was not one of the cities fortified by Solomon or Rehoboam (see 2 Chron. 11:5–11, for example, in which Gath but not Ekron is mentioned).

The evidence shows that during the Iron IIA period, the tenth to eighth centuries B.C. (beginning in David's time), Ekron shrunk to one-fifth of its previous size. What is to account for this? The directors of the excavation believe that this decrease in size must somehow be related to the ascendancy of Kings David and Solomon and the growing might of a united Israel (Gitin 1990, 34; Gitin and T. Dothan 1987, 214). "Some time afterward, David attacked the Philistines and subdued them" is an appropriate summary from 2 Samuel 8:1. Gezer, for whatever reason, was left alone by King David; Ekron became a small shell of its former self. What of Ekron's sister city, Timnah, during the same time frame? The excavators there believe that not only was Timnah taken from the Philistines but it was changed into an Israelite town (Kelm and A. Mazar 1989, 41f.). They base this opinion on the typical Israelite pottery (bowls and kraters with a thick red slip and hand burnish) found there, which dates from the tenth century B.C. This is true not only for Timnah but also for Beth-shemesh to the east. Beth-shemesh was mentioned in the 1 Samuel 6 story of the return of the ark by the terrified Philistines. Even though there was an Israelite population in Beth-shemesh at the time of the story (see 1 Sam. 6:10–21), the Israelites may have faced economic and political domination by the Philistines, a condition typical throughout the entire Sorek Valley during the period of the judges. Philistine domination ended for Beth-shemesh in the tenth century B.C., when it was captured by King David (T. Dothan 1982a, 51).

Whereas Ekron remained a Philistine town, its neighbor Timnah became an Israelite town. But like Ekron, Timnah was only partially built up in the tenth century B.C. (A. Mazar 1990, 387–90, lists and discusses Israelite towns). One of the interesting finds from this period in Timnah was a pottery sherd incised with a Hebrew name— *[Be]n Hanan* or "son of Hanan." Hebrew inscriptions from the times of David and Solomon are rare, the Gezer Calendar[5] being the major exception. The Timnah excavators point out that Hanan is included in Solomon's list of his governors and their districts in 1 Kings 4:9: "Ben-deker, in Makaz, Shaalbim, Beth-shemesh, and Elon-beth-hanan. . . ." Note the mention of the town of Beth-shemesh, and note as well that Elon has an additional form behind it, *beth-hanan*, meaning "house of Hanan." The town of Elon is mentioned in Joshua 19:43 as belonging to the tribe of Dan, along with

Field 1 at Ekron. In the foreground is the mudbrick wall with boulder-size stones on the top and ashlar facing. Note the fallen boulder and ashlar stones, part of the evidence of late Iron II destruction.

Timnah and Ekron. The excavators at Timnah suggest, therefore, that in the tenth century B.C. the family of Hanan resided in the area of Timnah, Ekron, and Beth-shemesh (Kelm and A. Mazar 1989, 42).

One final comment is in order concerning Ekron in this time period. As stated earlier, in 1984 a backhoe was in operation off the mound below the northeast acropolis. It was important to get at the soil underneath the erosion runoff from the tell and the wadi, and soil samples for flotation were planned. All of a sudden the backhoe struck huge, finely cut stones (referred to as ashlars) that formed the stone wall described in chapter 2. This wall turned out to be the facing for a twenty-two-foot-wide mudbrick tower attached to a new mudbrick wall, which may date to the tenth century B.C. city (Gitin 1990, 34). The city may have been reduced to ten acres in size, but it had a massive tower in its northeast sector. However, it was impossible in 1984 and is still impossible to excavate the tower because the water table is higher now than it was during the Iron Age. Water pumps were brought in in an attempt to drain the water so that the wall could be excavated to its base. However, the water came in as fast as it was pumped out, and some of the ashlar facing stones began to slide into what was fast becoming a frog pond—creating a dangerous situation, for the workers, not the frogs!

This tenth century B.C. ashlar-facing mudbrick wall is similar to what Oren describes at his excavation at Tel Sera' (Ziklag?), where he excavated mudbrick buildings faced with ashlar blocks from the same tenth-century period. At Tel Sera' the ashlars were used on only the three-course-high foundation levels, but at Ekron the workers have not yet been able to reach the foundation levels to compare them thoroughly with Tel Sera'. Another site that had a similar type of construction was Ashdod, where the ashlars were integrated into the tenth-century B.C. gate built after the city's destruction by David or Siamun. This rebuilding at Ashdod may have been due to the split of Israel after Solomon. At all three sites—Tels Sera', Ekron, and Ashdod—there was a continuity of the Philistine culture in the transition from Iron I to Iron II in spite of the defeats at Ekron and Ashdod, which were perhaps the work of King David. At Ekron especially, the decline of Philistine might and strength was clearly visible, but like the Greek phoenix, the Philistines would rise again. Philistine warriors even began to show up as David's professional soldiers, as we shall see in the next section.

The Royal Bodyguard

Benaiah son of Jehoiada was over the Cherethites and the Pelethites. . . .
[2 Sam. 8:18]

Who were these "Cherethites and Pelethites"? Digging through the early prophetical books of Samuel and Kings as well the as writings of the latter prophets, such as Ezekiel and Zephaniah, reveals a few references to these names or to variant forms of them. The first mention of the Cherethites is in 1 Samuel 30:14 in the passage dealing with David's return to Ziklag. Finding the city burned, and his wives and children taken captive, David gave chase and caught up with an Egyptian slave of the Amalekites, who stated that the Amalekites had gone raiding "on the Negeb of the Cherethites and . . . burned Ziklag down." The second reference is in 2 Samuel 8:18, quoted above, where David's officials are listed; the Cherethites are mentioned as part of David's bodyguard along with the Pelethites (see also 2 Sam. 15:18; 23:23).

The Cherethites were from the Negeb, in the same general area as Ziklag. It is logical to assume that David picked them up during his days as lord of Ziklag. The Pelethites are a bit more difficult to identify. They are mentioned only seven times in the Old Testament, and in every case they are the second part of a compound phrase connecting them with the Cherethites, as in 2 Samuel 8:18. Some scholars believe that *Pelethite* is a variant name for *Philistines* (Bright 1981, 205; McCarter 1984, 256), and McCarter believes that a specific place name in the Aegean or in Anatolia should be sought to reveal their origin. Since the Pelethites are tied in all seven biblical references with the Cherethites, let us focus on the Cherethites in order to determine who these professional bodyguards were.

Three biblical references to the Cherethites present them as a tribe. The first is the citation in 1 Samuel 30:14, in connection with David and Ziklag. The second can be found in Ezekiel, where a prophecy is stated against the Philistines:

> Thus says the Lord GOD: Because with unending hostilities the Philistines acted in vengeance, and with malice of heart took revenge in destruction; therefore thus says the Lord GOD, I will stretch out my hand against the Philistines, cut off the Cherethites, and destroy the rest of the seacoast. [Ezek. 25:15–16]

The third reference is in Zephaniah, where there is another prophecy of destruction:

> Gaza . . . Ashkelon . . . Ashdod . . . Ekron . . .
> Woe to you who live by the sea,
>   O Kerethite people;
> the word of the LORD is against you,
>   O Canaan, land of the Philistines.
> "I will destroy you,
>   and none will be left."
> The land by the sea, where the
>   Kerethites dwell,
> will be a place for shepherds and
>   sheep pens.
> [Zeph. 2:4–6]

174

These passages will be studied in more detail later in their historical contexts, but notice that in Ezekiel and Zephaniah the Cherethites are linked closely with the Philistines. Furthermore, many scholars link the name Cherethites to Crete (McCarter 1980, 435; 1984, 256; *ISBE* 1:610; A. Mazar 1990, 306; Elwell 1988, 1:415–16); therefore, the Anchor Bible commentary states that the phrase in 1 Samuel 30:14 may also be translated as the "Negeb of the Cretans" (McCarter 1980, 435). We know that these people lived somewhere in the area of Ziklag or towards the coast.

The mixture of the Philistines and Cherethites is somewhat analogous to the mixing of peoples that occurred when Israel left Egypt. As the Israelites left, they were joined by a "rabble" (Num. 11:4) and a "mixed crowd" (Exod. 12:38), but the entire multitude was called Israel. The Sea Peoples have always been viewed in the Egyptian records, as well as by scholars, as a confederation of peoples who invaded Egypt, of which the Philistines were a part. Along the southern coast of Canaan, the Philistines were evidently the dominant group in the confederation. According to the Bible, there were five Philistine lords; yet the Bible does not tell us whether these five lords had exactly the same heritage, only that they all operated in concert with each other in the days of the judges through David. It is clear, however, that within Philistia lived the Cherethites/Cretans, who became David's loyal bodyguards.

Just how loyal they were is seen in 2 Samuel 15, the story about Absalom's revolt against his father, King David. David is forced to flee from Jerusalem: "The king left, followed by all the people; and they stopped at the last house. All his officials passed by him; and all the Cherethites, and all the Pelethites, and all the six hundred Gittites who had followed him from Gath, passed on before the king" (vv. 17–18). Numerous people of Judah deserted David, as they had done before in the days when David was fleeing from Saul. Who remained loyal? The Philistine bodyguard and the Gittites from Gath. Like the Cherethites and Pelethites, the Gittites probably also joined David during his days with Achish of Gath (1 Sam. 27). Sadly (but fortunately perhaps for David), it was the Philistines who remained loyal to David while God's people shifted their loyalty like the wind.

Ittai, the commander of the Gittites, was released from his service obligation to David by David himself, but this "foreigner" who was in "exile" from Gath in Philistia (2 Sam. 15:19) responded with words similar to those of Ruth when she was told by Naomi to return to Moab. He said, "As the LORD lives, and as my lord the king lives, wherever my lord the king may be, whether for death or for life, there also your servant will be" (v. 21). The words of Ruth have been remembered through the ages, but here is another foreigner, a Philistine, who with other Philistines remained loyal to God's anointed.

Another strange episode involving a Gittite is found in 2 Samuel 6. David was returning the ark to Jerusalem and for some unknown reason was transporting it on a cart, rather than having the priests carry it with poles. Uzzah, at one point, steadied the ark and was struck dead for touching it. David was fearful of what had just transpired, and rather than taking the ark into Jerusalem, he left it at the house of Obed-edom the Gittite. Second Samuel 6:11 states, "the LORD blessed Obed-edom and all his household." Obed-edom's name betrays him as a foreigner, for it means "servant of (the deity) Edom" (McCarter 1984, 170). A later passage, 1 Chronicles 15:18, gave Obed-edom a Levitical genealogy. This Gittite, this Philistine, was blessed by the Lord in caring for the ark (see also NIV Study Bible 1 Chron. 13:13 footnote and McCarter 1984, 170).

Let us return to the Cherethites and the Pelethites of David's bodyguard. After Absalom's revolt, an even more dangerous revolt broke out against King David (2 Sam. 20:6). It was again "the Cherethites, the Pelethites, and all the warriors" who were called on to put this revolt down.

Later, shortly before David's death, a successor needed to be chosen and anointed as the next king. David's son Adonijah, born next after Absalom, felt that he was the proper choice. Joab, David's general, and Abiathar the priest took the side of Adonijah. Opposed to Adonijah were Nathan the prophet, Zadok the priest, David's warriors, and Benaiah, the man in charge of the Cherethites and the Pelethites. It was the king's Philistine bodyguard who took Solomon through the streets of Jerusalem to be anointed by Zadok at Gihon (1 Kings 1:44–45).

And so the hated enemy of Israel helped to save David, God's anointed, and also helped to put Solomon on the throne. The Philistines as a whole would continue to be castigated by Israel and the latter prophets; we will study this further, but let us not forget the Philistine bodyguard used by God to preserve those whom he had chosen.

The Empty Ark of the Covenant

There was nothing in the ark except the two tablets of stone
that Moses had placed there at Horeb. . . .
[1 Kings 8:9; see also 2 Chron. 5:10]

One of the reasons the Israelites saw the Philistines as more than
just a formidable enemy was related to the time the Philistines captured and kept the ark under their control (1 Sam. 4–6). Hebrews
9:3–4 states clearly, "Behind the second curtain [of the tabernacle]
was a tent called the Holy of Holies. In it stood the golden altar of
incense and the ark of the covenant overlaid on all sides with gold, in
which there were a golden urn holding the manna, and Aaron's rod
that budded, and the tablets of the covenant. . . ." Yet the verses
from Kings and Chronicles clearly state that only the tablets of the
law were in the ark at the time when Solomon put the ark into the
temple. What happened to the jar of manna and Aaron's staff? Did
the Philistines steal or destroy both the jar of manna and Aaron's
staff? Why didn't Solomon refer to those two items when he placed
the ark in the temple?

To answer this question, we need to go back to Exodus and
Numbers, where both the jar and staff are discussed.

And Moses said to Aaron, "Take a jar, and put an omer of manna in it, and
place it before the LORD, to be kept throughout your generations." As the
LORD commanded Moses, so Aaron placed it before the covenant, for safe-
keeping. [Exod. 16:33–34]

And the LORD said to Moses, "Put back the staff of Aaron before the
covenant, to be kept as a warning to rebels, so that you may make an end of
their complaints against me, or else they will die." [Num. 17:10]

Exodus 16:33 states that the jar was to be kept before the ark
"throughout your generations," and Numbers 17:10 states that the
staff was to be kept before the testimony "as a warning" for rebels.
The Numbers passage does not state explicitly that this warning was
to be kept for generations, but the Hebrews 9 passage does make it
clear that the staff was not only before the ark, but was within it. The
tablets of stone bearing the Ten Commandments were also placed in
the ark (Exod. 25:16, 21). The presence of the staff would have been
especially important for the descendants of Aaron as proof that the
Lord God had chosen them to be the priests. Its loss was a problem
for Israel.

One illustration of this problem is recorded in 1 Kings 2. Upon assuming the kingship, Solomon had two priests, Abiathar and Zadok. According to verse 35, one of Solomon's first duties as king was to remove Abiathar, since Abiathar had earlier supported Adonijah to be the next king after David. Imagine the role the staff of Aaron could have played in the conflict if Zadok could have carried it while he anointed Solomon as the king. Zadok, evidently, was related to Aaron through Eleazar, the oldest son of Aaron. Abiathar was related to Aaron through Ithamar, the younger son (1 Chron. 24:3–6). Eleazar had been the successor of Aaron. Possession of the staff could have cemented the case that Zadok was the proper priest in the line of Aaron and therefore had the right to anoint the next king. Alas, "There was nothing in the ark except the two tablets of stone. . . ."

After the Exodus and Numbers citations, the text of the Old Testament does not mention again either the gold urn of manna or Aaron's staff. Accounts of when Israel broke camp and moved towards the Promised Land make no mention of these two objects, leading one to assume that, at least while the people were on the move, the urn and the staff were placed in the ark. Then come the Kings and Chronicles passages, which state that the ark contained nothing but the two tablets of stone. The only break in the religious tradition of the ark between Israel's time in the desert and the time of Solomon occurred when the ark was captured by the Philistines. It was later returned to Israel but was ignored until David attempted to move it to Jerusalem.

So what happened to the urn of manna and the staff of Aaron? It is possible that they were lost to Israel when Israel lost the ark to the Philistines. Even if the two objects were not in the ark but were placed "before" the ark and had been left behind in the tabernacle in Shiloh (which was soon to be destroyed by the Philistines), a significant intrusion occurred in the way Israel worshiped God when the ark was captured. The urn and the staff no longer played a role in the nation's worship. Directly or indirectly, the Philistines were responsible for this loss, a crucial element in Israel's enduring hatred of the Philistines.[6]

⊰6⊱

The Philistines
from Solomon to Hezekiah

Solomon's Territory[1]

He [Solomon] ruled over all the kings from the Euphrates to
the land of the Philistines, and to the border of Egypt.
[2 Chron. 9:26]

The remains being excavated at Tel Miqne-Ekron support the
words of the biblical writer above. The tenth century B.C., the time
frame of Solomon's reign, was a period of decline at Ekron, during
which it shrank from fifty to ten acres in size. It became a small fortified town, no rival to the city that stopped the Israelites from further
pursuing the Philistines after the slaying of Goliath by David. The
only impressive finding from this period has been the mudbrick
tower with the ashlar facade described earlier. Evidently, this tower
remained in use to the end of the seventh century B.C. Are these
meager remains indicative of the plight of the Philistines at other sites
as well? Did Solomon rule only *to* "the land of the Philistines" or *in*
the land of the Philistines? The answers to these questions are the
focus of this section.

During King David's reign, the Philistines seem to have pulled back to their original boundaries along the Mediterranean coast. They may have become a second-rate power, as the evidence at Ekron seems to indicate. The Bible is silent concerning the Philistines of the tenth century B.C.; this silence lasts until finally a reference is made to their activities during the reign of Judah's King Jehoshaphat in the mid-ninth century. We know from other sources that tenth-century Philistia was the focus of a power play between Egypt and Judah that would soon involve the up-and-coming power Assyria, as well. Recall the example cited in chapter 5 about Solomon receiving the city of Gezer as part of a dowry when he married a daughter of the Egyptian pharaoh (1 Kings 3:1; 9:15–16). The pharaoh came north, burned Gezer, and then said, in effect, "Here, Solomon, it's yours now." This could have been the pharaoh's way of demonstrating that this land was still his. He was still able to control it (especially since David was dead by that time), and it was his choice to give Gezer away.

Gath (possibly Tell es-Safi) and Gaza, as noted earlier, are not being excavated currently; therefore, we cannot determine archaeologically what was happening there during the tenth-eighth centuries B.C. According to 1 Chronicles, 18:1, however, David captured Gath and 2 Chronicles 11:8 tells us that Gath was one of the cities to the west that Rehoboam fortified, probably against the Philistines. Ashkelon is being excavated presently, and we will need to wait some time before we have extensive knowledge about the tenth-eighth centuries at this site.

Tel Ashdod, site of the fifth of the major Philistine cities, has yielded interesting finds from this period. Sometime during the second half of the eleventh century B.C., Ashdod expanded down off the tell into a "lower city" and became a city of one hundred acres. It was fortified during these years but during the first half of the tenth century was destroyed, perhaps by David or by Pharaoh Siamun. Then late in the tenth or early ninth century it was rebuilt and refortified. Its tenth-century gate was unique, but was similar to the multi-chambered gates of Solomon's era at Gezer, Hazor, and Megiddo. As at Tel Sera' (Ziklag?) the gate and tower had ashlar corner stones. Ashdod's gate and tower both stood until approximately the beginning of the eighth century, when they may have been destroyed by Judah's king Uzziah:

He [Uzziah] went out and made war against the Philistines, and broke down the wall of Gath and the wall of Jabneh and the wall of Ashdod; he built cities in the territory of Ashdod and elsewhere among the Philistines. God helped him against the Philistines. . . . [2 Chron. 26:6–7a]

Ashdod's gate was rebuilt and continued to be in use until the days of the Assyrian Sargon II in the final quarter of the eighth century B.C. A partial inscription by Sargon II was found in the ruins of Ashdod on fragments of a stele. Thousands of skeletons were also found, coinciding with the information given in the Bible about the Assyrian invasions of Palestine.

Other biblical references to the Philistines, such as in 2 Chronicles 17:11, mention that the Philistines were paying tribute in silver to King Jehoshaphat of Judah (ca. 870 B.C.). This situation was altered during the rule of his son King Jehoram, the one who married Athaliah, daughter of King Ahab of Israel:

The LORD aroused against Jehoram the anger of the Philistines and of the Arabs who are near the Ethiopians. They came up against Judah, invaded it, and carried away all the possessions they found that belonged to the king's house. . . . [2 Chron. 21:16–17]

The evidence at Ashdod indicates that, unlike at Ekron, Philistine rule there expanded, especially after the division of Israel's united kingdom. Records also indicate that Ashdod had its own king, as did Gaza, Ashkelon, and Ekron (A. Mazar 1984, 52; Porten 1981, 39). But Ashdod, as well as the rest of Philistia, had its ups and downs. The Iron II period after David and Solomon was a period of transition; the old Philistine culture with its bichrome pottery was gone, and there seems to have been a greater adaptation to the local Canaanite/Semitic culture (A. Mazar 1990, 533).

Tel Ashdod provides some information about this adaptation. Even though no Philistine archives have yet been uncovered, certain seals have been found there. Some of the writing on the early seals resembles the Cypro-Minoan script of the thirteenth-twelfth centuries B.C.; still other early seals resemble different styles out of the Aegean. Some of the latest Ashdod seals are dated to the eleventh century B.C., but are also undeciphered. Still other inscriptions, dated to the ninth and eighth centuries, are in a script resembling Hebrew, Canaanite, and Phoenician or, in other words, a West Semitic script. Thus, even the inscriptions demonstrate a transition occurring at Ashdod during the tenth century B.C. (Oded 1979, 237–38; M. Dothan 1969, 245).

Next, let us move back to Tell Qasile, the seaport founded by the Philistines on the Mediterranean coast and now within the city limits of modern-day Tel Aviv. The fate of Qasile during the Iron II period seems to have been similar to that of Ekron. Ashdod had expanded and was flourishing, leading A. Mazar to suggest that, although the port city of Qasile was destroyed, the heart of Philistia to the south was prospering somewhat (1985b, 123).

David evidently conquered the area around Qasile up to the coast, but left much of Philistia alone. Perhaps he took back part or all of the old tribal area of Dan, which included the section of the coast from Joppa to the Yarkon River. We discussed Qasile's temples earlier, but now we will see what was happening there during the tenth–seventh centuries B.C. Qasile was a small, four-acre site located on the north side of the Yarkon River, just east of its estuary into the Mediterranean. It was founded in the twelfth century B.C., at the height of Philistine expansion preceding the years of their struggles with Samuel, Saul, and David. The early years of the eleventh century have been dubbed as "Pax Philistea" by B. Mazar (A. Mazar 1985b, 123). Vibrant growth continued at Qasile until the beginning of the tenth century B.C., when the site suffered a violent destruction. A. Mazar (1980, 46–47; 1985b, 127) suggests that this destruction may have been due to an earthquake causing the buildings to collapse and burn. The other alternative, the more probable one, according to A. Mazar, is that the destruction was due to King David's defeat of the Philistines mentioned in 2 Samuel 8:1.

Although Tell Qasile is not a site that can be identified with any site mentioned in Scripture, its role on the coast during the Pax Philistea period (eleventh century), as well as later in the days of Solomon, may be identified. Using the Yarkon River for irrigation, the Philistines had great success with agriculture in this region. The excavation exposed grain pits, silos, presses, and storerooms containing jars. Since Qasile's deep port provided shelter for ships, A. Mazar suggests that it may have been used as a port for cedars from Lebanon, floated down the Mediterranean "as rafts by sea to Joppa," as is mentioned concerning the days of Solomon (2 Chron. 2:16) and Zerubbabel (Ezra 3:7). A couple of pieces of burned wood found in the ruins of the elaborate tenth-century B.C. temple (possibly burned by David) have been identified as cedars of Lebanon (T. Dothan 1982a, 58).

If David did burn the stratum X city of Tell Qasile, what happened later at this site? Stratum IX there was not as elaborate as the earlier town. The temple was partially rebuilt, but how much of it was used could not be determined clearly due to the poor state of the remains. The radical changes in the layout of the town of stratum IX demonstrate that, even though it was resettled, it was not as prosperous as it had been during the reign of David.

B. Mazar states that the stratum IX holds an Israelite city built on the ruins of the Philistine one (A. Mazar 1985b, 127). A. Mazar agrees that Qasile was in Israelite hands during the tenth-century B.C. days of the united kingdom. Since the Philistine temple, as well as other buildings, had been partly rebuilt, it is postulated that the Israelites were now the overlords and that some of the local peoples were able to continue living and worshiping there. We know that Israel was not a seafaring nation and, in this area, as well as in the area of metalwork, may have had to rely on Philistine expertise. We also know that David and Solomon relied on the Phoenicians for building projects and that both of these kings relied on Philistine bodyguards.

Tell Qasile was to suffer more attacks by the end of the tenth century, believed to have been by the Egyptian pharaohs Siamun and Shishak. It was not the only site so troubled, for attacks on it coincided with attacks on several sites along the coast. Qasile was abandoned about this time, perhaps due to the breakup of Israel under King Rehoboam. Other port cities suffered the same fate, but the inland Philistine site of Ashdod was not abandoned. At Qasile, the pottery from this layer is badly weathered, indicating that it had been lying on the surface for a long time. There was a brief revival at Qasile late in the seventh century B.C. The pottery from the corresponding stratum may be Judean, which leads A. Mazar to suggest that the revival may have been due to an expansion of Judah during the days of good King Josiah (640–609 B.C.), who spread his reforms into the former territories of old Israel (2 Chron. 34:1–7). After this brief revival, Qasile ceased to exist.

Now let us move on to Timnah, the town discussed earlier in connection with Samson and his wife. It is located just to the east of Ekron. Did it, like Ekron, suffer a decrease in population? Timnah was a small Philistine site (just six acres) that flourished during the Iron I period (ca. 1200–1000 B.C.). However, around 1000 B.C., at the same time that neighboring Ekron shrank from fifty acres to ten, Philistine Timnah died. The site became an Israelite town, partially built up with typical Israelite artifacts. The pottery that has been found is Judean and is similar to the Israelite pottery from other sites such as Lachish and Beth-shemesh. A sherd found at Timnah bearing an incised Hebrew inscription is the most precious artifact from this period. The fact that Timnah appears have been an Israelite town during the tenth century and that neighboring Ekron greatly decreased in size may reflect the expansion of the Israelite kingdom under David.

However, David's successor, Solomon, died around 922 B.C., and his kingdom split in two. According to both Egyptian and biblical records (1 Kings 14:25–28), Pharaoh Shishak then invaded Judah. This pharaoh was the one with whom Jeroboam sought refuge while fleeing from Solomon (1 Kings 11:40). Since Solomon was dead, the pharaoh tested Rehoboam: "In the fifth year of King Rehoboam, King Shishak of Egypt came up against Jerusalem; he took away the treasures of the house of the LORD and the treasures of the king's house; he took everything. He also took away all the shields of gold that Solomon had made . . ." (1 Kings 14:25–26). According to the excavators, Timnah was destroyed near the end of the tenth century B.C., and this destruction fits in with Shishak's description of his military campaign into Palestine. Although the pharaoh does not mention Timnah on his temple walls at Karnak, he does mention nearby cities.

Timnah did not regain its full strength until the eighth-seventh centuries B.C.,when it was rebuilt on a grand scheme, as was Ekron. According to 2 Chronicles 28:18–19, sometime near the end of the eighth century, "the Philistines had made raids on the cities in the Shephelah and the Negeb of Judah, and had taken Beth-shemesh . . . [and] Timnah with its villages . . . because of King Ahaz of Israel [Judah], for he had . . . been faithless to the LORD." We do not know how long prior to the time indicated by these two verses that Judah or Israel controlled Timnah. Second Chronicles 26:6 mentions that King Uzziah (783–742 B.C.) had earlier declared war on the Philistines, going up against Gath, Ashdod, and "elsewhere among the Philistines." Timnah would have lain in the path of such an advance, but the text does not say that Uzziah took Timnah. The archaeological record neither shows that Uzziah took the town nor that the Philistines recaptured it during Ahaz's time, as stated in 2 Chronicles 29. Apparently as a result of the raids by the Philistines and by the Edomites (vv. 16–18), King Ahaz tried to make a coalition with Assyria, which was becoming a growing menace during the

"Solomonic" gateway at Gezer.

eighth century. The archaeological record does show that the Philistine cities of Timnah and Ekron and others had a rebirth under the Assyrians (which we will study later in detail, along with the admonitions of Amos and other prophets).

Let us move on to examine Gezer, beginning in the tenth century B.C. We have mentioned that an Egyptian pharaoh gave this city to Solomon as a dowry for his daughter (1 Kings 9:15–16). Evidently, Gezer had been in Canaanite hands and had had a Philistine overlord who had a vassal relationship with Egypt (Lance 1967, 41). The passage in 1 Kings also states that Solomon fortified Jerusalem, Hazor, Megiddo, and Gezer. It is interesting to see that the gates of Hazor, Megiddo, and Gezer are so similar that it is generally accepted that all three came from the same blueprints—Solomon's. Several of the chambers in the Gezer gate complex are lined with benches, some still covered with plaster.

The gateway at Gezer brings to mind several biblical stories. Absalom, for example, waited in the city gate to talk to the people who were coming to Jerusalem to plead a case in front of his father,

No.
Hen
Israel
in
He
North

185

Iron II (ninth/eighth century B.C.) industrial sector at Gezer.

King David (2 Sam. 15:1–6). Boaz also sat in the gate while meeting with the city elders at Bethlehem in order to fulfill his obligations concerning Ruth (Ruth 4:1–11).

The gate at Gezer attributed to Solomon was destroyed at the end of the tenth century B.C. Even today the destruction is clearly visible, since several of the limestone ashlars became so hot during the burning that they calcined, or melted into one another. This destruction is again attributed to Pharaoh Shishak, who reasserted his authority over Philistia and tested Rehoboam. We know that it occurred circa 918 B.C., for when Shishak returned home to Karnak, he carved on the walls of Amon's temple the names of towns that he had conquered; Gezer was one of them. Gezer's gateway was later rebuilt, but the calcined limestone remained in place, with additional stones placed alongside for buttressing. Today, therefore, the entryway of the main gate appears off balance and is narrower than that of the original Solomonic gate. The city continued to have inhabitants, and the gate continued to be used throughout the ninth and eighth centuries to the time when the Assyrians invaded and destroyed much of Israel, Judah, and Philistia.

And what about Tel Sera' and Tel Halif, the main candidates for David's Ziklag? What happened to these Philistine sites during the tenth-eighth centuries, down to the time of Assyrian ascendancy? We have already described them as they were during the Iron I period with the coming of the Philistines (pp. 154–59). We have also mentioned the limestone ashlars at Tel Sera' in connection with the use of ashlars in the gates at Ashdod and Ekron and with the architecture at the Solomonic gateways in Jerusalem, Gezer, Megiddo, and Hazor.

According to Oren, the large-scale building projects taking place at Tel Sera' during the tenth century B.C. should most likely be credited to Solomon or Rehoboam (1982, 163). The destruction that occurred there during the same century would then be attributed to the well-known Pharaoh Shishak, the troublemaker during King Rehoboam's reign. An alternative hypothesis that Oren mentions is that the building at Tel Sera' may have been due to Rehoboam's grandson, Asa, still in the tenth century. Asa, like Rehoboam (2 Chron. 11:5–12), fortified numerous cities in Judah (2 Chron. 14:5–7). During Asa's reign there was trouble with Zerah the Ethiopian, and some of the battles against him took place in the area of Tel Sera'. Thus the destruction at Tel Sera' could have been due to the invasion by this Ethiopian, and King Asa perhaps used his encounter with Zerah in southern Judah to reestablish control in the region separating Judah from Philistia and Egypt.

Eight miles to the east of Tel Sera' lies Tel Halif. It too witnessed a building project during the latter part of the tenth century, and this revival may be attributed to Solomon or his successors, as well. Tel Halif flourished along with Tel Sera' during the late tenth or early ninth century. Tel Sera' seems to have been abandoned for approximately 150 years beginning around 850 B.C. but was inhabited again circa 700 B.C., the period of Assyrian ascendancy. On the other hand, Tel Halif shows continued occupation throughout the ninth, the eighth, and the beginning of the seventh centuries, but it did not survive through the Assyrian period (Seger 1984, 51–52).

Now back to the question asked at the beginning of this chapter: Did Solomon rule only *to* "the land of the Philistines" or *in* the land of the Philistines as well? We have seen in our examination that, clearly, Solomon ruled *in* the land of the Philistines, but the situation changed under his son Rehoboam. The heartland of Philistia, exemplified by Ashdod, had its ups and downs but remained strong. It was during Rehoboam's time that Israel/Judah lost control of Philistia. This control would be regained only sporadically, under kings Asa, Jehoshaphat, and Uzziah, who successfully raided Philistia periodically.

Baal-zebub

"Go, inquire of Baal-zebub, the god of Ekron. . . ."
[2 Kings 1:2]

The Assyrians marched into history during the ninth century B.C. and built a reputation for fierceness in the use of their ruthless fighting machine (see, for example, Bleibtreu 1991 and Yadin 1963, 2:394–403). Shalmaneser III (859–824 B.C.) was the second king in this renaissance of Assyrian military might. The Assyrians had had an empire already around 1100 B.C., but then they declined in power for a two-hundred-year period. Extrabiblical Assyrian records of the ninth century speak of Israel, sometimes referring to it as the House of Omri, in deference to Ahab's father. The same Assyrian records also relate encounters with "Ahab, the Israelite" (*ANET*, 279). In another Assyrian record of an assault not mentioned in the Bible, Shalmaneser III campaigned against Syria and Israel, and Ahab committed two thousand chariots and ten thousand soldiers into the fray. This commitment is substantial when compared with Syria's twelve hundred chariots, twelve hundred cavalrymen, and twenty thousand soldiers (*ANET*, 278–79). King Ahab was listed third out of twelve kings on this inscription, but all of them suffered overwhelming defeat at the hands of Shalmaneser, by his account.

Still another one of Shalmaneser's records states that he crossed the Euphrates for the sixteenth time to fight Syria and collected tribute "of the inhabitants of Tyre, Sidon, and of Jehu, son of Omri" (*ANET*, 280). This was to have happened in his eighteenth year, or 841 B.C. Yet another record of Shalmaneser is found on the famous Black Obelisk, which was excavated at the Assyrian capital of Nimrud. Israel's King Jehu is pictured bowing down to Shalmaneser in the second of five panels on one of the four sides of the obelisk. The Assyrian gods Ashur and Ishtar are witnesses of the event (Yadin 1963, 2:395 for picture). The following text accompanies the picture:

> The tribute of Jehu, son of Omri; I received from him silver, gold, a golden *saplu* bowl, a golden vase with a pointed bottom, golden tumblers, golden buckets, tin, a staff for a king, (and) a wooden [word unknown]. [*ANET*, 282; Finegan 1959, 205]

These stories of Assyria's encounters with Israel set the stage for much of the rest of this book. Although the Assyrian campaigns through Tyre, Sidon, Israel, Judah, and Philistia led to the downfall of Israel and the weakening of Judah, Assyria's march south meant renewed growth for Philistia.

One of Israel's kings who ruled between Ahab and Jehu, not mentioned in any Assyrian text but important to our study, was Ahaziah.

> Ahaziah had fallen through the lattice in his upper chamber in Samaria, and lay injured; so he sent messengers, telling them, "Go, inquire of Baal-zebub, the god of Ekron, whether I shall recover from this injury." But the angel of the LORD said to Elijah the Tishbite, "Get up, go to meet the messengers of the king of Samaria, and say to them, 'Is it because there is no God in Israel that you are going to inquire of Baal-zebub, the god of Ekron?' Now therefore thus says the LORD, 'You shall not leave the bed to which you have gone, but you shall surely die.'" So Elijah went. [2 Kings 1:2–4]

Ahaziah of Israel was the son of King Ahab who became king upon Ahab's death in battle against the Syrians at Ramoth-gilead in 853 B.C. Ahaziah apparently reigned in two different years, but his rule lasted less than twelve months (1 Kings 22:51; 2 Kings 3:1). This short reign was due to an injury received through a fall. When Ahaziah died, Joram (also called Jehoram), another son of Ahab, became the next king. Jehu, of course, was not Omri's biological son (as the Assyrian text quoted above states), but in fact killed Ahab's true son, Joram, Ahaziah's brother (2 Kings 9). The Assyrian record may simply intend to say, Jehu of Israel or Jehu the Successor (Bright 1981, 254 n. 64; Pfeiffer 1973, 332).

Ahaziah's injury led him to send messengers to consult Baal-zebub, a god at the Philistine city of Ekron. An accurate picture of this god is still impossible, since the original meaning of the name is not yet known. One hopes continued excavations at Ekron will recover more information about the god. Scholars presently believe that Baal-zebub was a local, Philistine version of the Canaanite god Baal (Cogan and Tadmor 1988, 25). The last part of the name, *zebub,* means "flies," and so the complete name means "Baal of the flies" or "Lord of the flies," which is a form of Baal that has not been found elsewhere in the Near East.

Some scholars have gone to the classical world to attempt to link Baal-zebub to Zeus Apomuios, "fly-averting Zeus" or "flycatcher Zeus" (Cogan and Tadmor 1988, 25; *ISBE* 1:381). Since it is difficult to explain naming a god after the flies that buzz around a sacrifice or around any decaying carcass, many scholars mention that perhaps Baal-zebub is a pejorative of the name Baal-zebul. Baal-zebul is known from the Canaanite religion; the name refers to the god Baal as Lord Prince (Cogan and Tadmor 1988, 25) or "lord of the lofty abode" (Achtemeier 1985, 86; *ISBE* 1:381). The Lord God of Israel was upset with Ahaziah for wanting to consult a rival god (2 Kings 1:3), and so perhaps through Elijah this Baal-zebul, or "Lord Prince," was mocked by being called "Lord of the Flies." Scholars, though, have reached no firm conclusion on the identification of Baal-zebub/zebul. At the site of Ekron pieces of male figurines (perhaps idols) have been unearthed, but there, too, nothing firm has been learned concerning the identification of the gods of Ekron—not yet.

Jesus used the name Beel-zebub/zebul in reference to the Prince of Demons (Matt. 10:25; 12:24, 27; Mark 3:22; Luke 11:15, 18–19), but no direct link can be made between Beel-zebul or Satan, the New Testament Prince of Demons, and Baal-zebub, the Old Testament god of Ekron.

Ekron during Ahaziah's time was not very impressive, just the small ten-acre site in the upper portion of the city. Soon however, the Assyrians would come south to stay, which would do much for the rebirth of Ekron and other parts of Philistia.

Jehoiada and the Carites[2]

> But in the seventh year Jehoiada summoned the captains of
> the Carites and of the guards . . .
> [2 Kings 11:4]

The Assyrians left Palestine for the remainder of the ninth century, since Shalmaneser III (859–824 B.C.) and his successor had to put down revolts in Armenia, Babylonia, and elsewhere. Second Kings and 2 Chronicles have much to say about problems between

190

Israel, Judah, and Syria at the time. The Philistines, however, do not figure into these chapters except in 2 Chronicles 21:16–17 and 2 Kings 11. One of the problems in Judah concerns Queen Athaliah, the daughter of Ahab and Jezebel. A marriage alliance had been arranged between King Jehoshaphat of Judah and King Ahab of Israel (2 Chron. 18:1). To seal the alliance, Jehoshaphat's son Jehoram (also called Joram) married Ahab's daughter Athaliah (2 Kings 8:16ff.). The land of Judah suffered during Jehoram's brief reign of eight years, perhaps due in part to the fact that he killed his brothers as competitors for the throne (2 Chron. 21:1–4). Jehoram may have done this at the urging of his wife, the daughter of Ahab. Athaliah was probably the one who had the house of Baal built in Jerusalem (2 Kings 11:18). God allowed Edom to revolt against Judah, and the Philistines as well as Arabs to the east and southwest made forays into Judah "and carried away all the possessions they found that belonged to the king's house" (2 Chron. 21:17). These forays were probably into royal cities on the outskirts of Judah and not into Jerusalem itself. The Philistines were thereby able to reverse the situation that had existed in the time of Jehoram's father, Jehoshaphat. Then, some of the Philistines had had to bring tribute to Jehoshaphat, the king of Judah (2 Chron. 17:11). Jehoram died in 841 B.C. of a painful abdominal disease, and "he departed with no one's regret" (2 Chron. 21:20).

Jehoram's son Ahaziah then took over the throne of Judah. This son was later killed by Jehu at the same time that Jehu killed Joram (Jehoram) of Israel (Ahab's son and Athaliah's brother) in the dramatic story recited in 2 Kings 9. When Jehu entered Jezreel, he also killed Jezebel by having her thrown over the palace wall.

Back in Judah, Jezebel's daughter Athaliah heard about the death of her brother, mother, and son at the hands of King Jehu of Israel, and she then performed a sickening deed in a fashion that would have made her mother proud. Athaliah killed off the royal house and became queen. She missed one young member of the royal house of David who had been hidden, but nonetheless she was able to rule Judah for six years. In the seventh year of Athaliah's reign, Jehoiada, a priest loyal to the Lord, took steps to put this young survivor, Joash, on the throne. In order to restore the house of David to the throne in Jerusalem, Jehoiada called in the Carites. Who were these Carites?

Caria was located in the southwest corner of Anatolia, that is, modern-day Turkey. Miletus was one of its major cities. As has been explained, it is one possible location for the origins of the Sea Peoples. The Carites were very well known in extrabiblical sources from the seventh century B.C.. They were mercenaries hired by the Egyptians (Pfeiffer 1973, 398–99; Miller and Hayes 1986, 370; Herodotus 2.150f.). Herodotus, in reference to an oracle, calls the Carians (and their companions, the Ionians) "bronze men from the sea." Due to these references to the Carians of the seventh century, some scholars conclude that the Carites of 2 Kings 11 of the ninth century B.C. were probably mercenaries from Caria hired somehow by Jehoiada or by a previous king of Judah. I disagree, but I will refer to Herodotus's Carians again when we discuss King Josiah of Judah.

The Carites of 2 Kings 11 were part of the royal guard, similar in function to the Cherethites and the Pelethites back in the days of David and Solomon. Is it possible to link the Carites to David's Philistine bodyguard? It is, and I believe that the biblical text itself gives us a clue. If the Carites had always been part of the royal bodyguard, why did they turn on Athaliah? The logical answer is that they recognized that Athaliah was not of the house of David to whom they first swore allegiance. Since Joash was a direct descendant of David, Jehoiada did not have to do any arm-twisting to get them to help place Joash on the throne.

Carites, in transcription from Hebrew, is *kari*, and the transcription for the Cherethites of David's bodyguard is *kereti* (see 2 Sam. 8:18; 15:18; 20:7 for examples of *kereti*; see also p. 67). Yet in 2 Samuel 20:23, the Hebrew word translated "Cherethites" is *kari* and not *kereti*. Thus the word *kari* seems to be interchangeable in the minds of translators with the word *kereti* and probably refers to the same people. This then leads to the suggestion that the Carites in the Joash story of 2 Kings 11 had been in the employ of David's royal house for generations, much like the Swiss Guard (Cogan and Tadmor 1988, 126) that has protected the pope in Rome for generations.

> But in the seventh year Jehoiada summoned the captains of the Carites and of the guards and had them come to him in the house of the LORD. He made a covenant with them and put them under oath in the house of the LORD; then he showed them the king's son. He commanded them, "This is what you are to do: . . . surround the king, each with weapons in hand; and whoever approaches the ranks is to be killed. Be with the king in his comings and goings." [2 Kings 11:4–8]

Notice that Jehoiada showed the Carites the king's son, and then commanded them to protect the rightful heir to the throne. The

Carites agreed to this alliance with Jehoiada, which would have been the natural response for them as the royal bodyguard.

Then Jehoiada, with a stroke of genius, "delivered to the captains the spears and shields that had been King David's, which were in the house of the LORD; the guards stood, every man with his weapons in his hand. . . " (2 Kings 11:10–11). If the Carites were the "Swiss Guard," then giving them the spears and shields of King David's time was indeed a brilliant move, since this would have been enough to remind them where their loyalty should lie. "Then he [Jehoiada] brought out the king's son, put the crown on him, and gave him the covenant; they proclaimed him king, and anointed him; they clapped their hands and shouted, 'Long live the king!'" (2 Kings 11:12). Yes, the Carites were doing for Joash as their predecessors had done for David (2 Sam. 15:13–18) and Solomon (1 Kings 1:38–40). "He [Jehoiada] took the captains, the Carites, the guards, and all the people of the land; then they brought the king down from the house of the LORD, marching through the gate of the guards to the king's house. He took his seat on the throne of the kings" (2 Kings 11:19). It must have been an emotional moment for all, but especially for the proud Philistine bodyguard, who more than once in its history had saved the life of the king.

Uzziah

God helped him against the Philistines. . . .
[2 Chron. 26:7]

In 2 Chronicles 26 we again reach a time from which a good deal of biblical as well as extrabiblical information about the Philistines and their role in Palestine is available. We are coming to the days of Amos and Isaiah, who recite words of prophetic judgment not only against God's people, the Jews, but against the Philistines, too. In this section, the data from Chronicles, the prophets, and the extrabiblical texts will be joined together with the archaeological data presently being retrieved from the major Philistine sites and from a few additional ones.

The eighth century B.C. opened with a resurgence of both Israel and Judah, and the amount of territory gained through their military might nearly rivaled that of Solomon's day. The respective kings were Jeroboam II in the north and Uzziah in Jerusalem. It was Uzziah who battled the Philistines:

193

He went out and made war against the Philistines, and broke down the wall of Gath and the wall of Jabneh and the wall of Ashdod; he built cities in the territory of Ashdod and elsewhere among the Philistines. . . . He built towers in the wilderness and hewed out many cisterns, for he had large herds, both in the Shephelah and in the plain, and he had farmers and vinedressers in the hills and in the fertile lands, for he loved the soil. . . . Uzziah provided for all the army the shields, spears, helmets, coats of mail, bows, and stones for slinging. In Jerusalem he set up machines, invented by skilled workers, on the towers and the corners for shooting arrows and large stones. And his fame spread far, for he was marvelously helped until he became strong. [2 Chron. 26:6, 10, 14–15]

All these military adventures resulted not only in the expansion of Uzziah's kingdoms, but also in a time of prosperity that no one in the divided kingdoms had previously witnessed. This prosperity would lead to words of condemnation from the prophets, due to the kings' lack of *misphat,* or justice towards the people. But what was this period like for the Philistines, since the verses above state that Uzziah captured Gath and Ashdod and built cities in the area of Ashdod and elsewhere in Philistia?

The words of Amos, who was among the shepherds of Tekoa, which he saw concerning Israel in the days of King Uzziah of Judah and in the days of King Jeroboam son of Joash of Israel, two years before the earthquake. . . .
Thus says the LORD:
For three transgressions of Gaza,
    and for four, I will not revoke the punishment;
because they carried into exile entire communities,
    to hand them over to Edom.
So I will send a fire on the wall of Gaza,
    fire that shall devour its strongholds.
I will cut off the inhabitants from Ashdod,
    and the one who holds the scepter from Ashkelon;
I will turn my hand against Ekron,
    and the remnant of the Philistines shall perish,
                    says the Lord GOD.
[Amos 1:1, 6–8]

Notice that, of the five chief Philistine cities, Gath is absent from the list. In Amos 6, the prophet warns the inhabitants of Jerusalem and Samaria not to take it for granted that the thick walls of their cities will save them from divine retribution. Amos then reminds God's people of three other sites:

> Cross over to Calneh, and see;
> from there go to Hamath the great;
> then go down to Gath of the Philistines.
> Are you better than these kingdoms?
> Or is your territory greater than their territory? . . .
> [Amos 6:2]

Amos seems to be saying that the three sites had been destroyed, Calneh (see Na'aman 1974, 37) and Hamath by Jeroboam II (2 Kings 14:25 on Hamath) and Gath by Uzziah (2 Chron. 26:6). Is it possible to date the destruction of these sites before looking at the archaeological data? Amos 1:1 gives us a clue; Amos is prophesying "in the days of King Uzziah . . . and . . . King Jeroboam . . . two years before the earthquake." Zechariah 14 refers to the time when the Lord would return to Jerusalem and when the people would "flee as you fled from the earthquake in the days of King Uzziah of Judah" (14:5). Both Zechariah and Amos seem to have been be referring to a major earthquake.

It must have been a memorable event for the eighth-century Amos to have said that his prophecy from God came two years before the quake, and even more memorable for the sixth-century Zechariah to have used the quake as a reference point for his audience, saying that the earth would again shift and split as in the days of Uzziah. Josephus dates this earthquake to the day that Uzziah committed his sin against the Lord in the temple (2 Chron. 26:16–21) and was made a leper (*Antiq.* 9.215f. in Maier 1988, 171). The earthquake probably occurred in 749 B.C. (Yeivin 1979, 162, 168). Since Amos did not include Gath in his prophecy, and since Uzziah must have gone out and "made war against the Philistines" (2 Chron. 26:6) before he contacted leprosy, Gath must have been destroyed (not to be mentioned again) and Ashdod must have been attacked around 750 B.C., before the earthquake.

Gath, if it is Tell es-Safi, still needs to be excavated, but Ashdod has been excavated, and its tell should shed light on the days of Uzziah. According to the excavator, M. Dothan, its brick gateway with the ashlar block facade was destroyed about this time, and he attributes this destruction to Uzziah (Yadin 1979, 218; Oded 1979, 240; Myers 1986b, 152–53). Second Chronicles 26:6 also mentions that Uzziah "built cities" in the area around Ashdod. The port city of Ashdod's territory, Tel Mor, and its fortress show development during this time period. By fighting his way towards the coast, Uzziah no doubt gained control over trade going north and south, but he also was able to use the Philistine plain to expand his flocks, herds, and farms, "for he loved the soil" (2 Chron. 26:10).

Ekron at this time was still a tiny, ten-acre town and probably was controlled along with Gaza by Uzziah (Yeivin 1979, 165). At Ekron, the pottery forms from this century are the typical coastal forms and the forms common in Judah (Gitin 1990, 35).

Ashkelon evidently was not a part of Uzziah's plans, especially since he had gained a segment of the coastline at Ashdod. But it is probably also true that he would have been unable to take it, since it was a huge city and was directly on the coast. Uzziah had no navy to blockade Ashkelon (Yeivin 1979, 165). The former Philistine port at Tell Qasile was abandoned at this time, but Timnah (east of Ekron), which had become an Israelite city during the tenth century and then had been destroyed at the end of the same century, was rebuilt on a grand scale during the time of Uzziah.

More information about Uzziah and Philistia is available through Assyrian records. Right around the turn of the ninth/eighth century, an Assyrian king by the name of Adad-nirari III took the throne. At least one of his military campaigns apparently took him down into Philistia, since he included Philistia on an inscription at Nimrud as one of his tribute-paying clients (Oded 1979, 241). It is in sources from a later king, Tiglath-pileser III (745–727 B.C.), that a most interesting reference appears. This king took the Assyrian throne a few years before the end of Uzziah's reign. Beginning with him, Assyria not only campaigned for tribute but also for conquest and direct control over its subject nations. Tiglath-pileser III recorded his campaigns in clay, and from these documents we can today read the names of kings who had to pay him tribute, as well as kings who dared to oppose him. We must recognize, however, that this is his own version of events. Some of the names in his records are Jehoahaz of Judah as well as Menahem of Samaria and the kings of Ashkelon and Gaza (*ANET*, 282–83; 2 Kings 15:19, 29; 16:7, 9; see Yadin 1963, 2:404–13 for pictures of the reliefs).

The intriguing reference mentioned above is found in a text that concerns a coalition of kings who opposed Tiglath (*ANET*, 282). The coalition was headed by an "Azriau of Yaudi," which is understood by several scholars to be "Azariah of Judah," the other name of Uzziah. This text is generally dated to 743 B.C., within the long reign of Uzziah and after the death of Israel's Jeroboam II. It is possible that Uzziah took control of parts of Israel. Second Chronicles 26 definitely presents him as a successful king and military leader "as long as he sought the LORD" (v. 5; see also vv. 14–15; Myers 1986b, 153; Wright 1966, 86; Oded 1979, 242f.; Pfeiffer 1973, 352; Bright 1981, 270). It should be mentioned, though, that there is not total agreement that Tiglath's text refers to Uzziah of Judah (see Pfeiffer 1973, 352; Na'aman 1974, 38–39). However, if it does indeed, then events it relates would have happened during the years that Uzziah was afflicted with leprosy. Most likely, Uzziah still held the power while his son Jotham co-reigned with him.

The texts relate that Tiglath was interested in controlling the maritime trade routes through Philistia and Phoenicia. Common "gifts" to the Assyrian king besides the expected gold and silver were "linen garments with multicolored trimmings, garments of their native (industries) (being made of) dark purple wool . . ." (*ANET*, 282–83). The kings of Ashkelon, Gaza, Ekron (possibly, according to Tadmor 1966, 89), Judah, and Israel were among those who sent these "gifts" to Assyria. The gift of linen garments reflects very well the scene at Ekron, where textiles would soon become a major industry. This industry will be described more fully later. First, though, let us consider what happened in Philistia after the reign of Uzziah and his son Jotham.

Words of Amos[3]

Woe to those who . . .
    drink wine in bowls,
    and anoint themselves with the finest oils. . . .
[Amos 6:4, 6 RSV]

Now that more than one hundred olive oil presses have been excavated at Tel Miqne-Ekron and others at Tel Batash-Timnah, biblical scholars have used the finds to reexamine biblical texts. One such scholar is Philip King, who has reexamined the Book of Amos in the light of this new data. Since our focus here is on the Philistines, I will present a synopsis of Dr. King's study only as it relates to Philistia.

Amos of Judah prophesied to Israel during its heyday under King Jeroboam II in the mid-eighth century B.C. Through its production of olive oil, Ekron was soon to become prosperous and a good source of revenue for its Assyrian overlords. (Neither Egypt nor Assyria cultivated olives.) Dr. King uses findings from the Ekron excavations in his study of Amos and the *marzeah* ritual of Amos 6:1–7, specifically verse 6. This ritual was a pagan one known in the Near East already in the fourteenth century B.C. It served both a religious and a social

197

function, and it could commemorate either joyful or sorrowful occasions, but, in both cases, excessive eating and drinking were involved. The ritual required wealth, and Amos castigated complacent affluence in his prophecy (chap. 6). Israel and Judah (6:1) were prosperous—for the rich.

Sometimes the marzeah was used as part of a funerary cult (as in Jer. 16:5, 7–8), where a feast was held for the departed loved ones. King is not sure if this is the way the marzeah was used in Amos 6:4–6, but any reading of the text indicates that overindulgence by the rich and famous was predicated. Amos attacked the complacency of both Israel and Judah in verses 1–6, as well as their mistaken notion that because they were God's people, nothing would happen to them.

The marzeah ritual is broken down into five components, and it is the fifth one, "and anoint themselves with the finest oils," that involves the olive presses of Tel Miqne-Ekron, Timnah, and, no doubt, other sites where these oil presses have been recovered. The initial phase of crushing the olives is what produces the finest oils, or virgin oil as it is presently marketed in our stores. During the eighth-seventh centuries B.C., the olives for oil were placed in a shallow stone basin and then crushed with a stone roller. Once they were of a paste-like consistency, the mess was washed with water. After the material in the basin was stirred, the oil would float to the top. The oil that was skimmed off at this stage was the virgin oil, or as the New Revised Standard Version calls it, the "finest oil," with which people anointed themselves.

Here then we have used the material culture found at Philistine sites to better understand a facet of the economic life of the people mentioned in Amos 6. The Lord warns his people here that economics is related to their religious life, and unless they act with justice, as a holy people, they will go the way of "Gath of the Philistines" (v. 2).

Ahaz[4]

And the Philistines had made raids on . . . Judah. . . .
[2 Chron. 28:18]

We are now within ten years of the collapse of Israel as a nation. In Judah, Ahaz (735–715 B.C.), the son of Jotham and grandson of Uzziah, was crowned king. Whereas Uzziah had been able to take over parts of Philistia, Ahaz lost territory, and the Philistines raided

Judah. Ahaz also encountered difficulties with Edom to the south and Israel and Syria to the north. All these troubles for Judah occurred presumably because Ahaz "did not do what was right in the sight of the LORD his God, as his ancestor David had done, but he walked in the way of the kings of Israel" (2 Kings 16:2–3).

It was during a direct assault on Jerusalem by Syria and Israel that the prophet Isaiah went to Ahaz and told him to have faith in the Lord and to ask the Lord for a sign. Ahaz refused to ask for a sign, but Isaiah gave him one anyway: "Behold, a young woman shall conceive and bear a son, and shall call his name Immanuel" (Isa. 7:14 RSV). Isaiah also prophesied that Assyria would attack Syria and that both Syria and the Philistines would attack Israel (Isa. 9:11–12). However, Ahaz refused to believe the word of the Lord and appealed to Assyria for aid. Tiglath-pileser III did not need an invitation to invade Israel, but he probably used Ahaz's appeal as an excuse. The precise chronology is difficult (*ANET*, 282–83; Tadmor 1966, 88–89; Pfeiffer 1973, 334–35; Bright 1981, 273–74), but after attacking Phoenicia, Tiglath-pileser invaded Philistia, destroying Gaza and causing its king, Hanno, to flee south to Egypt (*ANET*, 283). Hanno had previously been required to pay tribute to Assyria. An Assyrian list reveals that Ammon, Moab, "Mitinti of Ashkelon, Jehoahaz [Ahaz] (Ia-u-ha-zi) of Judah (Ia-u-da-a-a)," as well as Edom and a Mu-she-hu (or Mu-su-[ri]) of Ekron or Ashdod were also required to pay (*ANET*, 282; Tadmor 1966, 89). Other texts speak of the Assyrian invasion of Syria and Israel. These texts fit accurately the description recorded in 2 Kings 16 of Ahaz's trip to Damascus, the former Syrian capital, to pay homage to the Assyrian conqueror. It was then that Ahaz, impressed by an altar in Damascus, ordered one like it to be constructed and placed in the temple courtyard in Jerusalem.

Ahaz was not the only ruler paying homage and tribute in Damascus. Gezer, which had by then come under the influence of Ekron (Tadmor 1966, 89 n. 15), also is depicted on one of Tiglath-pileser's reliefs. Isaiah predicted that Judah would again swoop down on the Philistines (Isa. 11:14); this did not happen in Ahaz's lifetime, but Isaiah's prediction remains:

> In the year that King Ahaz died this oracle came:
> Do not rejoice, all you Philistines,
>> that the rod that struck you is broken,
> for from the root of the snake will come forth an adder,
>> and its fruit will be a flying fiery serpent.

The firstborn of the poor will graze,
　　and the needy lie down in safety;
but I will make your root die of famine,
　　and your remnant I will kill.
Wail, O gate; cry, O city;
　　melt in fear, O Philistia, all of you!
For smoke comes out of the north,
　　and there is no straggler in its ranks.
[Isa. 14:28–31]

When Tiglath-pileser died, Israel was dying and almost dead, but the Philistines and others could not relax, for another Assyrian king, one perhaps harsher than Tiglath, was coming south—Sargon II (see Yadin 1963, 2:414–27 for pictures of Sargon's reliefs). Although the prophets of God, such as Isaiah, had told the people to lean on the Lord and not on the Assyrians, Judah probably viewed the destruction of Israel as merely a direct result of Ahaz's unwise cooperation with Tiglath-pileser.

Sargon II[5]

Egypt, Philistia, and other countries made an attempt to oppose this new Assyrian king, which is reflected in Isaiah 19–20 and in Assyrian accounts (*ANET*, 284–86; Tadmor 1966, 90f.; Yadin 1963, 2:417–18). The destruction of Israel is also described in Sargon's own records, as are the various assaults on Philistia, namely Ashdod, Gaza, and Ekron. Sargon II proclaimed his conquest of

> . . . Samaria (Sa-mir-i-na) and of the entire (country of) Israel (Bit-Hu-um-ri-a) who despoiled Ashdod (and) . . . who declared Hanno, king of Gaza, as booty. . .

> Iamani from Ashdod, afraid of my armed force (lit.: weapons), left his wife and children and fled to the frontier of M[usru]. . . . I conquered and sacked the towns of Shinuhtu (and) Samaria, and all Israel (lit.: Omri-Land Bit Hu-um-ri-ia). [*ANET*, 284–85]

Assyria, by controlling Gaza and other parts of Philistia, would control and develop the north-south trade routes linking Egypt and Arabia with Europe and Asia. Sargon II evidently had to make repeated forays into Philistia, with Ashdod perhaps being the ringleader in opposition to him. At the time that the fortunes of Israel were declining after its division, the fortunes of Ashdod had

The siege of Ekron depicted on a wall relief at Sargon's palace at Khorsabad. "Ekron" is written in cuneiform on the towers.

been generally improving. In the late tenth century, Ashdod had grown in power and expanded so much that it moved off the tell. It had grown from twenty to one hundred acres. From the tenth century to Sargon II's day it had experienced and survived one partial destruction, perhaps by King Uzziah (ca. 750 B.C.).

Gaza and final references to Gath are also mentioned in a few of the Assyrian inscriptions (*ANET*, 284–86), and one inscription, dated to after 716 B.C., notified Sargon II that foreign chieftains from Egypt, Judah, Gaza, Ashdod, Ekron, and Ashkelon, among others, had arrived with their tributes (Tadmor 1966, 92–93).

Still another Assyrian document—a letter that may have been sent by Sennacherib, the crown prince—describes in detail the fixed annual tribute from two Philistine cities. The tribute, as well as additional gifts, came from Ashdod and perhaps Ashkelon or Gaza (the letter is broken). Besides the usual precious metals, textiles again figured importantly, as well as dried fish (Tadmor 1966, 92–93).[6] Sargon II assaulted Ashdod and its neighbors in 713 and 712 B.C. Ashdod, in preparation for the attack, constructed a moat (*ANET*, 287). The assault is referred to in Isaiah 20:1–2: "In the year that the commander-in-chief, who was sent by King Sargon of Assyria, came to Ashdod and fought against it and took it—at that time the LORD had spoken to Isaiah son of Amoz. . . . " A fragment of an Assyrian cuneiform tablet also refers to an attack on Azekah (southeast of Ekron), which, if dated to this assault, may have been launched to keep King Hezekiah in check (Tadmor 1966, 94). To commemorate the conquest, Sargon II erected a stele, pieces of which have been found in the Ashdod excavations. Ashdod became an Assyrian province, ruled by an Assyrian governor and a local prince (Tadmor 1966, 94; Oded 1979, 243–44).

One of Sargon II's wall reliefs in his palace at Khorsabad not only shows the siege of Ekron but also names the city (Porten 1981, 46–47; Tadmor 1966, 90, 94; Yadin 1963, 2:418–19). Discussion of these military campaigns into Philistia brings us to the close of the eighth century B.C. and into the reign of King Hezekiah, who also had important encounters with the Philistines. Ashdod had become an important city-state for Assyria, but as the excavations at Ekron show, the sun would also rise on Ekron and its olive oil industry.

The destructive military campaign of Sargon II through Philistia and down into Egypt led Isaiah to make his warning to Judah in chapter 20 not to look to Egypt for aid against Assyria. Both Ashkelon and Gaza were crushed, but Ashdod and Ekron survived to become powerful city-states for Assyria in the seventh century BB.C. Ashdod would even have its own king again by the time of Sennacherib (ca. 700 B.C.).

The city revived after Sargon II's conquest. The excavated areas show that the streets, houses, and courtyards were rebuilt, and commerce resumed and continued down throught he first half of the seventh century. Inscriptions as well as inscribed weights have been excavated, dating to the end of the eight and into the seventh centuries. The recovery of a *pim* weight (see pp. 142–43) as well as others has led scholars to ponder whether the Ashdod inscriptions are in Hebrew (Negev 1986, 42), due to contacts with people of Judah, or Canaanite/West Semitic, again indicative of Philistine adaptation to the local culture (Oded 1979, 238). Some of this material might date to the time of Josiah, who may have taken over the area following the destruction of Ashdod by Pharaoh Psamtik I.

Tell Qasile lies to the north of Tel Ashdod. As described earlier, Qasile was uninhabited during the Iron II period, except perhaps for a brief revival in the late seventh century (according to Judean ceramics), when King Josiah may have used it as a port.

When last we looked to the south at Tels Sera' and Halif, we noted that Tel Halif flourished during the late tenth or early ninth through the eighth centuries B.C. This city did not survive the Assyrian period. Tel Sera', on the other hand, was abandoned for approximately 150 years beginning around 850 B.C. and was revived, evidently by the Assyrians, cica 700 B.C. That was the final fortified city at this site, and its citadel contained Assyrian "palace ware" ceramics and Assyrian bronzes, indicating to Oren, the excavator, that the citadel was occupied by Assyrian troops, perhaps during the reign of Esarhaddon (681–669).

Some of the interesting artifacts at Tel Sera' include a crescent-shaped bronze standard, which may symbolize the Asyrian moon-god, Sin, and a socketed bronze spearhead. This type of spearhead can be seen on Assyrian palace reliefs. The Egyptian goddess Sekhmet was also found on a faience (a fine grade of painted and glazed pottery) satuette, and East Greek pottery and both Hebrew and Aramaic ostraca were uncovered as well. The ceramic repertoire at Tel Sera' corresponds to the seventh-century repertoire found at Ashdod, Mesad Hashavyahu (see pp. 230–34), and Ekron. The late seventh-century B.C. destruction of Tel Sera' may have been due to either the Babylonian Nebuchadnezzar, the Egyptian pharaoh Neco, or Judah's King Josiah.

7

(handwritten margin note: Where is Assyria today?)

The Philistines from Hezekiah to Josiah

Hezekiah[1]

> He [Hezekiah] rebelled against the king of Assyria and would
> not serve him. He attacked the Philistines as far as Gaza and
> its territory, from watchtower to fortified city.
> [2 Kings 18:7–8]

Hezekiah not only reversed his father's policy of appeasement with the Assyrians, but also "did what was right in the sight of the LORD" (18:3). Second Kings 18–20 and portions of Isaiah are filled with graphic information about the results of Hezekiah's religious reform and his revolt against the Assyrians. Numerous Assyrian records that speak of the revolts in Philistia and Judah and the Assyrian response to them are also available (see Ussishkin 1979 and Yadin 1963, 2:428–38 for pictures of reliefs concerning Sennacherib and Hezekiah).

The time was right for Hezekiah to assert some independence, for after the fall of Samaria, Assyria's king Sargon II was busy putting down problems in Babylonia (foreshadowing the defeat of Nineveh by Babylon), Syria, Asia Minor (ruled then by the legendary King

Midas, according to Pfeiffer 1973, 364), and other places. Chapter 6 described the problems Sargon II was having in Philistia, especially in Ashdod and Ekron. Egypt, as well, was beginning to flex its muscles again.

The time was also right for Hezekiah to institute his religious reforms as described in 2 Kings 18:1–6, which included his destruction of the bronze serpent Nehushtan, the serpent Moses had made in the wilderness so long ago, but which evidently had become an

Nehushta

The Lachish prism, a six-sided prism of baked clay with cuneiform inscriptions. The side facing the reader refers to Sennacherib's campaign against Hezekiah.

206

object of worship. According to 2 Chronicles 30 Hezekiah also issued a call to the survivors of the ten northern tribes of Israel to come to Jerusalem to worship the Lord God.

> "O people of Israel, return to the LORD, the God of Abraham, Isaac, and Israel, so that he may turn again to the remnant of you who have escaped from the hand of the kings of Assyria. Do not be like your ancestors and your kindred, who were faithless to the LORD God of their ancestors. . . . Do not now be stiff-necked as your ancestors were, but yield yourselves to the LORD and come to his sanctuary . . . and serve the LORD your God, so that his fierce anger may turn away from you. . . . "
>
> So the couriers went from city to city through the country of Ephraim and Manasseh, and as far as Zebulun; but they laughed them to scorn, and mocked them. Only a few from Asher, Manasseh, and Zebulun humbled themselves and came to Jerusalem. [vv. 6–8, 10–11]

It was at this time that the Assyrians allowed an Israelite priest to return to what had been Israelite territory, to Bethel, to teach the people placed there by the Assyrians how to worship the God of Israel. This, however, resulted in a mixed religion for the mixed people in Samaria (2 Kings 17:24–33).

Hezekiah was able to keep out of harm's way until Sennacherib (705–681 B.C.) ascended to the Assyrian throne after Sargon II. It is during the reign of this Assyrian king that biblical historians place 2 Kings 18:7, "He [Hezekiah] rebelled against the king of Assyria and would not serve him" (Bright 1981, 284 and Pfeiffer 1973, 365, for example). According to the Assyrian records (*ANET*, 287–88), Hezekiah allied himself with the Philistine city of Ashkelon, as well as with an anti-Assyrian segment of Ekron that overthrew their king Padi and turned him over to Hezekiah.

Sennacherib could not march down immediately to teach Hezekiah and the others a lesson, so Hezekiah had time to strengthen his defenses (2 Chron. 32:1–8, 30). He strengthened Jerusalem's walls, raised towers, and "made weapons and shields in abundance" (2 Chron. 32:5). To secure his people's water supply, he also constructed a water tunnel within the walls of the city of David, a tunnel that still today is called "Hezekiah's water tunnel." A translation of the Hebrew inscription that once adorned its ceiling is as follows:

> [. . . when] (the tunnel) was driven through. And this was the way in which it was cut through:—While [. . .] (were) still [. . .] axe(s), each man towards his fellow, and while there were still three cubits to be cut through, [there was

207

heard] the voice of a man calling to his fellow, for there was an overlap in the rock on the right [and on the left]. And when the tunnel was driven through, the quarrymen hewed (the rock), each man toward his fellow, axe against axe; and the water flowed from the spring toward the reservoir for 1,200 cubits, and the height of the rock above the head(s) of the quarrymen was 100 cubits. [*ANET*, 321]

It is still a treat to walk in the cool waters of the unlit tunnel (see 2 Kings 20:20 and 2 Chron. 32:30).

Finally, after settling the troubles in Babylon, Sennacherib was able to come down to Philistia and Judah in 701 B.C. According to Sennacherib's own record (in cuneiform on a clay prism), several kings, including the king of Philistine Ashdod, traveled north to meet him, kissed his feet, and offered their loyalty. Evidently Ashkelon continued to resist; its king was captured (though perhaps without a battle) and deported, along with his family, to Assyria. Heavy tribute was imposed upon Ashkelon, and a new king loyal to Assyria was placed on the throne there. Sennacherib moved next against Ekron and was able to occupy it (as well as nearby Timnah). The rulers of the city were impaled, and captives were taken; at some point Hezekiah was forced to return Padi, the former king, to Ekron. Then Sennacherib invaded, occupied, and plundered much of Judah. What happened to Hezekiah and Judah can be read in vivid detail in 2 Kings 18:13–19:36 and Isaiah 36–37.

It is interesting to note some of the similarities between the biblical text and that of Sennacherib. Sennacherib spoke of Hezekiah's hope that help might come from Egypt:

> . . . Hezekiah, the Jew . . . had become afraid and had called (for help) upon the kings of Egypt . . . and the cavalry of the king of Ethiopia (Meluhha), an army beyond counting—and they had come to their assistance. [*ANET*, 287]

Compare this with 2 Kings 18:19–21.

> The Rabshakeh [field commander] said to them, "Say to Hezekiah: Thus says the great king, the king of Assyria: On what do you base this confidence of yours? . . . See, you are relying now on Egypt, that broken reed of a staff, which will pierce the hand of anyone who leans on it."

Relying on Egypt is exactly what the prophet Isaiah warns against in 30:1–2:

> Oh, rebellious children, says the LORD,
> who carry out a plan, but not mine;

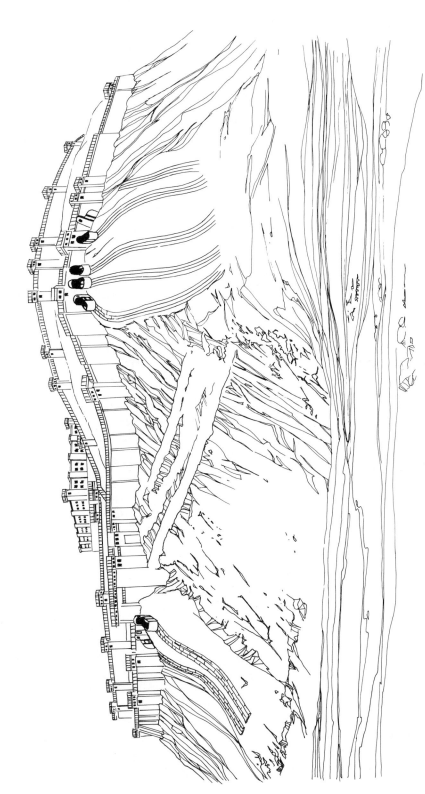

These reliefs (pp. 209–13) graphically picture how the Assyrians attacked and destroyed cities. Note the armor, weapons, and battering ram.

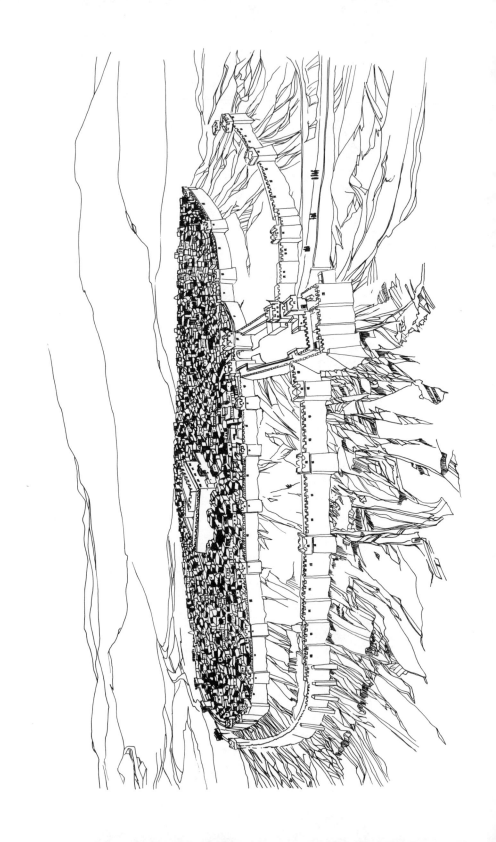

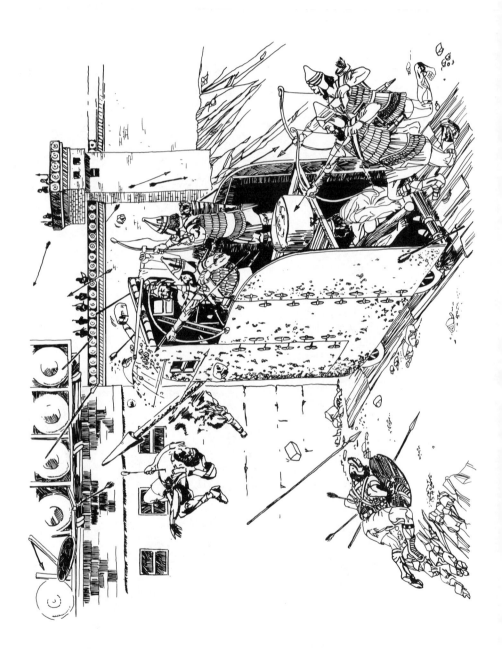

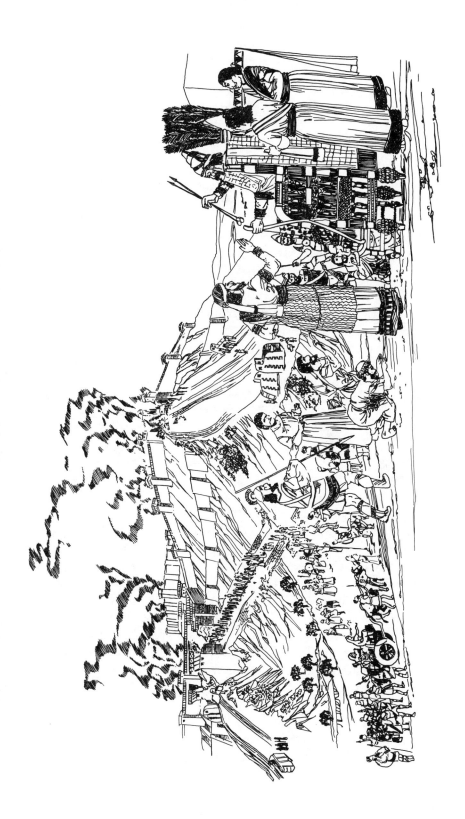

who make an alliance, but against my will,
adding sin to sin;
who set out to go down to Egypt
without asking for my counsel,
to take refuge in the protection of Pharaoh,
and to seek shelter in the shadow of Egypt. . . .

In 2 Kings 19:8–9, we read that soldiers from Ethiopia were indeed moving up to Canaan. Sennacherib met and defeated this force at Eltekeh, near Ekron, and then said of Hezekiah:

> As to Hezekiah, the Jew, he did not submit to my yoke, I laid siege to 46 of his strong cities, walled forts and to countless small villages in their vicinity. . . . Himself [Hezekiah] I made a prisoner in Jerusalem, his royal residence, like a bird in a cage. [*ANET*, 288]

Sennacherib described specifically how he captured the cities and all the booty, how he took prisoners, and how Hezekiah paid him forced tribute:

> [Hezekiah] did send me, later, to Nineveh, my lordly city, together with 30 talents of gold, 800 talents of silver, precious stones, antimony, large cuts of red stone . . . his own daughters, concubines, male and female musicians. [*ANET*, 288]

Second Kings 18:14–17 states that Hezekiah was required to give the Assyrian king "three hundred talents of silver and thirty talents of gold." This is not as much as in the Assyrian account, but it is a hefty amount, especially considering that one talent equaled about seventy-five pounds of either precious metal. In fact, the temple of the Lord and Hezekiah's treasury had to be stripped to gather together that much gold and silver.

According to the biblical account, Sennacherib was not able to capture Jerusalem. This may be confirmed by the fact that he recorded on his palace walls in Nineveh the graphic conquest of Lachish, a city of Judah, but nowhere recorded a siege or conquest of Jerusalem. Second Kings 19:35–36 comments that divine intervention sent Sennacherib back to Nineveh a defeated man, as prophesied by Isaiah.

Interestingly, the Greek historian Herodotus also records (bk. 2. 141) a defeat of Sennacherib at about this time on the Egyptian-Palestinian border, due to divine intervention—the intervention of an Egyptian god. Reportedly, a plague of mice was sent, causing an

The author in a guardroom at the city gate of Lachish. Sennacherib watched the destruction of the city from the hill in the background.

Assyrian retreat and heavy loss of life to the Assyrians. There is no way to be certain, but this story could have been the backdrop for Sennacherib's attack on Ashkelon and southern Philistia. In any event, Sennacherib broke off his attack on Philistia and Judah and returned to Nineveh, having had a successful campaign, by his account. Apparently, he did punish Hezekiah further, however: "His towns which I had plundered, I took away from his country and gave them (over) to Mitinti, king of Ashdod, Padi, king of Ekron, and Sillibel, king of Gaza. Thus I reduced his country. . . " (*ANET*, 287–88). There were no more rebellions against Assyria in Philistia until the final quarter of the seventh century. Egypt continued to be a problem, necessitating Assyrian military campaigns through Philistia, but these campaigns seem to have assumed Philistine cooperation, and the region was used as the staging area for attacks on Egypt. Let us now go to the archaeological record to see more clearly what was happening at some of the Philistine sites at the end of the eighth and beginning of the seventh centuries B.C.

Ekron figures prominently in the Assyrian records of Sargon II and Sennacherib, and it probably was one of the cities captured by Hezekiah when the biblical record states, "He attacked the Philistines as far as Gaza and its territory, from watchtower to fortified city" (2 Kings 18:8). You may recall that the archaeological record thus far reveals that Ekron was not, evidently, a major

215

Philistine city from the days of King David until the end of the eighth century B.C., in King Hezekiah's day. The evidence thus far seems to indicate that perhaps only the upper city of approximately ten acres was occupied continuously during this two-hundred-year period. Evidence at Ekron of occupation by King Hezekiah late in the eighth century B.C. includes storage jars that bear the stamp *l'melekh* on the handles. This Hebrew phrase means "belonging to the king." Most of the more than one thousand stamped handles that have been found thus far have been found in Judah and are dated stratigraphically to the reign of Hezekiah. These royally owned vessels, which contained olive oil, grain, or wine, held food supplies that probably were part of Hezekiah's preparations to stand against the Assyrians (see for example Kelm and A. Mazar 1989, 43, for brief discussion and picture of those found at Timnah; A. Mazar 1990, 455–58; Ussishkin 1985, 142–44). The storage jar stamps sometimes contain the name of a city, and one of the stamps found at Ekron has the name Hebron on it.

At some point near the end of the eighth century B.C., Ekron passed into the hands of the Assyrians. As has been mentioned, Sargon II both pictured the siege of Ekron on his wall reliefs at Khorsabad and also mentioned Ekron's name. He pictured the city as having been fortified by a low crenelated (notched) outer wall as

Handle of a storage jar stamped *l'melekh* (belonging to the king).

216

well as a crenelated inner wall with towers holding archers who were defending Ekron with their arrows. Ekron's role in Hezekiah's revolt against Sennacherib, with Hezekiah holding Padi, king of Ekron, hostage in Jerusalem has also been mentioned. The wall that both Sargon II and Sennacherib encountered in their campaigns against Ekron is presently visible at the site. This is the ashlar-faced wall that was uncovered by accident through the aid of a backhoe in 1984. The upper city on its highest point also had a citadel tower of boulder-sized stones constructed during the last half of the eighth century B.C.

Under Assyrian control, Philistine Ekron began its period of greatest growth and wealth. The summer excavations of 1990 confirmed that the seventh-century city expanded well beyond the mound on its northwest side to the vicinity of the Wadi Timnah. The evidence shows that Ekron in the seventh century B.C. covered seventy to eighty acres.

Hezekiah's Jerusalem was also expanding during this period of time. It was growing in part due to the flow of refugees from the north after the fall of Israel in 722/1 B.C. Due to the nature of the artifacts found at Tel Miqne-Ekron from the seventh century and the end of the eighth, it is thought that some Israelites also moved, voluntarily or otherwise, to Ekron.

Clearly, time and money were spent rebuilding the city early in the seventh century B.C. Approaching the tell from the southwest, one can see the remains of the stone wall at the base of the tell that may be pictured on Sargon II's reliefs at Khorsabad. The remains of the stone wall are also visible at the crest of the mound, and in between the two walls is a long line of what used to be the stables for many horses. The entryway into the city was on the south side, and the gateway was protected by a gatehouse to the south making the complex similar to the entryways found at Gezer, Lachish, and Philistine Ashdod. The gateway had a guard tower and chambers on each side. Only the east side of the gate has been excavated, leaving the west side, which is poking through the surface, for future archaeologists.

Just inside the gateway is ample evidence of the industry that must have filled Assyrian coffers—olive oil production. This was Ekron's industrial zone. Presence of a street with industrial buildings on both sides is obvious. More than one hundred olive oil presses have been found there, which, as we have said, would have enabled Ekron to produce one thousand tons (290,000 gallons) of olive oil in a season;

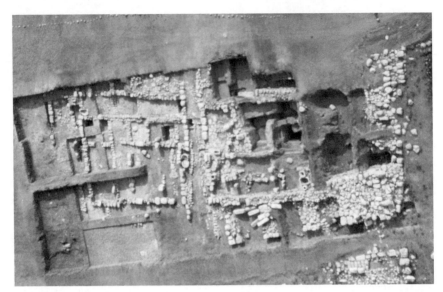

Industrial area at Ekron.

this is one-fifth of the olive oil currently produced for export in Israel![2]

Many of these olive presses are visible right at surface level. There are also several that can be seen in the area off the tell to the north-west. The nearby Kibbutz Revadim has based its reconstruction of the olive oil industry at Ekron on the complex excavated near the gateway. The rectangular buildings in this complex are divided into three rooms: the olive oil production room, the storage/work room, and an anteroom that is just off the street.

Stone weight used to press oil from olives.

218

Reconstruction of an olive press room.

In the production room is a large rectangular stone basin where the olives were first crushed with a stone roller. Probably the pulp was then washed, and the oil that was skimmed off was the finest oil, or virgin oil. To obtain more oil, the pulp would then have been placed in woven baskets on top of the vats on either side of the crushing basin. The vats have a circular hole in them so that, as the pulp was crushed, the oil would have flowed into the vats. To apply pressure to the pulp, a wooden beam, with one end anchored in a hole in the wall of the building, was placed over the pulp bag, with stone weights at the end of the beam opposite the wall. The people of the seventh century B.C. had developed a simple machine similar to a nutcracker (but bigger). The pressure applied on the beam by the weights would have slowly squeezed additional oil from the olives through the woven baskets into the vats below. Since the stone vats do not have a plugged hole in them, the oil must have been dippered out, or perhaps the vat was lined with a bag that was then lifted out when full.

As the production rooms were excavated, numerous storage jars, some crushed, some not, were taken out. In one oil production room, more than one hundred restorable vessels were extracted, plus thirty-four conical ceramic stoppers for the storage jars, numerous small jugs, and other finds. The adjacent storage/work room held at least eighty-eight restorable vessels, eight well-preserved iron agricultural tools hidden in a ceramic jar below the floor, and the most unexpected find of all, a stone niche with a four-horned altar inside it.

I remember when this particular altar was found. We were beginning to close down the site for the season, when two flat, parallel upright stones with dirt between them were uncovered. The area supervisor suspected a burial, and everyone was surprised when an altar was uncovered instead (more information on this altar will be given in the following section).

The anterooms leading to the street contained ceramic vessels used for food preparation and hundreds of loom weights. Since the finds mentioned above were somewhat typical for many of the production rooms, it is hypothesized that textiles were a secondary industry at Ekron. Olive harvest and the pressing of olive oil is seasonal (lasting approximately four months of the year), so it appears that these rooms had another function during the off season. This supports the Assyrian records of kings Esarhaddon (681–669) and Ashurbanipal (668–627), who recorded that some of the items they valued for booty or tribute from their subjects were "linen garments with multicolored trimmings" (*ANET*, 290–95; see Yadin 1963, 2:440–53, for the reliefs).

It was precisely during the reigns of Esarhaddon and Ashurbanipal and their predecessor, Sennacherib, that Ekron grew to its greatest extent in the approximately six hundred years of Philistine history in Canaan. The Assyrians had created a kind of "Pax Assyriaca," allowing Ekron to become the largest known center of olive oil production in the ancient Near East (Gitin 1990, 39).

Ekron was ideally suited for such a distinction. Due to a persistent problem with Egypt throughout the reigns of Sennacherib, Esarhaddon, and Ashurbanipal, a stable Philistia was important for the logistical movement of Assyrian men and supplies. The highways between Assyria and Egypt went through Philistia. It appears that Philistia was exempt from the usual practice of deporting the native inhabitants of a conquered state (such as was done with Israel) and moving a foreign people in. In Philistia the enemy king was simply replaced, without a major movement of peoples. Philistia was the linchpin between the Assyrian empire and Egypt (Eph'al 1979, 276–89).

Economically, Philistia was linked to trade between Egypt and Arabia as well as linked to trade to the north with Syria, Assyria, and points beyond. Assyria may have realized that the economy of the empire could be affected by damaging the social fabric of Philistia. Ekron had olive oil, a commodity that could be sold to help finance wars, and the Assyrian empire had the markets to sell the oil. Ekron was located on the eastern edge of the coastal plain near the hills where the olives were grown. It was also close enough to the coast for access to shipping the product throughout the Near East. The labor force was kept intact by the Assyrians, and at least two kings of Ekron were subject to Assyria in the seventh century B.C. King Padi was put back on the throne by Sennacherib, and a king named Ikausu governed during at least part of Esarhaddon's reign, according to Assyrian records (*ANET*, 291). Ekron and some other parts of Philistia lived a privileged life during the seventh century; this was not true, however, of the forty-six cities of Judah that Sennacherib boasted about destroying.

The properous life is dramatically evident in the upper city in the northern sector of Ekron. Here a new industrial sector was constructed, but since this area was higher than other parts of the mound and not flat, terrace walls were needed. Huge field stones, two and one-half feet in diameter, were stacked, creating walls the remains of which are at least ten feet high. Industrial rooms were placed alongside these walls, eventually creating terraces of buildings stepping down towards the center of the town.[3]

Field IV in the center of the tell, sometimes referred to as the elite zone, has also yielded olive presses. There, typical olive presses, though perhaps in secondary use, have been found alongside four-horned altars. Now is perhaps an appropriate time to discuss these altars further.

Incense Altars[4]

Was it not this same Hezekiah who took away his high places and his altars and commanded Judah and Jerusalem, saying, "Before one altar you shall worship. . . ."
[2 Chron. 32:12]

An intriguing feature of Tel Miqne-Ekron is the fifteen (thirteen of them four-horned) altars found there (as of the 1990 season). Before the Ekron finds, the entire Near East had yielded only twenty-five of these incense altars. Five of those had been uncovered in Judah, nineteen in Israel, and one in Nineveh. All of the twenty-five, as well as the fifteen from Ekron, are from the tenth through the seventh centuries B.C. Fourteen of the Ekron altars are from the seventh century, the period during which Assyria dominated Ekron but which also witnessed Ekron's greatest growth; the fifteenth one came from an eleventh/tenth-century fill. During the last quarter of the eighth century B.C., Israel was conquered by Assyria and led away into captivity. The deportation of Israel's ten tribes may account for the one incense altar found at Nineveh; Israelite captives may have made it, trying to worship as they had in Israel. It could also have been imported to Nineveh from Israel for the same purpose.

The fact that nineteen of these altars were found in Israel brings to mind another question concerning the Ekron altars. Is it possible

House temple (ninth century B.C.) at Arad. Two incense altars flank the sacred niche.

that Israelites from the ten tribes were connected with these altars at the Philistine city of Ekron? The Bible records that some refugees from Israel traveled south to Judah (2 Chron. 30:11, 18, 21, 25). Is it possible that some Israelites also fled to Philistia or were placed there by the Assyrians as part of the labor pool for the olive oil industry? How are the Ekron incense altars, quite often found in the industrial buildings, tied in to the olive oil industry? Are they related to the religious cult?

Typology, that is, classifying artifacts by type, is an important tool for archaeologists. When these incense altars began to be excavated at Ekron, they were studied in context with all of the other incense altars mentioned above. Other than one incense altar found at Lachish in Judah, the oldest altars came from Israelite shrines (temples or high places) at Megiddo and Dan. Dan was one of the two locations for the golden calves set up by Jeroboam in the tenth century B.C. (1 Kings 12:27–29). At Megiddo, a royal Israelite city, the earliest altars are from the tenth century, and at Dan the earliest ones are from the ninth century.

Down to the south in Judah, the incense altars were found in four locations. At Lachish, a Judean city during the reigns of the kings following Solomon, one altar in a cult room was found and dated to the tenth century B.C. Its closest parallel is thought to be the altars excavated at Megiddo. The large altar found at Beer-sheba was recovered in pieces, for the stones of the altar had been used for other functions, but it is believed to be from the ninth/eighth century B.C. Two incense altars without horns have been found at Arad. These were found *in situ*, where they had been used in what is believed to have been a Judean temple dedicated to Yahweh. They were positioned at the entrance of the Holy of Holies of the temple. Then, just outside the Arad temple, in the courtyard, a square sacrificial altar that corresponds in size and type of stones used to the divine requirement in Exodus 20:21–25 and 27:1–2a was also uncovered. It appears that that altar was no longer used during the days of Hezekiah, the reformer king (2 Chron. 31:1). The two incense altars at the entrance to the temple, however, remained in use through the seventh century, possibly until the days of Josiah (640–609 B.C.), another reformer king. Josiah's reforms, mentioned in 2 Kings 23, probably included the demolition of the temple at Arad, but the incense altars had first been placed reverently on their sides and then been covered with dirt. The other altar of the five found in Judah comes from Tell en-Nasbeh, some six miles north of Jerusalem. It was recovered in the 1930s, but the find was not published until 1947, and not much is said of it. The site may be the Mizpah of 1 Samuel 7:5–16, 2 Kings 25:23–26, and Jeremiah 40–41.

The incense altars found at Ekron are different from the ones mentioned above in several ways. First of all, they are the latest altars found thus far. Fourteen of them originated at the time of the Babylonian Nebuchadnezzar's military campaign at the end of the seventh century, a time from which no horned altars have been found in Judea. Secondly, these altars came from a Philistine site, though the ethnic composition of seventh-century Ekron is not yet completely understood. In addition, the other altars described above were found in shrines, temples, or high places, but at Ekron they were found in a completely different context and quite often in industrial buildings.

Due to the large number of incense altars found, as well as the contexts in which they were found, it is believed that the altars wee somehow used in the operation of the industry at Ekron by the priestly class, who held royal authority. Inscriptions were found on large storage jars near some of these altars. The storage jars were of the type used to hold and ship olive oil. The inscriptions at Ekron include "sanctified to Asherat," "for the shrine," and "oil." Asherat, or Asherah, is the same Canaanite goddess that is named in many places in the Bible, including 2 Kings 21:7: "The carved image of Asherah that he had made he set in the house of which the LORD said to David and to his son Solomon, 'In this house, and in Jerusalem, which I have chosen out of all the tribes of Israel, I will put my name forever. . . .'" This passage refers to Judah's King Manasseh, who ruled about the time of these altars and inscriptions at Ekron. Because both chalices and altars were found in the room with the storage jars, it is thought that perhaps this room did have some cultic significance. Too much oil, however, was produced at Ekron for all of it to have been used solely for cultic or religious purposes.

Ekron's altars have also been compared with the others from Israel and Judah in terms of size and construction technique, and whether they were freestanding, finished, or unfinished. According to that study (Gitin 1989a, 61f.), the earliest altars, such as those from Megiddo in the north, were built to the specifications and instructions found in Exodus 27:1–2a; 30:1–2; and 37:25, except that these altars were made of stone. Most of Ekron's incense altars, however, reflect "the earlier tradition of horned altars at Megiddo in the tenth century . . ." (Gitin 1989a, 62). When all characteristics of the altars are compared and contrasted, the conclusion is that Ekron's incense altars "were derived from the northern tradition" (Gitin 1989a, 63).

What does all this mean for our study of the Philistines? The incense altars from Ekron are related typologically to the altars from the northern territory that once was Israel. It has even been conjectured that former Israelites might have made Ekron's incense altars (Gitin 1990, 40). In addition, the inscriptions on the storage jars found near some of them are in a Semitic script that can be read by those who know Hebrew characters. These inscriptions could be Hebrew, Phoenician, or Philistine. Not enough inscriptions have been found at Philistine sites to determine definitively what the Philistine language was. Sufficient artifacts without inscriptions have been recovered to enable us to say that the people living at Ekron

224

were living in the same Philistine coastal traditions as their forebears of the twelfth century B.C. Both biblical and extrabiblical texts consider this area still to have been occupied by the Philistines during the late seventh century B.C., and not by some other people.

However, because of the incense altars and the Semitic inscriptions (especially the reference to the Canaanite goddess Asherah in a Semitic script) found at Ekron, another biblical passage comes to mind.

> Then the king of Assyria commanded, "Send there [to Israel] one of the priests whom you carried away from there; let him go and live there, and teach them the law of the god of the land." So one of the priests whom they had carried away from Samaria came and lived in Bethel; he taught them how they should worship the LORD. [2 Kings 17:27–28]

Perhaps Israelite laborers were helping to maintain the olive industry at this Philistine site of Ekron and were also able to worship, at least in part, as they had in the north.

Philistine Raids[5]

> And the Philistines had made raids on the cities in the Shephelah and the Negeb of Judah, and had taken Beth-shemesh, Aijalon, Gederoth, Soco with its villages, Timnah with its villages, and Gimzo with its villages; and they settled there. [2 Chron. 28:18]

This verse comes from the time of King Ahaz back in the mid-eighth century B.C., but I want to use it to describe Timnah in the days of Ahaz's son, Hezekiah, who reigned at the end of the eighth and into the seventh centuries (715–687 B.C.). Timnah, remember, was the hometown of Samson's wife in the twelfth century B.C. After King Solomon (tenth century), it was contested by Judah and Philistia. In King Ahaz's time, Timnah was in Philistine hands, and then, with his son King Hezekiah, it may have returned to Judah's control. There is no fiery evidence of a violent takeover during this time, according to the excavators, but, as at neighboring Ekron, there is evidence of the later destructive campaign of Sennacherib.

The previous section on Ekron during this same time period mentioned Judean stamped jar handles now generally associated with King Hezekiah's preparations against Sennacherib's planned assault on Judea. Eight of these smashed jars with the royal Judean stamp (*l'melekh*) on the handle have also been found at Timnah. Some of

Gates at Timnah.

the smashed jars surrounded a human skeleton, testifying to the violent end of the city, as described in Sennacherib's account: "I besieged Eltekeh (and) Timnah, conquered (them) and carried their spoils away. I assaulted Ekron. . . " (*ANET*, 288).

Timnah, like Ekron, had an impressive wall and gate. Timnah's defenses were composed of a massive, two-part gate complex (Kelm and A. Mazar 1989, 45). An ramp led to the gateway, and if an enemy survived past the first gate, he had to make a ninety-degree turn in order to proceed through a second gate. In addition, six guardroom chambers were located just prior to the passage through the second gate, three on either side of the passageway. The impressive ruins at Timnah apparently indicate that the defenses did some good, but the city fell to the Assyrians nonetheless, as Ekron did. According to Sennacherib's cuneiform campaign prism, Timnah was taken before Ekron. The stamped Judean storage jars found at both sites probably held supplies for the Judean garrisons. Remember, Hezekiah had forced the Philistine king of Ekron, Padi, to join the revolt against Assyria and had imprisoned Padi in Jerusalem. If the Judean storage jars may be used as evidence, they may indicate that Hezekiah was able to force Timnah to join the revolt also.

The destruction of Timnah by Sennacherib led to an Assyrian reconstruction of the city in the seventh century B.C. similar to that of Ekron, but on a smaller scale. Here, the remains of an olive oil industry have also been uncovered. Here, too, the seventh-century B.C. city flourished, and, like Ekron, it was destroyed by Nebuchadnezzar a century later. The process of making olive oil at Timnah was the same as at Ekron, except for two distinct differences. First, Timnah's oil presses are of smaller capacity than Ekron's; and second, no incense altars are present with the oil presses at Timnah. One hypothesis concerning the presence of numerous altars in association with the olive oil industry at Ekron is that the burning of incense would have masked the bad odor of producing olive oil. However, if that were true, incense altars should also then have been present at Timnah. This difference may provide additional proof that foreigners, in this case Israelites, were present at Ekron (see Nielsen 1991 for information on incense and altars). There was evidently a good deal of home industry in Timnah, since both olive oil presses and loom weights were found in homes. However, the excavators feel that at Timnah, too, the oil production was greater than would have been needed for local use.

227

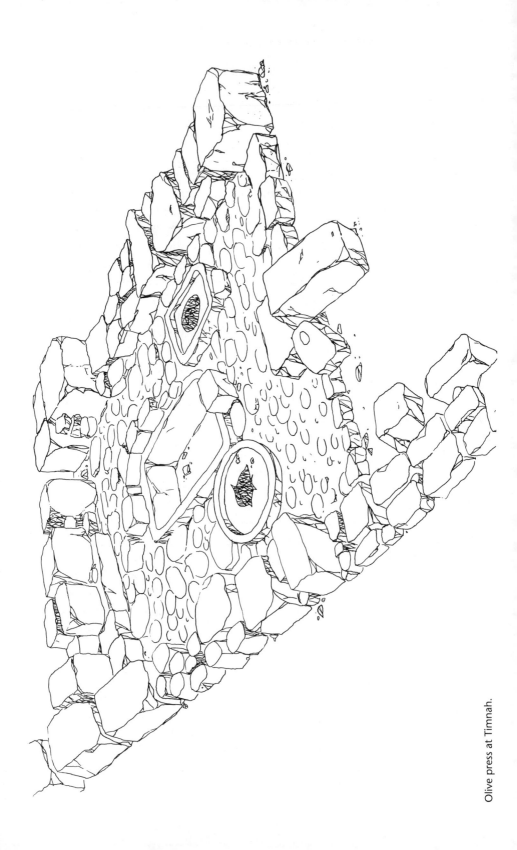

Olive press at Timnah.

Assyria (and not Judah) was in control of Timnah during the seventh century B.C., according to its excavators. An Assyrian administrative center may have been at Gezer (Tadmor 1966, 101), just six miles north of Timnah, and Timnah may have been tied to Ekron as a daughter city. An important obstacle to this conclusion about Assyrian control, however, is the fact that the Judean system of weights was used for Timnah's commercial relations. An assortment of stone shekel weights has been found there, including a weight inscribed with the word *pim* (*PYM*) or *payim*. Only a few of these weights have been found anywhere in Palestine (see pp. 142–43), and they come from Philistine sites or sites with Philistine occupation layers, such as Gezer, Ashdod, Ekron, and Timnah.

According to the archaeological record, both Timnah and neighboring Ekron were prosperous throughout the seventh century B.C. This prosperity was to last until the collapse of Assyria's might, and then both cities faced destruction by Nebuchadnezzar around 600 B.C. Both suffered the destruction that came to Jerusalem as well and was prophesied by Jeremiah—a contemporary of Nebuchadnezzar.

> For thus the LORD, the God of Israel, said to me: Take from my hand this cup of the wine of wrath, and make all the nations to whom I send you drink it. They shall drink and stagger and go out of their minds because of the sword that I am sending among them.
>
> So I took the cup from the LORD's hand, and made all the nations to whom the LORD sent me drink it: Jerusalem and the towns of Judah, its kings and officials, to make them a desolation and a waste, an object of hissing and of cursing, as they are today; . . . all the kings of the land of the Philistines—Ashkelon, Gaza, Ekron, and the remnant of Ashdod. . . . [Jer. 25:15–20]

Jeremiah did not mention Timnah. Perhaps he did not do so because it was small and was not as important as Ashdod, Ashkelon, Gaza, and Ekron. On the other hand, Timnah probably was associated closely with Ekron. Therefore, it may not have been necessary for Jeremiah to mention it in his prophecy. One mentioned Timnah when one mentioned Ekron.

Josiah[6]

In his [Josiah's] presence they [men of Judah] pulled down the altars of the Baals; he demolished the incense altars that stood above them.
[2 Chron. 34:4]

Oren has mentioned that the ceramic typology of seventh-century Tel Seraʿ fits in well with the ceramic typology at another site, that of Mesad Hashavyahu. This site is north of Ashdod, near where the Nahal Sorek of Ekron and Timnah empties into the Mediterranean. He has also mentioned that the person who destroyed Tel Seraʿ late in the seventh century may have been King Josiah of Judah. Earlier, we linked this king to the destruction of the incense altars at Arad. This reformer king of 2 Kings 22–23 and 2 Chronicles 34–35 has also been linked to Mesad Hashavyahu. This site was occupied only in the last third of the seventh century B.C. In addition, it was a small settlement, covering only about one and one-half acres, with an L-shaped fortress enclosing a courtyard area of approximately one acre. Why include mention of this site in our study of the Philistines? At least two things make Mesad Hashavyahu significant—the abundance of East Greek pottery found there and the presence of ostraca with Hebrew inscriptions.

King Manasseh (687–642) and his son Amon (642–640) were evidently vassals to Assyria, but by Josiah's time (640–609) Assyria was weak enough for Josiah to try to make Judah independent once again. (Nineveh, Assyria's capital, would fall to Babylon in 612 B.C.) This process of seeking independence may have started already in Josiah's father's time, and this may have been the reason for Amon's death. "The people of the land" (2 Kings 21:24) in turn killed Amon's assassins, perhaps because they felt that Judah was not yet ready for independence from Assyria (Bright 1981, 316). However, Josiah, Amon's son, felt strong enough in 628 B.C. to spread his religious reforms throughout Judah (2 Kings 23:15–20; 2 Chron. 34:1–7) and into what once was the land of Manasseh, Ephraim, and Naphtali. Perhaps Mesad Hashavyahu fits into the historical framework of this period.

Josiah appears to have taken over Samaria, Megiddo (2 Kings 23:30; 2 Chron. 35:22), and perhaps the northern coastal plain south to Mesad Hashavyahu (Aharoni 1982a, 270–71; Miller and Hayes 1986, 389). Mesad Hashavyahu is a fortress that was in existence only from approximately 630 to 609 B.C., within the years of

Josiah's reign. From the abundance of Greek pottery found, as well as the Hebrew ostraca, it is generally assumed that Greeks were there as well as Josiah's men. The excavator, Joseph Naveh, believes that, since the structure was a fortress and since there was a workshop for producing iron, the Greek inhabitants were soldiers, not merchants. Some of the other scholars using Naveh's reports refer to the Greeks as mercenaries of Egypt (Miller and Hayes 1986, 389; Aharoni 1968, 11, 14), but Naveh points out that neither Egyptian pottery nor scarabs have been found at Mesad Hashavyahu. He also believes that the Greek soldiers were there first, and that Josiah's men then took the fortress at some point before 609 B.C., the year of Josiah's death. E. Stern believes that this fortress was Judean from its inception, with Josiah using the Greeks as mercenaries until his death in battle against the Egyptian army (Stern 1975, 37). The fortress, on Josiah's Judean border facing the Philistine city of Ashdod, was abandoned in 609 or shortly thereafter.

Along with the beautiful and distinctive East Greek pottery found at Mesad Hashavyahu, locally manufactured pottery was uncovered as well, and this pottery is readily identifiable as typical seventh-century ware (Naveh 1962, 100–103). Throughout Naveh's preliminary report are references to the East Greek pottery in its various forms (1962, 104–13, figs. 6–10). It is referred to as East Greek since much of it comes from western Turkey (Anatolia) where the Greeks had established colonies such as at Ionia. Quite a few Ionian cups, for example, were found in various areas of the fortress. Similar pottery from this period can be seen in numerous museums on Cyprus, Rhodes, and other Aegean and Eastern Mediterranean islands. Also, quite a bit of this East Greek pottery is being recovered at Ekron and Ashkelon. A few fragments were also excavated at Tel Batash-Timnah, and at Timnah the excavators suggest that the pottery was unloaded at Mesad Hashavyahu and then transported inland (Kelm and A. Mazar 1989, 49). Remember that Mesad Hashavyahu is located at the end of the Wadi Sorek and on the road that leads inland to Timnah and Ekron. It is exciting to dig up this East Greek pottery, because it comes out of the dirt very clean, is a shiny black, and is decorated with striking paint or etched drawings. We will return to this pottery later when we return to Ekron.

The Greek historian Herodotus records that the Egyptian king Psamtik I (664–610 B.C.) often used Ionians and their neighbors, the Carians, as mercenary troops, and for this reason it is sometimes suggested that the Greeks of Mesad Hashavyahu were mercenaries in

231

An "East Greek" vase purchased in the eastern Aegean. It is a replica of the beautiful East Greek pottery found on the Philistine coast.

the employ of Egypt. Psamtik I apparently did used Ionian and Carian mercenaries in his twenty-nine-year siege of Ashdod, which lies just to the south of Mesad Hashavyahu (Herodotus 2.152, 154, 157, Rieu 1954, 163–64; Naveh 1962, 98). However, as I mentioned earlier, Naveh did not find any Egyptian artifacts at Mesad Hashavyahu, which one would expect if its Greek soldiers were in the employ of the Egyptians. It is possible that the Greeks there were mercenaries hired by Josiah to guard his access to the sea from the Philistines (see also Tadmor 1966, 102 n. 59). Additional support for this theory may be found at Arad, where some Hebrew ostraca have been recovered that date to this period, the end of the seventh century, towards the end of Josiah's reign. Several of these ostraca refer to a "Kittim" people and the rations that should be given them at Arad. The Kittim are probably Greeks from the Aegean or perhaps from the Kition site on Cyprus (Aharoni 1968, 13–14). The presence of Greek mercenaries at both Arad and Mesad Hashavyahu should not be a surprise, for the Judean kings perhaps were continuing a tradition dating back to David and his Aegean Philistine body-guard from Ziklag.

The other distinctive artifacts from Mesad Hashavyahu are its Hebrew ostraca. Naveh surmises that Josiah quartered his soldiers at the fortress, and also placed a governor there to administer the area. What follows is a translation of one of the ostraca, which may be the most important one found yet and is composed of fourteen lines in Hebrew. It opens with a formula phrase that can also be found in 1 Samuel 26:19, where David makes a plea to Saul.

> Let my lord the governor hear the words of his servant. Thy servant [behold], thy servant was reaping in Hasar-Asam, and thy servant reaped and finished and there came Hoshayahu son of Shobai, and he took thy servant's garment: And all my brethren will witness on my behalf, they who reap with me in the heat [of the sun], my brethren will witness on my behalf "Verily" I am free of the guilt. [Negev 1986, 184]

So a picture emerges from the soil of this small settlement. In the second half of the seventh century B.C. a fortress was erected at the northern extent of Philistia, perhaps even to guard against Philistine encroachment. It was inhabited by Greek soldiers, possibly merce-nary, and at some point also by Hebrews of King Josiah's day, before its destruction and abandonment soon after 609 B.C. The Hebrew ostraca found in the guardroom seem to indicate that biblical princi-ples were practiced; the ostracon cited above brings to mind Old Testament law:

> If you take your neighbor's cloak in pawn, you shall restore it before the sun goes down; for it may be your neighbor's only clothing to use as cover; in what else shall that person sleep? [Exod. 22:26–27]

> If the person is poor, you shall not sleep in the garment given you as the pledge. You shall give the pledge back by sunset, so that your neighbor may sleep in the cloak and bless you; and it will be to your credit before the LORD your God. [Deut. 24:12–13]

It appears that a reaper had had his garment confiscated by his over-seer, who may have thought that the worker had skipped some work. The worker appealed to the governor in the fortress that he indeed was working, in the heat of the day, and that his fellow workers would witness to this. Old Testament law required that the garment be returned before sunset, since it may be needed as a blanket.

The Egyptians killed Josiah at Megiddo (2 Kings 23:28–30) and quite possibly destroyed Mesad Hashavyahu shortly before or after they did so. Egyptian presence can also be detected at Philistine sites in the final years of Assyrian control over Philistia and Judah. It was not Egypt, however, but was the rising star of Babylon that caused the destruction of Assyria and the Philistine sites that will be the focus of our final chapter.

Woe to the Philistines[7]

For Gaza shall be deserted,
     and Ashkelon shall become a desolation;
Ashdod's people shall be driven out at noon,
     and Ekron shall be uprooted.

Ah, inhabitants of the seacoast,
     you nation of the Cherethites!
The word of the LORD is against you,
     O Canaan, land of the Philistines;
     and I will destroy you until no inhabitant is left.
[Zeph. 2:4–5]

According to the opening verses of this Old Testament book, these dire words were spoken by Zephaniah, a prophet of the Lord during the reign of King Josiah. Things were going well in Philistia at the time. It was evidently a major money-maker for Assyria, besides being a buffer against and a staging area for Assyrian attacks on Egypt. However, Zephaniah's pronouncement of approaching doom was not aimed at the Philistines alone. Judah would have to face "the day of the Lord" (1:4–18) for its idolatry, and Assyria would also have to face the Lord's wrath (2:13–15).

Zephaniah 1:1 calls the prophet a fourth-generation descendant of King Hezekiah, the king who rebelled against Assyria. Assyria had been the ascending power of the Near East by the end of the eighth century B.C. This power was evident in our discussion of Sennacherib (705–681 B.C.) and his encounter with Hezekiah. Philistia had been subdued by Sennacherib and did not attempt to break away from Assyria during either the reigns of Esarhaddon (681–669) or of Ashurbanipal (668–627). Assyria's star kept rising through the reign of Esarhaddon and into the first half of Ashurbanipal's reign (Eph'al 1979, 281). One source refers to the first three-fourths of the seventh century as "Pax Assyriaca" (Miller and Hayes 1986, 365). However, to enforce this "pax," the two Assyrian kings made at least five campaigns against Egypt within an eleven-year period, using Philistia as the staging area for the attacks. Around the year 650 B.C., Babylon began to trouble Assyria to the extent that Assyrian forces needed to be on alert on their eastern border. Babylon was to be the power to bring about the destruction of Assyria and Philistia prophesied by Zephaniah.

There is an interesting text from Esarhaddon that names the Philistine kings of Ashdod, Ashkelon, Ekron, and Gaza, as well as Manasseh, the king of Judah at this time, and seven additional kings from the seacoast. This particular text of Esarhaddon dates to 677 B.C. and describes how these kings, as well as twenty-two other vassal kings and kingdoms, were required to provide labor and supplies for a palace in Nineveh, the Assyrian capital city.

> I called up the kings of the country. . .: Ba'lu, king of Tyre, Manasseh, king of Judah, Qaushgabi, king of Edom, Musuri, king of Moab, Sil-Bel, king of Gaza, Metinti, king of Ashkelon, Ikausu, king of Ekron, . . . Ahimilki, king of Ashdod. . . . all these I sent out and made them transport under terrible difficulties, to Nineveh, the town (where I exercise) my rulership, as building material for my palace: big logs, long beams (and) thin boards from cedar and pine trees. . . . [ANET, 291]

At this time there were four surviving Philistine city-states. The Bible does not give us the names of their kings, but we have the names of all four from the Assyrian record. According to one source (Tadmor 1966, 98), only Ekron's Ikausu has a name that is possibly Philistine, whereas the other kings have Canaanite/Semitic or Assyrian names. This is not an unusual revelation, since the Philistines were very adaptive. The 1990 season at Tel Miqne-Ekron uncovered a late-seventh-century ostracon with the name Ahimilk on it (Gitin 1991, 7, 15). That is a common Semitic name, so it is not presently known if it refers to the Ahimilki of Ashdod from the Assyrian records, to someone at Ekron, or to a ruler elsewhere. Ahimilk could also have been an assigned throne name of the kings and could, therefore, refer to kings over many decades.

Ten years after the 677 B.C. document of Esarhaddon, these four Philistine kings, Judah's Manasseh, and the other kings were called upon to help the new Assyrian king Ashurbanipal in one of his attacks against Egypt by land and sea (ANET, 294 for the text; Yadin 1963, 2:462 for the relief). Ashurbanipal attacked Egypt a second time in 663, and this attack was very successful, for he was able to sack Thebes, the capital in Upper (that is, southern) Egypt. This may have been the event the biblical prophet Nahum had in mind when he prophesied that Nineveh would fall as Thebes had fallen.

> Are you [Nineveh] better than Thebes
> that sat by the Nile,
> with water around her,
> her rampart a sea,
> water her wall?
> Ethiopia was her strength,
> Egypt too, and that without limit;
> Put and the Libyans were her helpers.
>
> Yet she became an exile,
> she went into captivity;
> even her infants were dashed in pieces
> at the head of every street;
> lots were cast for her nobles,
> all her dignitaries were bound in fetters. [Nah. 3:8–10]

None of the Philistine kings nor King Manasseh are mentioned together again in any other Assyrian document yet recovered, but we know that Philistia was still a money-maker for Assyria during Ashurbanipal's reign, and we also know from legal documents found at Gezer (Tadmor 1966, 101) that Ashurbanipal still had some control over that city. Egypt was able during his reign to shake off Assyrian domination, and as Assyria retreated back toward the land of two rivers to fend off Babylon, Egypt moved into Philistia and the hearts and minds of Judah.

A new Egyptian king, Psamtik I, came to the throne in 664 B.C. He continued the attempt to liberate Egypt from Assyria and finally was successful. After that, he invaded Philistia with the aid of the Greek mercenaries mentioned earlier. Psamtik I was the Egyptian king who besieged Ashdod for twenty-nine years and conquered it about the time that the Assyrian Ashurbanipal died (Herodotus 2.156, Rieu 1954, 165). Egypt and Babylon were now to become the new power brokers in Palestine.

Keeping the activities of Psamtik I in mind, let us look at the actions of Judah's king, Manasseh (687–642 B.C.; 2 Kings 21 and 2 Chron. 33) during the same time frame. Whereas King Hezekiah rebelled against Assyria, his son Manasseh became Assyria's vassal. The account of this in 2 Chronicles links Assyria and Babylon without any accompanying explanation:

The LORD spoke to Manasseh and to his people, but they gave no heed. Therefore the LORD brought against them the commanders of the army of the king of Assyria, who took Manasseh captive in manacles, bound him with fetters, and brought him *to Babylon.* [2 Chron. 33:10–11, emphasis mine]

A̶s̶s̶y̶r̶i̶a̶ ̶w̶a̶s̶ ̶f̶i̶g̶h̶t̶i̶n̶g̶ ̶a̶n̶ ̶e̶x̶h̶a̶u̶s̶t̶i̶n̶g̶ ̶w̶a̶r̶ ̶w̶i̶t̶h̶ ̶B̶a̶b̶y̶l̶o̶n̶ ̶e̶v̶e̶n̶ ̶t̶o̶ the g̶a̶t̶e̶s̶ ̶o̶f̶ ̶B̶a̶b̶y̶l̶o̶n̶ ̶i̶t̶s̶e̶l̶f̶ (Reviv 1979, 200; Porten 1981, 48). The Assyrian records do not record that Manasseh was taken to the Assyrian king Ashurbanipal there but it is logical to assume that Manasseh had displeased his lord king, who then summoned him to pay a visit and to swear allegiance once again. Manasseh did so, was able to return to Jerusalem, and then did what at first may seem strange:

While he [Manasseh] was in distress he entreated the favor of the LORD his God and humbled himself greatly before the God of his ancestors. He prayed to him, and God received his entreaty and heard his plea, and restored him again to Jerusalem and to his kingdom. Then Manasseh knew that the LORD indeed was God. [2 Chron. 33:12–13]

Manasseh probably was unable to return to Jerusalem until he swore allegiance to the Assyrian king, but after he was released he then rejected the Assyrian and Canaanite gods and found the God of his fathers. He realized that the Assyrians needed him, as well as Philistia, because of the encroachment of the Egyptians. Manasseh might have felt after his appearance in Babylon that he could be more independent and had been given more latitude by Ashurbanipal. It was during Manasseh's reign that Egypt, with the aid of the Greek mercenaries, besieged Ashdod. Manasseh fortified Judah (2 Chron. 33:14), and if he did so as a vassal of Assyria, he was making Judah a factor that Egypt could not ignore in its conflicts with Assyria. A few years later the Egyptian king Psamtik I made an agreement with Assyria (Porten 1981, 48–49) that would later prove to be deadly to Manasseh's grandson Josiah (2 Kings 23:29–30).

The Egyptians controlled Gaza and Ashkelon (Jer. 47:1–7), had conquered Ashdod, and may also have taken over Ekron about the time of Ashurbanipal's death. Some of the artifacts uncovered at Ekron that date approximately to this time include a scarab of the twenty-sixth Egyptian dynasty, from Pharaoh Neco II, the slayer of the Judean king Josiah (2 Chron. 35:20–27). A beautiful Egyptian image of a goddess and a large fragment of an Egyptian sistrum (musical instrument) decorated with hieroglyphics have also been recovered.

In spite of Egypt's increased influence in Philistia, the Judean king Josiah had been able to gain at least a toehold on the Mediterranean coast at Mesad Hashavyahu, the site inhabited by the Greek "mercenaries" that was described earlier. The Egyptians, however, had made an alliance with the Assyrians, and Pharaoh Neco II came to their aid when the events of 2 Kings 23:29–30 took place. Assyria had already lost its capital, Nineveh, to the Babylonians three years earlier, but Pharaoh Neco was rushing north to help Assyria when King Josiah, on the side of the Babylonians, intercepted him.

> But Neco sent envoys to him, saying, "What have I to do with you, king of Judah? I am not coming against you today, but against the house with which I am at war; and God has commanded me to hurry. Cease opposing God, who is with me, so that he will not destroy you." But Josiah would not turn away from him, but disguised himself in order to fight with him. He did not listen to the words of Neco from the mouth of God, but joined battle in the plain of Megiddo. [2 Chron. 35:21–22]

Josiah died by Egyptian hands, but the Egyptians in turn were not successful in aiding Assyria; Babylon was the victor. Judah became the vassal of Egypt (2 Chron. 36:1–4; Bright 1981, 324–25) for a few years, as Philistia did for a short while. Babylon was the new rising star, and this empire would bring about the destruction of the Philistines, as Zephaniah had foretold.

The Final Destruction of Philistia[1]

Ashkelon shall see it and be afraid;
    Gaza too, and shall writhe in anguish;
    Ekron also, because its hopes are withered.
The king shall perish from Gaza;
    Ashkelon shall be uninhabited;
a mongrel people shall settle in Ashdod,
    and I will make an end of the pride of Philistia.
I will take away its blood from its mouth,
    and its abominations from between its teeth;
it too shall be a remnant for our God;
    it shall be like a clan in Judah,
    and Ekron shall be like the Jebusites.
[Zech. 9:5–7]

Nebuchadnezzar is a name known to all students of the Bible. Children listening to Bible stories know that Nebuchadnezzar was the one who destroyed David's city of Jerusalem and its temple and led the Jews away to captivity in Babylon for seventy years. We learn other stories as well about Nebuchadnezzar, such as the account in the Book of Daniel about the fiery furnace. What we learn from extrabiblical sources is that Nebuchadnezzar made at least

239

Workers at Ekron excavated pottery, limestone sherds, and animal bones that attested to the devastation Nebuchadnezzar caused at the site.

three military campaigns into Palestine, that Jerusalem and Judah were not alone in being attacked and destroyed, and that Ezekiel and Daniel and his friends were taken to Babylon in one of the earlier campaigns. It was also in one of the earlier campaigns, probably the one in which Daniel was taken, that Philistia was attacked, ravaged, and destroyed. That destruction is the focus of this final chapter.

I learned the Bible stories as a youth, but it was not until the summer of 1990 that the devastation caused by Nebuchadnezzar became very real to me. One of the areas that I supervised at Ekron that summer was in field INW, the upper city. Due to the steep slope of this area, the Ekronites built huge terrace walls and then constructed their buildings against the walls in a stepped-down fashion. We began excavating a room built against one of these terrace walls and almost immediately dug into destruction debris. The students took out vessel after vessel of pottery, many of them whole forms and the others all restorable.

But the effects of the fire that destroyed this room made at least as lasting an impression on us as the abundance of good pottery specimens. The fire next to this terrace wall had been hotter than the fire in the middle of the room, and as the flames shot up against the wall the soil on the other side of it was blackened. We found sherds of limestone everywhere in the room, and we wondered where they had come from. It took a few days to figure out that the fire had been so intense and the limestone the walls were made of had become so hot

240

that sherds of it began to pop off the boulders and shoot across the room until eventually its side walls collapsed. We also recovered a large quantity of animal bones there, many of them distinguished by their hardness and grey color, which are additional signs of an extremely hot fire.

Finding large quantities of pottery was a daily experience for us for the first three and a half weeks, until we got below the destruction debris, which was all, we determined, caused by a military campaign of Nebuchadnezzar. Our experience, minus the huge boulders of the terracing, was duplicated at other points of the tell where evidence of Nebuchadnezzar's destruction was also being excavated. In all of these places, the destruction debris layer was nearly one meter deep and was packed with ceramic vessels and animal bones.

The huge city of Ekron and its olive oil industry had been completely destroyed, and the evidence of this destruction could be seen wherever we excavated. Ekron has not been occupied again as a city or even as a village in the twenty-six hundred years since, and for this reason the olive industry vats and basins, the four-horned altars, the thousands of ceramic vessels, and other seventh-century artifacts lie close to the surface or are even poking through the surface.

When did the destruction happen? Can all this destruction that was foretold by the prophets be attributed to Nebuchadnezzar? Was what was true for Ekron also true for the other Philistine cities mentioned in the prophecies? Again, sources other than the Bible can be used to obtain a clearer picture.

King Josiah lost his life to the Egyptians in 609 B.C. (2 Chron. 35), and after that the Egyptians were again able to exert some influence over Judah (2 Kings 23:31–35; 2 Chron. 36:1–4), even in choosing the king. The Egyptians were also able to gain control over Philistia again for a short time (Gitin 1990, 42; Malamat 1979, 207). Egypt had already made two recent campaigns into the Euphrates area (616, 610 B.C.) to aid the ailing Assyrians (Malamat 1979, 205). In 605 B.C., however, before Nebuchadnezzar became king over Babylonia, he defeated the Egyptians in Syria. After assuming the kingship, Nebuchadnezzar journeyed into Philistia. His records specifically mention the capture of Ashkelon (see also Jer. 47:1–7) since it had not delivered tribute, whereas other cities, including Philistine cities, had apparently brought tribute (Malamat 1979, 207–8; Thomas 1958, 78–79; Miller and Hayes 1986, 380–81). "All the kings of the Hatti-land came before him and he received their heavy tribute. He marched to the city of Askelon and captured it in the month of Kislev. He captured its king and plundered it and carried off . . ." (Miller and Hayes 1986, 381).

The defeat of Pharaoh Neco by Nebuchadnezzar at Carchemish in Syria in 605 B.C. is also reported in Jeremiah 46:2–12. Jeremiah predicted that Judah would be captured by Nebuchadnezzar in the same year Nebuchadnezzar assumed the throne (605 B.C.; see Jer. 25:1–14, esp. v. 1 and compare with 46:2) and that Judah would go into captivity for seventy years (Jer. 25:11–12). Jehoiakim (609–598), the king over Judah during these events, refused to heed Jeremiah's advice and burned the scroll on which God's prophecy was written (Jer. 36).

Nebuchadnezzar returned to Philistia and Judah in his second full year, 603, captured Jerusalem, and perhaps took Daniel, Ezekiel, and others at this time (Malamat 1979, 208–9; Gitin 1990, 42; 2 Kings 24:1ff.; 2 Chron. 36:5–8). The words of Jeremiah began to be fulfilled:

> So I took the cup from the LORD's hand, and made all the nations to whom the LORD sent me drink it: Jerusalem and the towns of Judah, its kings and officials, to make them a desolation and a waste, an object of hissing and of cursing, as they are today; Pharaoh king of Egypt, his servants, his officials, and all his people; all the mixed people; all the kings of the land of Uz; all the kings of the land of the Philistines—Ashkelon, Gaza, Ekron, and the remnant of Ashdod. . . . [Jer. 25:17–20]

The extant Babylonian Chronicles dealing with this period are partially broken (Malamat 1979, 208, 350 n. 14), but it is believed that Nebuchadnezzar did intend to conquer all of Philistia in preparation for an assault on Egypt. Ashkelon, according to the Chronicles, was conquered the first full year of his reign (December 604 B.C.), and the conquest of the other Philistine cities may have been mentioned on the missing segment. In any event, the destruction of the three remaining major Philistine cities must have occurred either in Nebuchadnezzar's 603 campaign or the campaign in 601 when Jehoiakim again rebelled against the Babylonian masters (2 Kings 24:1) and Nebuchadnezzar attacked Egypt. The Babylonian Chronicles relate Nebuchadnezzar's heavy losses and subsequent return to Babylon (Malamat 1979, 209).

The excavators of Ekron, Timnah, and Ashdod believe that these Philistine sites were destroyed around this time in order to enable Nebuchadnezzar to assault Egypt (T. Dothan and Gitin 1990, 25; Gitin 1990, 42; Kelm and A. Mazar 1989, 49; M. Dothan 1969,

245). Gath had already disappeared from the scene during the reign of Uzziah (mid-eighth century). Gaza still cannot be excavated in order to verify the date of its destruction, and not enough work has been completed at Ashkelon to clarify this period there.

The Adon letter, a significant find from this time period, shows that Judah was not alone in looking to Egypt for help against the Babylonians (Jer. 37:4ff.). This letter, sent by a King Adon to the pharaoh of Egypt, is a late-seventh-century B.C. document written in Aramaic on papyrus. It was found in Saqqarah, Egypt, near the stepped pyramid. In the nine lines of the letter King Adon, a vassal of Egypt, appealed for help, since the king of Babylon was already at Aphek in Palestine. It had been generally assumed that King Adon was from either a Philistine or a Phoenician city (Porten 1981, 38–41). Now, however, the latest study and translation presents a case that Adon was the king of Ekron (Porten 1981, 36–52):

1. To Lord of Kings Pharaoh, your servant Adon King of [Ekron. The welfare of my lord, Lord of Kings Pharaoh may the gods of]
2. Heaven and Earth and Beelshmayin, [the great] god [seek exceedingly at all times, and may they lengthen the days of]
3. Pharaoh like the days of (the) high heavens. That [I have written to Lord of Kings is to inform him that the forces]
4. of the King of Babylon have come (and) reach[ed] Aphek . . [. . . .
5. . . . they have seized . . .
6. for Lord of Kings Pharaoh knows that [your] servant [. . .
7. to send a force to rescue [me]. Do not abandon [me, for your servant did not violate the treaty of the Lord of Kings]
8. and your servant preserved his good relations. And as for this commander [. . .
9. a governor in the land. And as for the letter of Sindur . . . [Porten 1981, 36]

So when was this appeal written and sent? Porten lists all the Babylonian campaigns according to the Babylonian Chronicle and describes what is said to have happened during each campaign. He then concludes that there are two good dates for Adon's appeal to Egypt—either 604 or 603 B.C. (see also Miller and Hayes 1986, 384, 386).

Nebuchadnezzar did send an expedition against Egypt, and this is where 2 Kings 24:7 may best fit in. "The king of Egypt did not come again out of his land, for the king of Babylon had taken over all that belonged to the king of Egypt from the Wadi of Egypt to the River Euphrates." This verse indicates that Babylon, not Egypt, controlled all of Philistia (and Judah?) by the time of Jehoiachin's reign (598–97) at the beginning of the sixth century. Jehoiachin reigned only three months before he was taken captive to Babylon (2 Kings 24:8–17). Within the corpus of administrative documents found in the excavations of Babylon are some dating to the reign of Nebuchadnezzar. One broken document mentions providing rations to Jehoiachin, specifically named as the king of Judah, and to his sons. This same Babylonian document also mentions provisions for the Philistine king of Ashkelon, as well as for other kings (*ANET*, 308). A second document, also broken, mentions the kings of Gaza and Ashdod performing duties for Nebuchadnezzar (*ANET*, 308).

The predictions of Jeremiah, Zephaniah, and Zechariah about the destruction of Philistine cities came true according to the excavations at Ashdod, Ekron, and Timnah. Future excavating should reveal more about Philistine Ashkelon, but unfortunately Gaza will not be excavated in the foreseeable future.

However, does archaeology also reveal a problem with the Zechariah 9:5–7 passage? Zechariah was a contemporary of the prophet Haggai, both beginning ministry around 520 B.C. In Zechariah 9, quoted at the beginning of this chapter, the verb tense is future. Yet there is no way that the destruction of Timnah, Ekron, and Ashdod could have occurred after 520 B.C. The destruction of the sites happened during the days of King Nebuchadnezzar. So how can this problem be resolved?

Biblical scholars have always seen a break between Zechariah 8 and 9 (*ISBE* 4:1184; Elwell 1988, 2:2184–87; Meyers and Meyers 1987, xliv–xlviii; Achtemeier 1985, 1159–60; Bright 1981, 413 n. 20). Many of these scholars would date Zechariah 9 and following to a period still later than 520 B.C., but one source mentions Jeremiah's time as the appropriate date for portions of Zechariah 9–14 (*ISBE* 4:1185). There seems to be no definitive agreement on the time frame of these final chapters, but perhaps the excavations at Tel Miqne-Ekron are providing the solution—at least for parts of Zechariah 9.

I do not believe there can be any question about the final destruction of Ekron; it occurred at the end of the seventh century B.C. All of the destruction material from Nebuchadnezzar's day is either at or just below the surface. There is some evidence of occupation on the site after Nebuchadnezzar, but *not* as a city or even as a village. It appears that part of the mound may have been the location for a villa in the Roman period, and this may corroborate literary evidence from 1 Maccabees 10:89 and Josephus's *Antiquities* (Naveh 1958, 169). There is also some sherd evidence from the late Roman or Byzantine period that fits, in part, with a fourth-century A.D. reference by Eusebius to a village near Ekron and the village of Ekron itself. However, there is no evidence of an actual village on the mound or just off it at that late date. The few Roman, Byzantine, and Islamic period sherds found in field XI where I excavated in the 1990 season were found near the wadi to which people for centuries have gone for water (T. Dothan and Gitin 1990, 25). This evidence of no significant settlement at Ekron after the seventh century B.C. demonstrates that the Zechariah 9 passage, at least verses 5–8, must belong to an earlier period and may perhaps be from the same time as Zephaniah and Jeremiah.

Philistia disappeared as a nation after the destruction by Nebuchadnezzar, its people taken into captivity. It never recovered its glory of the previous six hundred years. Timnah, like Ekron, ceased to exist. The remains at Ashdod from the Persian period following the Babylonian destruction are sparse, but that city did recover during the Hellenistic period in the fourth century B.C. and later. To what extent Ashdod was "Philistine" during the Persian and Hellenistic periods cannot be determined precisely, but Nehemiah (mid-fifth century B.C.) did refer to the foreign women of Ashdod and to "the language of Ashdod" (Neh. 13:23–24), which scholars believe was a Canaanite language (Oded 1979, 237–38, using the work of M. Dothan at Ashdod). Strata from the Hellenistic and Roman periods are clearly identifiable, although Ashdod was now known by a new name, Azotus. In the first century B.C., Ashdod/Azotus belonged to Herod, and it probably was destroyed during the first Jewish revolt against Rome, around A.D. 67. The remains following this period are sparser still. Ashdod is gone and is covered with weeds today.

Ashkelon fared better, since it was located on the coast and continued to be important as a port. Following the city's destruction by Nebuchadnezzar in 604 or 603, Ashkelon's last Philistine king, Aga, was taken to Babylon along with his nobles and sailors. Babylon, in turn, was conquered by the Persians, and Cyrus the Great of Persia allowed those captured by the Babylonians to be resettled "in their sacred cities" (*ANET*, 316). Whereas some of the Jews returned to Jerusalem, there is no record of Philistines returning home. No doubt, as in Judah, some Philistines had been able to avoid being taken to Babylon, but nonetheless Ashkelon clearly became Persian in 538 B.C. and remained so until 332 B.C. The Philistines "simply disappear from history" (Stager 1991b, 28). Persia gave Ashkelon to the Phoenicians of Tyre. According to Stager, Ashkelon of the fifth through fourth centuries B.C. had a very mixed population: "Persians, Phoenicians, Philistines . . . Egyptians, Greeks, and perhaps Jews" (Stager 1986, 4). The city continued to flourish during the Hellenistic, Roman, and Byzantine periods to the present (Stager 1991b and c).Today it is a Mediterranean resort city.

We have seen that the material culture of the Philistines can be traced for a six-hundred-year period from the days of Joshua through those of Nebuchadnezzar. As a people, they disappeared from the historical scene after Nebuchadnezzar's campaigns into Philistia. However, their name lives on in the word *Palestine*, which in the centuries before Christ referred to the coastal homeland of the Philistines, but now includes the Judean, Samarian, and Galilean hills as well. Their name also lives on in cartoons and jokes as a pejorative for uncultured people. However, as we have seen, this concept of the Philistines has always been false.

Starting with Joshua, the Philistines were viewed by the Israelites as the enemy, but they played an important role in the redemptive history of God's people by testing Israel. All too often the Israelites lost their confidence due to the giants or the fortified cities in the land. The Philistines were a foil used by God. Sometimes they even rescued God's people, as they did when protecting David or as they did when the Philistine bodyguard put Solomon and Joash on the throne. Both Jews and Philistines adapted to the local Canaanite culture, but when both peoples went into captivity, the Philistines left the stage of Near Eastern history and disappeared, as the northern ten tribes of Israel had disappeared earlier. Zechariah 9:6–7 says that the once-proud Philistines shall go the way of the Jebusites. Where are they today?

Mycenae, Troy, Kition, Achilles and Hector, Ziklag, Ashdod, Ekron, Achish, Goliath, David, and Jonathan—all are of ages long gone. Up until fairly recently these names of cities and people were thought of as parts of two separate worlds. We live in a world today that seems to grow smaller due to instant communication and swift transportation. Now our investigations into the past have revealed that the ancient Near East was also a smaller world than it was once believed to have been. Playing a unifying role in the history of that time and place were the Sea Peoples, of which the Philistines were a part. Some of the cities and persons mentioned were formerly thought of as part of legend, the other cities and persons as part of inspired history. Now, however, archaeology is linking them together. The descendants of the legends from the Aegean were used by the Lord God to test his people Israel and at times to save them.

Chronological Chart for Chapters 5–8

	Egypt	Israel				Assyria
1000 B.C.		David ca. 1000–961				
		Solomon ca. 961–922				
950 B.C.						
	XXII Dyn. ca. 935–725 Shishak I ca. 935–914					
		Schism 922				
		Judah Rehoboam	**922–587** 922–915	**Israel** Jeroboam I	**922–722/1** 922–901	
900 B.C.		Abijah	915–913			Adad-nirari II 912–892
		Asa	913–873	Nadab	901–900	
				Baasha	900–877	Ashurnasirpal II 884–860
				Elah	877–876	
		Jehoshaphat	873–849	Zimri Omri Ahab	876 876–869 869–853	
850 B.C.						Shalmaneser III 859–824
		Jehoram Ahaziah Athaliah Joash	849–843/2 843/2 842–837 837–800	Ahaziah Joram Jehu	853–852 852–843/2 843/2–815	
				Jehoahaz	815–802	Shamshi-adad V 824–812 Adad-nirari III 811–784
800 B.C.		Amaziah	800–783	Jehoash	802–786	
		Uzziah (Azariah)	783–742	Jeroboam II	786–746	(Assyria is weak)
	XXIII Dyn. ca. 759–715			Zechariah Shallum	746–745 745	
750 B.C.		Jotham Ahaz	742–735 735–715	Menahem Pekahiah Pekah	745–737 737–736 736–732	Tiglath-pileser III 745–727
	XXIV Dyn. ca. 725–709 XXV Dyn. (Ethiopian) ca. 716/5–664	Hezekiah	715–687	Hoshea (Fall of Samaria	732–723 722/1)	Shalmaneser V 727–722 Sargon II 722–705 Sennacherib 705–681
700 B.C.		Manasseh	687–642			Esarhaddon 681–669
	XXVI Dyn. 664–525 Psamtik I (Psammetichus I) 664–610					Ashurbanipal 668–627
650 B.C.		Amon Josiah	642–640 640–609			
				(Neo-Babylonian Empire rises)		Sin-shar-ishkun 627–612
	Neco II 610–594	Jehoahaz Jehoiakim	609 609–598	Nebuchadnezzar	605/4–562	(Nineveh falls 612)
600 B.C.	Psamtik II (Psammetichus II) 594–589	Jehoiachin Zedekiah (Fall of Jerusalem 587)	598/7 597–587			Ashur-uballit II 612–609

Conclusion

The objective of this book has been to present the armchair archaeologist with the most recent information on the Philistines, a people who have been much maligned throughout the millennia. The study has been based on the latest archaeological developments in Philistia, as well as on historical documents from Egypt, the Aegean, Anatolia, and Mesopotamia. Together these have been used to reexamine the biblical text in order to better understand the Philistines.

We have come to understand why God's people detested the Philistines, but we also now understand that God used these "pagans" not only to test but also to preserve his people at various times throughout the Iron I and Iron II periods. An added benefit of this study has been the discovery that some of the biblical Philistines were most likely descendants of the heroes of the epic tragic tale played out on the plains of Troy. Much more could be said of ties between the Philistine plains and the plains of Troy, but it is an interesting twist of history that due to our incomplete understanding of the biblical Philistines the offspring of the noble heroes of an epic tale came to be remembered as uncultured people.

We have seen that when the Philistines arrived in their new land in Canaan, they appear to have immediately adopted from and adapted to the cultures of their new neighbors. This perspective contradicts the dictionary definition of *Philistine*—a person who lacks or who is indifferent to culture. A key concept that ought to be associated with the Philistines may be assimilation, rather than the "smug conventionalism" that is the accepted definition of *Philistinism* (*New Am. Heritage Dict.* 1981). We have read, for example, how Israel's King

Ahaziah sent messengers to Ekron to consult the god Baal-zebub, who had been assimilated, evidently, into the Philistine pantheon from the Canaanites. We have also read of the numerous Israelite altars found at Ekron. Continued excavations at Tel Miqne-Ekron and at other Philistine sites such as Ashkelon will no doubt help reveal just how much of the Canaanite and Israelite cultures the Philistines assimilated.

For now, the Philistines have gone the way of the ten lost tribes of Israel, but the future holds promise for more information on both lost peoples, as excavations continue in the Near East.

250

Endnotes

Preface

1. "Tel" is the spelling used with Hebrew site names. "Tell" is used with Arabic site names and when referring to mounds in general.

Chapter 1: The Philistines in Scripture

1. These other names can be found on page 27 of this chapter but are addressed in depth in chapter 5, pp. 173–76, and chapter 6, pp. 190–93.

2. In chapter 3, in a discussion of Egyptian records, it is noted that the Philistines were one of a group of invading peoples most often referred to today as the Sea Peoples. These invaders were defeated and repulsed by the Egyptians, and they finally settled north of Egypt in various places along Canaan's coast. See also Mendenhall (1973, 10–12) and T. Dothan (1982a, 25) for a discussion of ethnic and cultural homogeneity.

3. This is the same plain where in later years Saul battled the Philistines, who controlled the plain at that time.

4. See chapter 6, pp. 190–93, as well as Naveh (1962).

5. See chapter 5, pp. 177–78, as well as Myers (1986b, 29).

Chapter 2: Ekron: The Archaeological Record

1. The primary published sources used for this chapter were T. Dothan (1982a and b, 1989, 1990), T. Dothan and Gitin (1990), Gitin (1989a and b, 1990), and Gitin and T. Dothan (1987).

2. More detailed description of Philistine pottery can be found in T. Dothan (1982a and b) and in A. Mazar (1990, 313–17, 364 n. 24).

Chapter 3: The Origins of the Philistines

1. The primary published sources used for this section were Bright (1981), M. Dothan (1989), T. Dothan (1982a and b), Gardiner (1961), A. Mazar (1990), Sandars (1978), Stager (1991a), Stiebing (1980), Wright (1966), and Yurco (1990).

2. The lists and discussion can be found in Albright (1950, 166–67), Barnett (1975, 366–67), Breasted (1906, 3:241ff.), Daniel and Evans (1975, 741–42), M. Dothan (1989, 63–64), and Gardiner (1961, 270ff.).

3. The lists and discussion can be found in Albright (1950, 170–72; 1975, 507ff.), *ANET,* 262–63, Barnett (1975, 371ff.), and Breasted (1906, 4:24, 38, 41, 48).

4. Numerous sources compare descriptions of the Sea Peoples with descriptions of Aegean peoples. Representative of them are T. Dothan (1982a, 5ff.), A. Mazar (1990, 304ff.), Mitchell (1967, 412ff.), Raban and Stieglitz (1991, 38–39), Sandars (1978,132ff.), and especially Yadin (1963, 2:248–53, 334–45).

5. The primary published sources for this section were Albright (1975), Barnett (1975), Desborough (1964), T. Dothan (1982a), A. Mazar (1990), Sandars (1978), Stiebing (1980, 1989), Vermeule (1972), and Wainwright (1961).

6. See Douglas (1962, 199), Elwell (1988, 1:415–16), *ISBE* (1:610), and Stiebing (1980, 14).

7. Although most current scholarship concerning Caphtor points to Crete, there are two other possible locations for Caphtor. One is in southwest Anatolia, which does have numerous ties to Crete, and the other is in southeast Anatolia or the Mediterranean coast of Syria. A basic reason for suggesting southwest Anatolia is that the Greek Septuagint translation of the Bible translates Caphtor in Deuteronomy 2:23 and Amos 9:7 as Cappadocia. T. Dothan believes this equation is an error, due perhaps to the fact that Cappadocia had a prominent position in southeast Anatolia at the time of the composition of the Septuagint. Remember, also, that the Ugaritic text just mentioned tells of a ship from Kapturi to Ugarit, whereas in all likelihood, land routes would have been utilized from Cappadocia to Ugarit rather than sea routes. For more information see T. Dothan (1982a, 21), *ISBE* (1:611–12), and Wainwright (1959, 73–84).

8. Cretan seals have been found near Gaza on the Philistine coast, the area directly linked with the Cretans. See Barnett (1975, 373) and Albright (1975, 511–12).

9. Stager predicts that when longer Philistine texts are uncovered—this is only a matter of time—the texts will be in Mycenaean Greek, since the Sea Peoples were originally Mycenaean Greek (1991a, 36).

10. Waldbaum has some serious detractors, however, concerning her conclusions about the Mycenaean antecedents of these cemetery 900 tombs. T. Dothan says that they contain too few Mycenaean artifacts for them to have been built by invaders of the Egyptian territory or mercenaries (1982a, 260). Stiebing states that the type of tomb is not unusual in the Near East (1970, 139).

11. Albright uses the study of names and the Luwian dialect to place the origin of the Philistines in southwest Anatolia.

12. The primary published sources used for this section were Karageorghis (1982, 1984) and Karageorghis and Demas (1985). The other main source was Dikaios (1979a–c). A. Mazar, T. Dothan, Sandars, and others use the findings of these individuals in their publications.

Chapter 4: The Philistines from Joshua to David

1. The high chronology was adapted from older sources, the low chronology from Wente and Van Siclen (1976).

2. The primary published sources used for this section were M. Dothan (1968, 1969, 1979, and 1989), T. Dothan (1985), and her respondents on pages 215–32 of the same book.

3. The primary published sources used for this section were Boling (1975), Kelm and A. Mazar (1985 and 1989), and A. Mazar (1985c and 1990).

4. Stager has said that when the "archives" are found "those texts will be in Mycenaean Greek (that is, in Linear B or some related script)" (1991a, 36). See T. Dothan (1982b, 31) and Kelm and A. Mazar (1982, 18–19; 1989, 41–42) for further discussion and pictures of the seals, bullae, and writing from the ancient Near East.

5. Beth-shemesh, meaning "House of the Sun (god)," at the eastern end of the Sorek Valley is another candidate for Delilah's home. It too had a Philistine presence (pottery) at one time. This will be addressed later.

6. The primary published sources used for this section were Boling (1975), Negev (1986, 315–17), and especially A. Mazar (1973, 1977, 1980, 1985b, 1990, 317–23).

7. The primary published sources used for this section were T. Dothan (1989, 1990) and Gitin and T. Dothan (1987).

8. The primary published sources used for this section were Bright (1981), McCarter (1980), Pfeiffer (1973), Wright (1966), and especially Finkelstein (1986) and Kaufman (1988).

9. The primary published sources used for this section were M. Dothan (1979, 1989), M. Dothan and Freedman (1967), M. Dothan et al. (1971), T. Dothan (1985), A. Mazar (1980, 1985b), McCarter (1980), and Negev (1986, 60–61).

10. For more information on Dagon, consult Achtemeier (1985), Curtis (1985), Douglas (1962), *ISBE* (vol. 1), A. Mazar (1985b), McCarter (1980), and Mitchell (1967).

11. Studies have determined that the population density of typical cities in Canaan would have been around 160–200 people per acre (Broshi 1978, 10; Broshi and Gophna 1984, 41–53). Qasile with its four acres, for example, would then have had approximately 640–800 people, of which about 200 would have been adult males. These 200 would have been able to assemble in the Qasile temple courtyard very nicely (A. Mazar 1985b, 130). A similar courtyard of their god Dagon in Ashdod, Gath, and Ekron might have been a fitting place for the Lord to afflict the Philistines with "tumors."

12. The primary published sources used for this section and not mentioned in the text were T. Dothan (1990), Gitin and T. Dothan (1987), *ISBE* (3:158), and A. Mazar (1990, 312).

Chapter 5: The Philistines from David to Solomon

1. Naveh (1985, 9, 13 n. 14) states that Ikausu, the name of the king of Ekron in the seventh century B.C., is a non-Semitic name that can be associated with that of the Achish of Gath in David's time. The name in the seventh century has a *shin* ending that is non-West Semitic.

2. The primary sources used for this section were T. Dothan (1982a, 81–82, 268–76; 1982b, 41–42), Fitzgerald (1967), A. Mazar (1990, 355–56), Negev (1986, 59–60), and Rowe (1940). Note that the NRSV translation has two different spellings for Beth-shean/Beth-shan, as do other major translations.

3. The primary sources used for this section were Bright (1981, 198–201) and McCarter (1984).

4. Primary published sources used for this section but not specifically cited in the text were Dever (1967), Gitin (1989b), and Wright (1966).

5. This is an incised limestone tablet (4 inches by 3 inches) with an alphabetic script found at Gezer and dated by scholars to the tenth century (925) B.C. It may have been a schoolboy's exercise copy, and it appears to be a mnemonic ditty in Hebrew of the agricultural calendar relating the seasons of the year to their agricultural activities. " . . . His month is hoeing up of flax, His month is harvest of barley . . . " [*ANET,* 320]. This tablet helps us understand the biblical references to months and seasons. The Hebrew script is written in horizontal lines reading from right to left.

6. Not all authorities agree that the two objects were placed in the ark; see, for example, Myers (1986b, 29), who states that this was a later tradition. Both *ISBE* (1:293) and Elwell (1988, 1:169) do state that the objects were in the ark. See also *ISBE* (4:1169–70) and Elwell (1988, 2:2176–77).

Chapter 6: The Philistines from Solomon to Hezekiah

1. The primary published sources used for this section but not specifically mentioned in the text were Bright (1981, 198f.), T. Dothan and Gitin (1986), Gitin (1990), A. Mazar (1977, 1984), Negev (1986, 41–43), and Shanks (1984).

2. The primary published sources used for this section but not specifically mentioned in the text were Bright (1981, 254–55), *ISBE* (1:617–18), and Yeivin (1979, 154–55).

3. The primary published source used for this section was King (1988a and 1988b).

4. The primary published sources used for this section but not specifically cited in the text were Bright (1981, 271–78), Myers (1986b), Oded (1979, 241–44), and Yeivin (1979, 174–78).

5. The primary published sources used for this section but not cited specifically in the text were M. Dothan (1968, 1969), A. Mazar (1990, 531–35), and Tadmor (1966, 90–102).

6. More about the textile industry in Philistia will be explained in chapter 7, but for now just a brief note about the fish is called for. While we excavate, we save all skeletal material. I remember that, already back in 1984 at Ekron, I excavated large fragments of what turned out to be Nile perch. The excavators at Ashkelon also found such remains, and we debated how the fish might have come to our sites and how the Nile perch might have been used in Philistine towns.

Chapter 7: The Philistines from Hezekiah to Josiah

1. The primary published sources used for this section but not specifically mentioned in the text were Bright (1981, 278–309, which contains an excursus on Sennacherib's campaigns), Gitin (1987, 1989b), Gitin and T. Dothan (1987), Oded (1979), Porten (1981), Reviv (1979), and Tadmor (1966, 95–102).

2. See especially Gitin (1990, 36–40) for additional information and pictures of the olive oil production process.

3. All the artifacts common to the industrial buildings were found in the industrial sector of the upper city, with one notable exception. No altars have been found there yet, but this area has not been excavated as fully as the area by the gate or the area in the center of the town.

4. The primary published source used for this section was Gitin (1989a, 52–57 and 1991, 1–18). Other published sources used were Herzog, Aharoni, and Rainey (1987, 16–35), A. Mazar (1990, 492–501), and Miller and Hayes (1986, 397–402, with pictures).

5. The primary published sources used for this section were Kelm and A. Mazar (1989) and A. Mazar (1990, 465–70, 489–91, 531–36).

6. The primary published source for this section was Naveh (1962, 89–113). Other sources used were Aharoni (1982a, 264, 270–71), Pfeiffer (1973, 371–74), and Tadmor (1966, 97–102).

7. The primary published sources used for this section but not cited specifically in the text were Bright (1981, 310–16, 320–21) and Pfeiffer (1973, 369–70, 376–77).

Chapter 8: The Final Destruction of Philistia

1. The following published sources were used for this chapter but were not specifically cited in the text: Bright (1981, 326–31), Pfeiffer (1973, 375–82), and Tadmor (1966, 102).

Bibliography

Achtemeier, Paul J., ed.
1985   *Harper's Bible Dictionary.* San Francisco: Harper and Row.

Aharoni, Yohanan.
1968   "Arad: Its Inscriptions and Temple." *Biblical Archaeologist* 31(1):2–32.
1982a   *The Archaeology of the Land of Israel.* Translated by Anson F. Rainey. Philadelphia: Westminster.
1982b   "The Israelite Occupation of Canaan." *Biblical Archaeology Review* 8(3):14–23.

Albright, William Foxwell.
1924   "Researches of the School in Western Judea." *Bulletin of the American Schools of Oriental Research* 15:8.
1925   "The Fall Trip of the School in Jerusalem: From Jerusalem to Gaza and Back." *Bulletin of the American Schools of Oriental Research* 17:4–9.
1950   "Some Oriental Glosses on the Homeric Problem." *American Journal of Archaeology* 54:162–76.
1975   "Syria, the Philistines, and Phoenicia." In *The Cambridge Ancient History,* 3d ed., edited by I. E. S. Edwards et al., vol. 2, pt. 2, 507–36. Cambridge: Cambridge University Press.

Andersen, Francis I., and David Noel Freedman.
1980   *Hosea.* The Anchor Bible, vol. 24. Garden City, N.Y.: Doubleday.

Avi-Yonah, Michael, and Emil G. Kraeling.
1962   *Our Living Bible.* New York: McGraw-Hill.

Barnett, R. D.
1975   "The Sea Peoples" and "Phyrgia and the Peoples of Anatolia in the Iron Age." In *The Cambridge Ancient History,* 3d ed., edited by I. E. S. Edwards et al., vol. 2, pt. 2, 359–78, 417–42. Cambridge: Cambridge University Press.

Betancourt, Philip P.
1985   *The History of Minoan Pottery.* Princeton: Princeton University Press.

Blegen, C. W.
1975   "Troy VII." In *The Cambridge Ancient History,* 3d ed., edited by I. E. S. Edwards et al., vol. 2, pt. 2, 161–64. Cambridge: Cambridge University Press.

Bleibtreu, Erika.
1991   "Grisly Assyrian Record of Torture and Death." *Biblical Archaeology Review* 17(1):52–61, 75.

Boling, Robert G.
1975   *Judges.* The Anchor Bible, vol. 6A. Garden City, N.Y.: Doubleday.

Boling, Robert G., and G. Ernest Wright.
1982   *Joshua.* The Anchor Bible, vol. 6. Garden City, N.Y.: Doubleday.

Borowski, Oded.
1988   "The Biblical Identity of Tel Halif." *Biblical Archaeologist* 51(1):21–27.

Breasted, James Henry.
1906   *Ancient Records of Egypt.* 5 vols. Chicago: University of Chicago Press.

Bright, John.
1980   *Jeremiah.* The Anchor Bible, vol. 21. Garden City, N.Y.: Doubleday.
1981   *A History of Israel.* 3d ed. Philadelphia: Westminster.

Bromiley, Geoffrey W., ed.
1979   *The International Standard Bible Encyclopedia (ISBE).* 4 vols. (vol. 1, 1979; vol. 2, 1982; vol. 3, 1986; vol. 4, 1988). Grand Rapids, Mich.: Eerdmans.

Broshi, Magen.
1978   "Estimating the Population of Ancient Jerusalem." *Biblical Archaeology Review* 4(2):10–15.

Broshi, Magen, and Ram Gophna.
1984   "The Settlements and Population of Palestine during the Early Bronze Age II–III." *Bulletin of the American Schools of Oriental Research* 253:41–53.

Buchholz, H.-G.
1974   "Grey Trojan Ware in Cyprus and Northern Syria." In *Bronze Age Migrations in the Aegean: Archaeological and Linguistic Problems in Greek Prehistory.* Proceedings of the First International Colloquium on Aegean Prehistory, Sheffield, 1970, edited by R. A. Crossland and Ann Birchall, 175–87. Park Ridge, N.J.: Noyes.

Burn, Andrew Robert.
1930   *Minoans, Philistines, and Greeks, B.C. 1400–900.* London: Kegan, Paul, Trench, Trubner, and Co.

Buttrick, George Arthur, ed.
1962   *The Interpreter's Dictionary of the Bible.* New York: Abingdon.

Catling, H. W.
1975   "Cyprus in the Late Bronze Age." In *The Cambridge Ancient History,* 3d ed., edited by I. E. S. Edwards et al., vol. 2, pt. 2, 188–216. Cambridge: Cambridge University Press.

Chadwick, John.
1976   *The Mycenaean World.* New York: Cambridge University Press.

Cogan, Mordechai, and Hayim Tadmor.
1988   *II Kings.* The Anchor Bible, vol. 11. Garden City, N.Y.: Doubleday.

Cook, J. M.
1974   "Bronze Age Sites in the Troad." In *Bronze Age Migrations in the Aegean: Archaeological and Linguistic Problems in Greek Prehistory.* Proceedings of the First International Colloquium on Aegean Prehistory, Sheffield, 1970, edited by R. A. Crossland and Ann Birchall, 37–40. Park Ridge, N.J.: Noyes.

1975 "Greek Settlement in the Eastern Aegean and Asia Minor." In *The Cambridge Ancient History*, 3d ed., edited by I. E. S. Edwards et al., vol. 2, pt. 2, 773–804. Cambridge: Cambridge University Press.

Cottrell, Leonard.
1957 *The Anvil of Civilization.* New York: New American Library, Mentor Books.
1963 *The Lion Gate.* London: Pan Books.

Curtis, Adrian.
1985 *Ugarit (Ras Shamra).* Grand Rapids: Eerdmans.

Daniel, Glyn, and J. D. Evans.
1975 "The Western Mediterranean." In *The Cambridge Ancient History*, 3d ed., edited by I. E. S. Edwards et al., vol. 2, pt. 2, 713–72. Cambridge: Cambridge University Press.

Desborough, V. R. d'A.
1964 *The Last Mycenaeans and Their Successors: An Archaeological Survey, c. 1200–c. 1000 B.C.* Oxford: Oxford University Press.

Dever, William G.
1967 "Excavations at Gezer." *Biblical Archaeologist* 30(2):47–62.

Dever, William G., H. Darrell Lance, and George Ernest Wright.
1970 *Gezer I: Preliminary Report of the 1964–66 Seasons.* Annual of the Nelson Glueck School of Biblical Archaeology. Jerusalem: Hebrew Union College.

Dever, William G., H. Darrell Lance, Reuben G. Bullard, Dan P. Cole, Anita M. Furshpan, John S. Holladay, Jr., Joe D. Seger, and Robert B. Wright.
1971 "Further Excavations at Gezer, 1967–71." *Biblical Archaeologist* 34(4):94–132.

Dever, William G., et al.
1986 *Gezer IV: The 1969–71 Seasons in Field VI, "The Acropolis."* Annual of the Nelson Glueck School of Biblical Archaeology 4. Jerusalem: Hebrew Union College.

Dikaios, P.
1979a *Enkomi.* vol. 1. Mainz am Rhine. (text).
1979b *Enkomi.* vol. 2. Mainz am Rhine. (text).
1979c *Enkomi.* vol. 3. Mainz am Rhine. (plates).

Dothan, Moshe.
1968 "Notes and News: Tel Ashdod." *Israel Exploration Journal* 18:253–54.
1969 "Notes and News: Tel Ashdod." *Israel Exploration Journal* 19:243–45.
1973 "The Foundations of Tel Mor and Ashdod." *Israel Exploration Journal* 23(1):1–17.
1979 "Ashdod at the End of the Late Bronze Age and the Beginning of the Iron Age." In *Symposia Celebrating the Seventy-fifth Anniversary of the Founding of the American Schools of Oriental Research (1900–1975)*, edited by Frank Moore Cross, 125–34. Cambridge, Mass.: American Schools of Oriental Research.
1989 "Archaeological Evidence for Movements of the Early 'Sea Peoples' in Canaan." In *Recent Excavations in Israel: Studies in Iron Age Archaeology*,

edited by Seymour Gitin and William G. Dever, 59–70. The Annual of the American Schools of Oriental Research 49. Winona Lake, Ind.: Eisenbrauns.

Dothan, Moshe, and David Noel Freedman.
  1967   "Ashdod I." *'Atiqot* 7. Jerusalem: Israel Department of Antiquities and Museums.

Dothan, Moshe, et al.
  1971   "Ashdod II–III." *'Atiqot* 9–10. Jerusalem: Israel Department of Antiquities and Museums.

Dothan, Trude.
  1973   "Philistine Material Culture and Its Mycenaean Affinities." In Acts of the International Archaeological Symposium, Nicosia 1973. *The Mycenaeans in the Eastern Mediterranean,* 187–88, 376. Nicosia: Department of Antiquities, Cyprus.

  1976   "Forked Bronze Butts from Palestine and Egypt." *Israel Exploration Journal* 26:21–34.

  1979   *Excavations at the Cemetery of Deir el-Balah.* Qedem 10. Jerusalem: The Hebrew University Press.

  1981   "The High Place of Athienou in Cyprus." In *Temples and High Places in Biblical Times,* edited by Avraham Biran, 91–95. Jerusalem: Hebrew Union College.

  1982a   *The Philistines and Their Material Culture.* New Haven, Conn.: Yale University Press.

  1982b   "What We Know about the Philistines." *Biblical Archaeology Review* 8(4):20–44.

  1982c   "Lost Outpost of the Egyptian Empire." *National Geographic* 162(6):739–69.

  1985   "The Philistines Reconsidered" In *Biblical Archaeology Today.* Proceedings of the International Congress on Biblical Archaeology, Jerusalem, April 1984, 165–76. Jerusalem: Israel Exploration Society.

  1989   "The Arrival of the Sea Peoples: Cultural Diversity in Early Iron Age Canaan." In *Recent Excavations in Israel: Studies in Iron Age Archaeology,* edited by Seymour Gitin and William G. Dever, 1–14. The Annual of the American Schools of Oriental Research 49. Winona Lake, Ind.: Eisenbrauns.

  1990   "Ekron of the Philistines, Part I: Where They Came From, How They Settled Down and the Place They Worshiped In." *Biblical Archaeology Review* 16(1):26–36.

Dothan, Trude, and Amnon Ben-Tor.
  1974   *Excavations at Athienou, 1971–1972.* Jerusalem: The Israel Museum, 116.

Dothan, Trude, and Seymour Gitin.
  1982   "Notes and News: Tel Miqne (Ekron) 1981." *Israel Exploration Journal* 32:150–53.

  1983   "Notes and News: Tel Miqne (Ekron) 1982." *Israel Exploration Journal* 33:128–29.

  1985   "Notes and News: Tel Miqne (Ekron) 1984." *Israel Exploration Journal* 35:67–71.

Bibliography

1986   "Notes and News: Tel Miqne (Ekron) 1985." *Israel Exploration Journal* 36:104–7, plates 16B–D.

1987   "Notes and News: Tel Miqne (Ekron) 1986." *Israel Exploration Journal* 37:63–68, plates 3–4.

1990   "Ekron of the Philistines: How They Lived, Worked and Worshiped for Five Hundred Years." *Biblical Archaeology Review* 16(1):20–25.

Douglas, J. D., ed.

1962   *The New Bible Dictionary.* Grand Rapids: Eerdmans.

Eitam, D., and A. Shomroni.

1987   "Research of the Oil Industry during the Iron Age at Tel Miqne." In *Olive Oil in Antiquity,* 37–56. Haifa University Conference Volume. Jerusalem: Albright Institute of Archaeological Research.

Elwell, Walter A., ed.

1988   *Baker Encyclopedia of the Bible.* 2 vols. Grand Rapids: Baker.

Eph'al, I.

1979   "Israel: Fall and Exile" and "Assyrian Dominion in Palestine." In *The World History of the Jewish People,* vol. 4, pt. 1, edited by Abraham Malamat, 180–91, 276–89. Jerusalem: Massada Press.

Faulkner, R. O.

1975   "Egypt: From the Inception of the Nineteenth Dynasty to the Death of Ramesses III." In *The Cambridge Ancient History,* 3d ed., edited by I. E. S. Edwards et al., vol. 2, pt. 2, 217–51. Cambridge: Cambridge University Press.

Finegan, Jack.

1959   *Light from the Ancient Past.* 2d ed. Princeton, N.J.: Princeton University Press.

Finkelstein, Israel.

1986   "Shiloh Yields Some, But Not All, of Its Secrets." *Biblical Archaeology Review* 12(1):22–41.

Fitzgerald, G. M.

1967   "Beth-shean." In *Archaeology and Old Testament Study,* edited by D. Winton Thomas, 185–96. Oxford: Clarendon.

French, D. H.

1974   "Archaeology of the Middle Bronze Age: Migrations and 'Minyan' Pottery in Western Anatolia and the Aegean." In *Bronze Age Migrations in the Aegean: Archaeological and Linguistic Problems in Greek Prehistory.* Proceedings of the First International Colloquium on Aegean Prehistory, Sheffield, 1970. Edited by R. A. Crossland and Ann Birchall, 51–55. Park Ridge, N.J.: Noyes.

Gardiner, Sir Alan.

1961   *Egypt of the Pharaohs.* Oxford: Clarendon.

Garstang, John, and O. R. Gurney.

1959   *The Geography of the Hittite Empire.* London: William Clows and Sons.

Gaster, Theodor Herzl, and Sir James George Frazer.

1969   *Myth, Legend, and Custom in the Old Testament.* New York: Harper and Row.

Gidal, Nachum T.
  1985   *Land of Promise: Photographs from Palestine 1850–1948.* New York: Alfred Van Der Marck.

Gitin, Seymour.
  1985   "Dramatic Finds in Ekron." *American Schools of Oriental Research Newsletter* 36(3): 2–3.
  1986   "Iron Age Research Group Formed in Jerusalem." *American Schools of Oriental Research Newsletter* 37(3):10.
  1987   "Comments on Presentations." In *Olive Oil in Antiquity.* Haifa University Conference Volume. Jerusalem: Albright Institute of Archaeological Research.
  1989a   "Incense Altars from Ekron, Israel and Judah: Context and Typology." *Eretz-Israel* 20. Yadin Memorial Volume, 52–67 (non-Hebrew section). Jerusalem: Israel Exploration Society and Hebrew University Press.
  1989b   "Tel Miqne-Ekron: A Type-Site for the Inner Coastal Plain in the Iron Age II Period." *Recent Excavations in Israel: Studies in Iron Age Archaeology,* edited by Seymour Gitin and William G. Dever, 23–59. The Annual of the American Schools of Oriental Research 49. Wiona Lake, Ind.: Eisenbrauns.
  1990   "Ekron of the Philistines, Part II: Olive-Oil Suppliers to the World." *Biblical Archaeology Review* 16(2):32–42, 59.
  1991   "Seventh Century B.C.E. Cultic Elements at Ekron." Address delivered at the Second International Congress on Biblical Archaeology, June 26, 1990. To be published in the congress volume by the Israel Exploration Society.

Gitin, Seymour, and Trude Dothan.
  1987   "The Rise and Fall of Ekron of the Philistines: Recent Excavations at an Urban Border Site." *Biblical Archaeologist* 50(4):197–222.

Gunneweg, Jan, Trude Dothan, Isadore Perlman, and Seymour Gitin.
  1986   "On the Origin of Pottery from Tel Miqne-Ekron." *Bulletin of the American Schools of Oriental Research* 264:3–16.

Gurney, O. R.
  1952   *The Hittites.* Baltimore, Md.: Penguin.

Herzog, Ze'ev, Miriam Aharoni, and Anson F. Rainey.
  1987   "Arad: An Ancient Israelite Fortress with a Temple to Yahweh." *Biblical Archaeology Review* 13(2):16–35.

Howell, R. J.
  1974   "The Origins of the Middle Helladic Culture." In *Bronze Age Migrations in the Aegean: Archaeological and Linguistic Problems in Greek Prehistory.* Proceedings of the First International Colloquium on Aegean Prehistory, Sheffield, 1970. Edited by R. A. Crossland and Ann Birchall, 73–100. Park Ridge, N.J.: Noyes.

Huxley, George Leonard.
  1960   *Achaeans and Hittites.* Belfast: The Queen's University.

Karageorghis, Vassos.
  1982   *Cyprus from the Stone Age to the Romans.* London: Thames and Hudson.

1984   "Exploring Philistine Origins on the Island of Cyprus." *Biblical Archaeology Review* 10(2):16–28.

Karageorghis, Vassos, and M. Demas, eds.
1985   *Excavations at Kition: The Pre-Phoenician Levels.* Vol. 5, pt. 1. Nicosia: Department of Antiquities, Cyprus.

Kaufman, Asher S.
1988   "Fixing the Site of the Tabernacle at Shiloh." *Biblical Archaeology Review* 14(6):46–52.

Kelm, George L., and Amihai Mazar.
1982   "Three Seasons of Excavations at Tel Batash—Biblical Timnah." *Bulletin of the American Schools of Oriental Research* 248:1–36.
1985   "Tel Batash (Timnah) Excavations: Second Preliminary Report (1981–1983)." *Bulletin of the American Schools of Oriental Research Supplement* 23:93–120.
1989   "Excavating in Samson Country: Philistines and Israelites at Tel Batash." *Biblical Archaeology Review* 15(1):36–49.

Kenyon, K. M.
1987   *The Bible and Recent Archaeology.* Revised by P. R. S. Moorey. Atlanta: John Knox.

King, Philip J.
1988a   *Amos, Hosea, Micah: An Archaeological Commentary.* Philadelphia: Westminster.
1988b   "The *Marzeaḥ* Amos Denounces: Using Archaeology to Interpret a Biblical Text." *Biblical Archaeology Review* 14(4):34–44.

Kochavi, Moshe.
1981   "The History and Archaeology of Aphek-Antipatris: a Biblical City in the Sharon Plain." *Biblical Archaeologist* 44(2):75–86.

Lance, H. Darrell.
1967   "Gezer in the Land and in History." *Biblical Archaeologist* 30(2):34–47.

Lattimore, Richmond.
1951   *The Iliad of Homer.* Chicago: University of Chicago Press.

Leaf, Walter, ed.
1923   *Strabo on the Troad.* Bk. 13, chap. 1. Cambridge: Cambridge University Press.

Lind, Millard C.
1980   *Yahweh Is a Warrior: The Theology of Warfare in Ancient Israel.* Scottdale, Penn.: Herald.

Livingstone, Sir Richard, ed.
1972   *Thucydides: The History of the Peloponnesian War.* New York: Oxford University Press.

Lorimer, Hilda Lockhart.
1950   *Homer and the Monuments.* London: Macmillan.

Macqueen, J. G.
1986   *The Hittites and Their Contemporaries in Asia Minor.* Rev. ed. London: Thames and Hudson.

Maier, Paul L.
1988   *Josephus: The Essential Writings.* Grand Rapids: Kregel.

Malamat, Abraham.
1975   "The Twilight of Judah: In the Egyptian-Babylonian Maelstrom."
         Supplements to Vetus Testamentum 28:123–45.
1979   "The Last Years of the Kingdom of Judah." In *The World History of the
         Jewish People,* vol. 4, pt. 1, edited by Abraham Malamat, 205–21, 350.
         Jerusalem: Massada Press.

Marinatos, S.
1974   "The First 'Mycenaeans' in Crete" and "Ethnic Problems Raised by
         Recent Discoveries on Thera." In *Bronze Age Migrations in the Aegean:
         Archaeological and Linguistic Problems in Greek Prehistory.* Proceedings of
         the First International Colloquium on Aegean Prehistory, Sheffield,
         1970. Edited by R. A. Crossland and Ann Birchall, 106–13, 199–201.
         Park Ridge, N.J.: Noyes.

Mazar, Amihai.
1973   "A Philistine Temple at Tell Qasile." *Biblical Archaeologist* 36(2):42–48.
1977   "Additional Philistine Temples at Tell Qasile." *Biblical Archaeologist*
         40(2):82–87.
1980   *Excavations at Tell Qasile: Part 1, The Philistine Sanctuary: Architecture
         and Cult Objects.* Qedem 12. Jerusalem: Hebrew University Press.
1984   "Archaeological Research on the Period of the Monarchy (Iron Age II)."
         In *Recent Archaeology in the Land of Israel.* Edited by Hershel Shanks and
         Benjamin Mazar. Jerusalem.
1985a "The Emergence of the Philistine Material Culture." *Israel Exploration
         Journal* 35:95–107.
1985b *Excavations at Tell Qasile: Part 2, The Philistine Sanctuary: Various Finds, the
         Pottery, Conclusions, Appendices.* Qedem 20. Jerusalem: The Hebrew University.
1985c "The Israelite Settlement in Canaan in the Light of Archaeological
         Excavations." In *Biblical Archaeology Today.* Proceedings of the
         International Congress on Biblical Archaeology, Jerusalem, April
         1984, 61–71. Jerusalem: Israel Exploration Society.
1990   *Archaeology of the Land of the Bible 10,000–586 B.C.E.* The Anchor Bible
         Reference Library. New York: Doubleday.

McCarter, P. Kyle, Jr.
1980   *I Samuel.* The Anchor Bible, vol. 8. Garden City, N.Y.: Doubleday.
1984   *II Samuel.* The Anchor Bible, vol. 9. Garden City, N.Y.: Doubleday.

Mellink, Machteld J.
1971   "Archaeology in Asia Minor." *American Journal of Archaeology*
         75(2):161–81.

Mendenhall, George E.
1973   *The Tenth Generation.* Baltimore, Md.: Johns Hopkins University Press.
1974   "Cultural History and the 'Philistine' Problem." Paper written while
         teaching at the University of Michigan.

Mercer, Samuel A. B., ed.
1939   *The Tell El-Amarna Letters.* 2 vols. Toronto: Macmillan.

Meyers, Carol L., and Eric M. Meyers.
1987   *Haggai, Zechariah 1–8.* The Anchor Bible, vol. 25B. Garden City:
         N.Y.: Doubleday.

Bibliography

Miller, James Maxwell, and John H. Hayes.
1986 *A History of Ancient Israel and Judah.* Philadelphia: Westminster.

Miller, R. D.
1939 *The Origin and Original Nature of Apollo.* Philadelphia: University of Pennsylvania.

Mitchell, T. L.
1967 "Philistia." In *Archaeology and Old Testament Study.* Edited by D. Winton Thomas. Oxford: Clarendon.

Molin, G.
1956 "What Is a Kidon?" *Journal of Semitic Studies* 1:334–37.

Muhly, James D.
1982 "How Iron Technology Changed the Ancient World—and Gave the Philistines a Military Edge." *Biblical Archaeology Review* 8(6):40–54.

Myers, Jacob M.
1986a *I Chronicles.* The Anchor Bible, vol. 12. Garden City, N.Y.: Doubleday.
1986b *II Chronicles.* The Anchor Bible, vol. 13. Garden City, N.Y.: Doubleday.

Na'aman, Nadav.
1974 "Sennacherib's 'Letter to God' on His Campaign to Judah." *Bulletin of the American Schools of Oriental Research* 214:25–39.

Naveh, Joseph.
1958 "Khirbat al-Muqanna'—Ekron." *Israel Exploration Journal* 8:87–100, 165–70.
1962 "The Excavations at Mesad Hashavyahu." *Israel Exploration Journal* 12:89–113.
1980 "The Greek Alphabet: New Evidence." *Biblical Archaeologist* 43(1):22–25.
1985 "Writing and Scripts in the Seventh-Century B.C.E. Philistia." *Israel Exploration Journal* 35:8–21.

Negev, Avraham, ed.
1986 *The Archaeological Encyclopedia of the Holy Land.* Rev. ed. Nashville, Tenn.: Thomas Nelson.

Nibbi, Alessandra.
1974 "The Identification of the Sea Peoples." In *Bronze Age Migrations in the Aegean: Archaeological and Linguistic Problems in Greek Prehistory.* Proceedings of the First International Colloquium on Aegean Prehistory, Sheffield, 1970. Edited by R. A. Crossland and Ann Birchall, 203–7. Park Ridge, N.J.: Noyes.

Nielsen, Ljeld.
1991 "Ancient Aromas Good and Bad." *Biblical Review* 7(3):26–33.

Oded, B.
1979 "Neighbors on the West." In *The World History of the Jewish People,* vol. 4, pt. 1, edited by Abraham Malamat, 222–46. Jerusalem: Massada Press.

Oren, Eliezer D.
1982 "Ziklag: A Biblical City on the Edge of the Negev." *Biblical Archaeologist* 45(3):155–66.

Pendlebury, J. D. S.
1965   *The Archaeology of Crete.* New York: W. W. Norton.

Pfeiffer, Charles F.
1973   *Old Testament History.* Grand Rapids: Baker.

Porten, Bezalel.
1981   "The Identity of King Adon." *Biblical Archaeologist* 44(1):36–52.

Pritchard, James B., ed.
1969   *Ancient Near Eastern Texts Relating to the Old Testament (ANET).* 3d ed. Princeton: Princeton University Press.

Raban, Avner.
1987   "The Harbor of the Sea Peoples at Dor." *Biblical Archaeologist* 50(2):118–26.

Raban, Avner, and Robert R. Stieglitz.
1991   "The Sea Peoples and Their Contributions to Civilization." *Biblical Archaeology Review* 17(6):34–42, 92.

Reviv, H.
1979   "The History of Judah from Hezekiah to Josiah." In *The World History of the Jewish People,* vol. 4, pt. 1, edited by Abraham Malamat, 193–204. Jerusalem: Massada Press.

Rieu, E. V., trans. and ed.
1946   *Homer: The Odyssey.* Baltimore, Md.: Penguin.
1950   *Homer: The Iliad.* Baltimore, Md.: Penguin.
1954   *Herodotus: The Histories.* Baltimore, Md.: Penguin.

Rowe, Alan.
1940   *The Four Canaanite Temples of Beth Shean.* Vol. 2, pt. 1. Philadelphia: University of Pennsylvania Press.

Sandars, N. K.
1978   *The Sea Peoples, Warriors of the Ancient Mediterranean, 1250–1150 B.C.* London: Thames and Hudson.

Schaeffer, Claude F. A.
1983   "The Last Days of Ugarit." *Biblical Archaeology Review* 9(5):74–75.

Seger, Joe D.
1983   "Investigations at Tell Halif, Israel, 1976–1980." *Bulletin of the American Schools of Oriental Research* 252:1–23.
1984   "The Location of Biblical Ziklag." *Biblical Archaeologist* 47(1):47–53.

Shanks, Hershel.
1984   "A New Generation of Israeli Archaeologists Comes of Age." *Biblical Archaeology Review* 10(3):46–61.

Shiloh, Yigal.
1979   "Iron Age Sanctuaries and Cult Elements in Palestine." In *Symposia Celebrating the Seventy-fifth Anniversary of the Founding of the American Schools of Oriental Research (1900–1975),* edited by Frank Moore Cross, 147–57. Cambridge, Mass.: American Schools of Oriental Research.

Speiser, E. A.
1964   *Genesis.* The Anchor Bible, vol. 1. Garden City, N.Y.: Doubleday.

Bibliography

Stager, Lawrence E.

1985a "The Archaeology of the Family in Ancient Israel." *Bulletin of the American Schools of Oriental Research* 260:1–35.

1985b "Merenptah, Israel, and Sea Peoples: New Light on an Old Relief." *Eretz-Israel* 18:56–64.

1986 "In the Footsteps of the Philistines: Excavations at Ashkelon, Israel, 1985–86." Read at Harvard University at Dr. Stager's installation as Dorot professor.

1987 "Notes and News: Ashkelon, 1985–86." *Israel Exploration Journal* 37(1):68–72.

1989 "The Song of Deborah: Why Some Tribes Answered the Call and Others Did Not." *Biblical Archaeology Review* 15(1):50–64.

1991a "When Canaanites and Philistines Ruled Ashkelon." *Biblical Archaeology Review* 17(2):24–43.

1991b "Why Were Hundreds of Dogs Buried at Ashkelon?" *Biblical Archaeology Review* 17(3):26–42.

1991c "Eroticism and Infanticide at Ashkelon." *Biblical Archaeology Review* 17(4):34–53.

Stern, Ephraim.

1975 "Israel at the Close of the Period of the Monarchy: An Archaeological Survey." *Biblical Archaeologist* 38(2):26–54.

Stiebing, William H., Jr.

1970 "Another Look at the Origins of the Philistine Tombs at Tell el-Far'ah (S)." *American Journal of Archaeology* 74(2):139–44.

1980 "The End of the Mycenean Age." *Biblical Archaeologist* 43(1):7–21.

1989 *Out of the Desert?: Archaeology and the Exodus/Conquest Narratives.* Buffalo, N.Y.: Prometheus.

Stieglitz, Robert R.

1982a "Did the Philistines Write?" *Biblical Archaeology Review* 8(4):31.

1982b "Philistines after David." *Biblical Archaeology Review* 8(4):33.

1982c "Philistines in the Patriarchal Age." *Biblical Archaeology Review* 8(4):28.

Stubbings, Frank H.

1975 "The Recession of Mycenaean Civilization." In *The Cambridge Ancient History,* 3d ed., edited by I. E. S. Edwards et al., vol. 2, pt. 2, 338–58. Cambridge: Cambridge University Press.

Tadmor, Hayim.

1958 "The Campaigns of Sargon II of Assur." *Journal of Cuneiform Studies* 12:22–40, 77–100.

1966 "Philistia under Assyrian Rule." *Biblical Archaeologist* 29(3):86–102.

1979 "The Decline of Empires in Western Asia ca. 1200 B.C.E." In *Symposia Celebrating the Seventy-fifth Anniversary of the Founding of the American Schools of Oriental Research (1900–1975).* Edited by Frank Moore Cross, 1–14. Cambridge, Mass.: American Schools of Oriental Research.

Ten Cate, H. J. Houwink.

1974 "Anatolian Evidence for Relations with the West in the Late Bronze Age." In *Bronze Age Migrations in the Aegean: Archaeological and*

Linguistic Problems in Greek Prehistory. Proceedings of the First International Colloquium on Aegean Prehistory, Sheffield, 1970, edited by R. A. Crossland and Ann Birchall, 141–60. Park Ridge, N.J.: Noyes.

Thomas, D. Winton, ed.
1958 *Documents from Old Testament Times.* New York: Thomas Nelson.

Tritsch, F. J.
1974 "The 'Sackers of Cities' and the Movement of Populations." In *Bronze Age Migrations in the Aegean: Archaeological and Linguistic Problems in Greek Prehistory.* Proceedings of the First International Colloquium on Aegean Prehistory, Sheffield, 1970. Edited by R. A. Crossland and Ann Birchall, 233–39. Park Ridge, N.J.: Noyes.

Ussishkin, David.
1978 "Excavations at Tel Lachish, 1973–1977." *Tel Aviv* 5:1–97.
1979 "Answers at Lachish." *Biblical Archaeology Review* 5(6):16–39.
1980 "The 'Lachish Reliefs' and the City of Lachish." *Israel Exploration Journal* 30(3–4):174–95.
1985 "Reassessment of the Stratigraphy and Chronology of Archaeological Sites in Judah in Light of Lachish III" In *Biblical Archaeology Today.* Proceedings of the International Congress on Biblical Archaeology, Jerusalem, April 1984, edited by J. Amitai, 142–44. Jerusalem: Israel Exploration Society.
1987 "Lachish: Key to the Israelite Conquest of Canaan?" *Biblical Archaeology Review* 13(1):18–39.

Vermeule, Emily.
1972 *Greece in the Bronze Age.* Chicago: University of Chicago Press.

Wainwright, G. A.
1956 "Caphtor, Cappadocia." *Vetus Testamentum* 6:199–210.
1959 "Some Early Philistine History." *Vetus Testamentum* 9:73–84.
1961 "Some Sea-Peoples." *Journal of Egyptian Archaeology* 47:71–90.

Waldbaum, Jane C.
1966 "Philistine Tombs at Tell Fara and Their Aegean Prototypes." *American Journal of Archaeology* 70:331–40.
1978 *From Bronze to Iron: The Transition from the Bronze Age to the Iron Age in the Eastern Mediterranean.* Studies in Mediterranean Archaeology, vol. 54. Göteborg, Sweden: Paul Åströms Förlag.
1990 "The Coming of Iron in the Eastern Mediterranean Basin." Lecture presented at Tel Miqne-Ekron.

Warren, P. M.
1974 "Crete, 3000–1400 B.C.: Immigration and the Archaeological Evidence." In *Bronze Age Migrations in the Aegean: Archaeological and Linguistic Problems in Greek Prehistory.* Proceedings of the First International Colloquium on Aegean Prehistory, Sheffield, 1970. Edited by R. A. Crossland and Ann Birchall, 41–47. Park Ridge, N.J.: Noyes.

Webb, Jennifer M.
1985 "Levels VII and VI at Tel Lachish and the End of the Late Bronze Age

in Canaan." In *Palestine in the Bronze and Iron Ages: Papers in Honour of Olga Tufnell,* edited by J. N. Tubb, 213–28. London: Institute of Archaeology, University of London.

1986   "The Incised Scapula." In *Excavations at Kition V.* Edited by V. Karageorghis and M. Demas. Nicosia: Department of Antiquities, Cyprus.

Wente, Edward F., and Charles C. Van Siclen III.
1976   "A Chronology of the New Kingdom." In *Studies in Honor of George R. Hughes.* Studies in Ancient Oriental Civilization 39, 217–61. Chicago: The Oriental Institute, University of Chicago.

Wood, Bryant G.
1991   "The Philistines Enter Canaan—Were They Egyptian Lackeys or Invading Conquerors?" *Biblical Archaeology Review* 17(6):44–52, 89.

Wood, Michael.
1986   *In Search of the Trojan War.* New York: Facts on File.

Wright, G. Ernest.
1966   "Fresh Evidence for the Philistine Story." *Biblical Archaeologist* 29(3):70–86.

Yadin, Yigael.
1963   *The Art of Warfare in Biblical Lands in the Light of Archaeological Study.* 2 vols. New York: McGraw-Hill.

1979   "The Archaeological Sources for the Period of the Monarchy." In *The World History of the Jewish People,* vol. 4, pt. 2, edited by Abraham Malamat. Jerusalem: Massada Press.

Yeivin, S.
1979   "The Divided Kingdom." In *The World History of the Jewish People,* vol. 4, pt. 1, edited by Abraham Malamat. Jerusalem: Massada Press.

Yellin, J., T. Dothan, and B. Gould.
1986   "The Provenience of Beer Bottles from Deir el-Balah: A Study by Neutron Activation Analysis." *Israel Exploration Journal* 36:68–73.

Yurco, Frank J.
1990   "3,200-Year-Old Picture of Israelites Found in Egypt." *Biblical Archaeology Review* 16(5):20–38.

1991   Israelites and Canaanites. In "Queries and Comments." *Biblical Archaeology Review* 17(1):21, 62.

Subject Index

Scripture Index

279